THE
SHAKESPEARE GARDEN

STRATFORD-UPON-AVON, NEW PLACE, BORDER OF ANNUALS

THE SHAKESPEARE GARDEN BY ESTHER SINGLETON ⚜ ⚜ WITH NUMEROUS ILLUSTRATIONS FROM PHOTOGRAPHS AND REPRODUCTIONS OF OLD WOOD CUTS ⚜ ⚜ ⚜ ⚜

PUBLISHED BY THE CENTURY CO.
NEW YORK ❧ ❧ M CM XX II

Republished by Gale Research Company, Book Tower, Detroit, 1974

Library of Congress Cataloging in Publication Data

Singleton, Esther, d. 1930.
    The Shakespeare garden.

        Bibliography: p.
        1. Shakespeare, William, 1564-1616–Knowledge–
Botany. 2. Gardens–History. 3. Gardening.
I. Title.
PR3041.S5   1974   822.3'3   74-8203
ISBN 0-8103-4048-8

To the memory of
MY MOTHER
WHOSE RARE ARTISTIC TASTES AND WHOSE CULTURED
INTELLECT LED ME IN EARLY YEARS TO THE APPRE-
CIATION OF SHAKESPEARE AND ALL MANIFESTATIONS
OF BEAUTY IN LITERATURE AND ART

PREFACE

In adding another book to the enormous number of works on Shakespeare, I beg indulgence for a few words of explanation.

Having been for many years an ardent and a devoted student of Shakespeare, I discovered long ago that there was no adequate book on the Elizabethan garden and the condition of horticulture in Shakespeare's time. Every Shakespeare student knows how frequently and with what subtle appreciation Shakespeare speaks of flowers. Shakespeare loved all the simple blossoms that "paint the meadows with delight": he loved the mossy banks in the forest carpeted with wild thyme and "nodding violets" and o'er-canopied with eglantine and honeysuckle; he loved the cowslips in their gold coats spotted with rubies, "the azured harebells" and the "daffodils that come before the swallow dares"; he loved the "winking mary-buds," or marigolds, that "ope their golden eyes" in the first beams of the morning sun; he loved the stately flowers of stately gardens—the delicious musk-rose, "lilies of all kinds," and the flower-de-luce; and he loved all the

new "outlandish" flowers, such as the crown-imperial just introduced from Constantinople and "lark's
heels trim" from the West Indies.

Shakespeare no doubt visited Master Tuggie's
garden at Westminster, in which Ralph Tuggie and
later his widow, "Mistress Tuggie," specialized in
carnations and gilliflowers, and the gardens of
Gerard, Parkinson, Lord Zouche, and Lord Burleigh. In addition to these, he knew the gardens
of the fine estates in Warwickshire and the simple
cottage gardens, such as charm the American visitor
in rural England. When Shakespeare calls for a
garden scene, as he does in "Twelfth Night,"
"Romeo and Juliet," and "King Richard II," it is
the "stately garden" that he has in his mind's eye,
the finest type of a Tudor garden, with terraces,
"knots," and arbors. In "Love's Labour's Lost" is
mentioned the "curious knotted garden."

Realizing the importance of reproducing an accurate representation of the garden of Shakespeare's
time the authorities at Stratford-upon-Avon have
recently rearranged "the garden" of Shakespeare's
birthplace; and the flowers of each season succeed
each other in the proper "knots" and in the true
Elizabethan atmosphere. Of recent years it has
been a fad among American garden lovers to set

apart a little space for a "Shakespeare garden," where a few old-fashioned English flowers are planted in beds of somewhat formal arrangement. These gardens are not, however, by any means replicas of the simple garden of Shakespeare's time, or of the stately garden as worked out by the skilful Elizabethans.

It is my hope, therefore, that this book will help those who desire a perfect Shakespeare garden, besides giving Shakespeare lovers a new idea of the gardens and flowers of Shakespeare's time.

Part One is devoted to the history and evolution of the small enclosed garden within the walls of the medieval castle into the Garden of Delight which Parkinson describes; the Elizabethan garden, the herbalists and horticulturists; and the new "outlandish" flowers. Part Two describes the flowers mentioned by Shakespeare and much quaint flower lore. Part Three is devoted to technical hints, instruction and practical suggestions for making a correct Shakespeare garden.

Shakespeare does not mention all the flowers that were familiar in his day, and, therefore, I have described in detail only those spoken of in his plays. I have chosen only the varieties that were known to Shakespeare; and in a Shakespeare garden only such specimens should be planted. For example, it would be an anachronism to grow the superb modern pansies, for the "pansy freaked with jet," as Milton so beautifully calls it, is the tiny heartsease, or "johnny-jump-up."

On the other hand, the carnations (or "sops-in-wine") and gilliflowers were highly developed in Shakespeare's day and existed in bewildering variety.

We read of such specimens as the Orange Tawny Gilliflower, the Grandpere, the Lustie Gallant or Westminster, the Queen's Gilliflower, the Dainty, the Fair Maid of Kent or Ruffling Robin, the Feathered Tawny, Master Bradshaw's Dainty Lady, and Master Tuggie's Princess, besides many other delightful names.

I have carefully read every word in Parkinson's huge volume, *Paradisi in Sole; Paradisus Terrestris* (London, 1629), to select from his practical instructions to gardeners and also his charming bits of description. I need not apologize for quoting so frequently his intimate and loving characterizations of those flowers that are "nourished up in gardens." Take, for example, the following description of the "Great Harwich":

I take [says Parkinson] this goodly, great old English Carnation as a precedent for the description of all the rest, which for his beauty and stateliness is worthy of a prime place. It riseth up with a great, thick, round stalk divided into several branches, somewhat thickly set with joints, and at every joint two long, green (rather than whitish) leaves turning or winding two or three times round. The flowers stand at the tops of the stalks in long, great and round green husks, which are divided into five points, out of which rise many long and broad pointed leaves deeply jagged at the ends, set in order, round and comely, making a gallant, great double Flower of a deep carnation color almost red, spotted with many bluish spots and streaks, some greater and some lesser, of an excellent soft, sweet scent, neither too quick, as many others of these kinds are, nor yet too dull, and with two whitish crooked threads like horns in the middle. This kind never beareth many flowers, but as it is slow in growing, so in bearing, not to be often handled, which showeth a kind of stateliness fit to preserve the opinion of magnificence.

It will amaze the reader, perhaps, to learn that horticulture was in such a high state of development. Some wealthy London merchants and noblemen, Nicholas Leate, for example, actually kept agents traveling in the Orient and elsewhere to search for rare bulbs and plants. Explorers in the New World also brought home new plants and flowers. Sir Walter Raleigh imported the sweet potato and to-

bacco (but neither is mentioned by Shakespeare)
and from the West Indies came the *Nasturtium Indicum*—"Yellow Lark's Heels," as the Elizabethans
called it.

Many persons will be interested to learn the quaint
old flower names, such as "Sops-in-Wine," the
"Frantic Foolish Cowslip," "Jack-an-Apes on Horse-
back," "Love in Idleness," "Dian's Bud," etc.

The Elizabethans enjoyed their gardens and used
them more than we use ours to-day. They went to
them for *re-creation*—a renewing of body and refreshment of mind and spirit. They loved their
shady walks, their pleached alleys, their flower-
wreathed arbors, their banks of thyme, rosemary,
and woodbine, their intricate "knots" bordered with
box or thrift and filled with bright blossoms, and
their labyrinths, or mazes. Garden lovers were criti-
cal and careful about the arrangement and grouping
of their flowers. To-day we try for masses of color;
but the Elizabethans went farther than we do, for
they blended their hues and even shaded colors from
dark to light. The people of Shakespeare's day were
also fastidious about perfume values—something
we do not think about to-day. The planting of
flowers with regard to the "perfume on the air," as
Bacon describes it, was a part of ordinary garden

lore. We have altogether lost this delicacy of gardening.

This book was the logical sequence of a talk I gave two years ago upon the "Gardens and Flowers of Shakespeare's Time" at the residence of Mrs. Charles H. Senff in New York, before the International Garden Club. This talk was very cordially received and was repeated by request at the home of Mrs. Ernest H. Fahnestock, also in New York.

I wish to express my thanks to Mr. Norman Taylor of the Brooklyn Botanic Garden, for permission to reprint the first chapter, which appeared in the "Journal of the International Garden Club," of which he is the editor. I also wish to thank Mr. Taylor for his valued encouragement to me in the preparation of this book.

I wish to direct attention to the remarkable portrait of Nicholas Leate, one of the greatest flower collectors of his day, photographed especially for this book from the original portrait in oils, painted by Daniel Mytens for the Worshipful Company of Ironmongers, of which Leate was master in 1616, 1626, and 1627.

The portrait of this English worthy has never been photographed before; and it is a great pleasure for me to bring before the public the features and personality of a man who was such a deep lover of horticulture and who held such a large place in the London world in Shakespeare's time. The dignity, refinement, distinction, and general atmosphere of Nicholas Leate—and evidently Mytens painted a direct portrait without flattery—bespeak the type of gentleman who sought *re-creation* in gardens and who could have held his own upon the subject with Sir Francis Bacon, Sir Thomas More, Sir Philip Sidney, Lord Burleigh, and Sir Henry Wotton—and, doubtless, he knew them all.

It was not an easy matter to have this portrait photographed, because when the Hall of the Worshipful Company of Ironmongers was destroyed by a German bomb in 1917 the rescued portrait was stored in the National Gallery. Access to the portrait was very difficult, and it was only through the great kindness of officials and personal friends that a reproduction was made possible.

I wish, therefore, to thank the Worshipful Company of Ironmongers for the gracious permission to have the portrait photographed and to express my gratitude to Mr. Collins Baker, keeper of the National Gallery, and to Mr. Ambrose, chief clerk and secretary of the National Gallery, for their kind cooperation; to Mr. C. W. Carey, curator of the

Royal Holloway College Gallery, who spent two days in photographing the masterpiece; and also to Sir Evan Spicer of the Dulwich Gallery and to my sister, Mrs. Carrington, through whose joint efforts the arrangements were perfected.

I also wish to thank the Trustees and Guardians of Shakespeare's Birthplace, who, through their Secretary, Mr. F. C. Wellstood, have supplied me with several photographs of the Shakespeare Garden at Stratford-upon-Avon, especially taken for this book, with permission for their reproduction.

E. S.

New York, September 4, 1922.

CONTENTS

PART ONE
THE GARDEN OF DELIGHT

PART TWO
THE FLOWERS OF SHAKESPEARE

PART THREE
PRACTICAL SUGGESTIONS

CONTENTS

II. The Small Garden 276
III. Soil and Seed 278
IV. The Gateway 280
V. The Garden House 281
VI. The Mount 282
VII. Rustic Arches 282
VIII. Seats 284
IX. Vases, Jars, and Tubs 284
X. Fountains 285
XI. The Dove-cote 287
XII. The Sun-dial 288
XIII. The Terrace 289
XIV. The Pleached Alley 292
XV. Hedges 293
XVI. Paths 294
XVII. Borders 295
XVIII. Edgings 297
XIX. Knots 298
XX. The Rock Garden 302
XXI. Flowers 302
XXII. Potpourri 324

A MASKE OF FLOWERS 325

COMPLETE LIST OF SHAKESPEAREAN FLOWERS WITH
BOTANICAL IDENTIFICATIONS 331

APPENDIX 333

ELIZABETHAN GARDENS AT SHAKESPEARE'S BIRTH-
PLACE 333

INDEX 347

LIST OF ILLUSTRATIONS

PART ONE

THE GARDEN OF DELIGHT

EVOLUTION OF THE SHAKESPEARE GARDEN

I

The Medieval Pleasance

SHAKESPEARE was familiar with two kinds of gardens: the stately and magnificent garden that embellished the castles and manor-houses of the nobility and gentry; and the small and simple garden such as he had himself at Stratford-on-Avon and such as he walked through when he visited Ann Hathaway in her cottage at Shottery.

The latter is the kind that is now associated with Shakespeare's name; and when garden lovers devote a section of their grounds to a "Shakespeare garden" it is the small, enclosed garden, such as *Perdita* must have had, that they endeavor to reproduce.

The small garden of Shakespeare's day, which we so lovingly call by his name, was a little pleasure garden—a garden to stroll in and to sit in. The garden, moreover, had another purpose: it was intended to supply flowers for "nosegays" and herbs for "strewings." The Shakespeare garden was a continuation, or development, of the Medieval "Pleasance," where quiet ladies retired with their embroidery frames to work and dream of their Crusader lovers, husbands, fathers, sons, and brothers lying in the trenches before Acre and Ascalon, or storming the walls of Jerusalem and Jericho; where lovers sat hand in hand listening to the songs of birds and to the still sweeter songs from their own palpitating hearts; where men of affairs frequently repaired for a quiet chat, or refreshment of spirit; and where gay groups of lords and ladies gathered to tell stories, to enjoy the recitation of a wandering *trouvère*, or to sing to their lutes and viols, while jesters in doublets and hose of bright colors and cap and bells lounged nonchalantly on the grass to mock at all things—even love!

In the illuminated manuscripts of old *romans*, such as "Huon of Bordeaux," the "Romaunt of the Rose," "Blonde of Oxford," "Flore et Blancheflore, Amadis de Gaul," etc., there are many charming miniatures to illustrate the word-pictures. From them we learn that the garden was actually within the castle walls and *very* small. The walls of the garden were broken by turrets and pierced with a little door, usually opposite the chief entrance; the walks were paved with brick or stone, or they were sanded, or graveled; and at the intersection of these walks a graceful fountain usually tossed its spray upon the buds and blossoms. The little beds were laid out formally and were bright with flowers, growing singly and not in masses. Often, too, pots or vases were placed here and there at regular intervals, containing orange, lemon, bay, or cypress trees, their foliage beautifully trimmed in pyramids or globes that rose high above the tall stems. Not infrequently the garden rejoiced in a fruit-tree, or several fruit-trees. Stone or marble seats invitingly awaited visitors.

The note here was *charming intimacy*. It was a spot where gentleness and sweetness reigned, and where, perforce, every flower enjoyed the air it breathed. It was a Garden of Delight for flowers, birds, and men.

To trace the formal garden to its origin would take us far afield. We should have to go back to the ancient Egyptians, whose symmetrical and magnificent gardens were luxurious in the extreme; to Babylon, whose superb "Hanging Gardens" were among the Seven Wonders of the World; and to the

Romans, who are still our teachers in the matter of beautiful gardening. The Roman villas that made Albion beautiful, as the great estates of the nobility and gentry make her beautiful to-day, lacked nothing in the way of ornamental gardens. Doubtless Pliny's garden was repeated again and again in the outposts of the Roman Empire. From these splendid Roman gardens tradition has been handed down.

There never has been a time in the history of England where the cultivation of the garden held pause. There is every reason to believe that the Anglo-Saxons were devoted to flowers. A poem in the "Exeter Book" has the lines:

> Of odors sweetest
> Such as in summer's tide
> Fragrance send forth in places,
> Fast in their stations,
> Joyously o'er the plains,
> Blown plants,
> Honey-flowing.

No one could write "blown-plants, honey-flowing" without a deep and sophisticated love of flowers.

Every Anglo-Saxon gentleman had a *garth*, or garden, for pleasure, and an *ort-garth* for vegetables.

In the *garth* the best loved flower was the lily, which blossomed beside the rose, sunflower, marigold, gilliflower, violet, periwinkle, honeysuckle, daisy, peony, and bay-tree.

Under the Norman kings, particularly Henry II, when the French and English courts were virtually the same, the citizens of London had gardens, "large, beautiful, and planted with various kinds of trees." Possibly even older scribes wrote accounts of some of these, but the earliest description of an English garden is contained in "De Naturis Rerum" by Alexander Neckan, who lived in the second half of the Twelfth Century. "A garden," he says, "should be adorned on this side with roses, lilies, the marigold, *molis* and mandrakes; on that side with parsley, cort, fennel, southernwood, coriander, sage, savory, hyssop, mint, rue, dittany, smallage, pellitory, lettuce, cresses, *ortulano*, and the peony. Let there also be beds enriched with onions, leeks, garlic, melons, and scallions. The garden is also enriched by the cucumber, which creeps on its belly, and by the soporiferous poppy, as well as by the daffodil and the acanthus. Nor let pot-herbs be wanting, if you can help it, such as beets, herb mercury, orache, and the mallow. It is useful also to the gardener to have anise, mustard, white pepper,

and wormwood." And then Neckan goes on to the
fruit-trees and medicinal plants. The gardener's
tools at this time were merely a knife for grafting,
an ax, a pruning-hook, and a spade. A hundred
years later the gardens of France and England were
still about the same. When John de Garlande (an
appropriate name for an amateur horticulturist) was
studying at the University of Paris (Thirteenth Century) he had a garden, which he described in his
"Dictionarus," quaintly speaking of himself in the
third person: "In Master John's garden are these
plants: sage, parsley, dittany, hyssop, celandine,
fennel, pellitory, the rose, the lily, the violet; and
at the side (in the hedge), the nettle, the thistle
and foxgloves. His garden also contains medicinal
herbs, namely, mercury and the mallows, agrimony
with nightshade and the marigold." Master John
had also a special garden for pot-herbs and "other
herbs good for men's bodies," i.e., medicinal herbs,
and a fruit garden, or orchard, of cherries, pears,
nuts, apples, quinces, figs, plums, and grapes. About
the same time Guillaume de Lorris wrote his
"Roman de la Rose"; and in this famous work of
the Thirteenth Century there is a most beautiful description of the garden of the period. *L'Amant* (the
Lover) while strolling on the banks of a river dis-

FIFTEENTH CENTURY GARDEN WITHIN CASTLE WALLS, FRENCH

covered this enchanting spot, "full long and broad behind high walls." It was the Garden of *Delight*, or Pleasure, whose wife was *Liesse*, or Joy; and here they dwelt with the sweetest of companions. *L'Amant* wandered about until he found a small wicket door in the wall, at which he knocked and gained admittance. When he entered he was charmed. Everything was so beautiful that it seemed to him a spiritual place, better even than Paradise could be. Now, walking down a little path, *bordered with mint and fennel*, he reached the spot where *Delight* and his companions were dancing a carol to the song of Joy. *L'Amant* was invited to join the dance; and after it was finished he made a tour of the garden to see it all. And through his eyes we see it, too.

The Garden of Delight was even and square, "as long as it was large." It contained every known fruit-tree—peaches, plums, cherries, apples, and quinces, as well as figs, pomegranates, dates, almonds, chestnuts, and nutmegs. Tall pines, cypresses, and laurels formed screens and walls of greenery; and many a "pair" of elms, maples, ashes, oaks, aspens, yews, and poplars kept out the sun by their interwoven branches and protected the green grass. And here deer browsed fearlessly and squirrels "in great plenty" were seen leaping from bough to bough.   Conduits of water ran through the garden and the moisture made the grass as thick and rich as velvet and "the earth was as soft as a feather bed."   And, moreover, the "earth was of such a grace" that it produced plenty of flowers, both winter and summer:

> There sprang the violet all new
> And fresh periwinkle rich of hue
> And flowers yellow, white and red,
> Such plenty grew there, never in mead.
> Full joy was all the ground and quaint
> And powdered as men had it paint
> With many a fresh and sundry flower
> That casteth up full good savor.

Myriads of birds were singing, too—larks, nightingales, finches, thrushes, doves, and canaries. *L'Amant* wandered on until he came to a marvelous fountain—the Fountain of Love—under a pine-tree.

Presently he was attracted to a beautiful rosebush, full of buds and full-blown roses.   One bud, sweeter and fresher than all the rest and set so proudly on its spray, fascinated him.   As he approached this flower, *L'Amour* discharged five arrows into his heart.   The bud, of course, was the woman he was destined to love and which, after many adventures and trials, he was eventually to pluck and cherish.

This fanciful old allegory made a strong appeal to the illustrators of the Thirteenth and later centuries; and many beautiful editions are prized by libraries and preserved in glass cases. The edition from which the illustration (Fifteenth Century) is taken is from the Harleian MS. owned by the British Museum.

II

The Garden of Delight

The old *trouveres* did not hesitate to stop the flow of their stories to describe the delights and beauties of the gardens. Many romantic scenes are staged in the "Pleasance," to which lovers stole quietly through the tiny postern gate in the walls. When we remember what the feudal castle was, with its high, dark walls, its gloomy towers and loop-holes for windows, its cold floors, its secret hiding-places, and its general gloom, it is not surprising that the lords and ladies liked to escape into the garden. After the long, dreary winter what joy to see the trees burst into bloom and the tender

flowers push their way through the sweet grass!
Like the birds, the poets broke out into rapturous
song, as, for instance, in *Richard Cœur de Lion:*

> Merry is in the time of May,
> Whenne fowlis synge in her lay;
> Flowers on appyl trees and perye;[1]
> Small fowlis[2] synge merye;
> Ladyes strew their bowers
> With red roses and lily flowers;
> Great joy is in grove and lake.

In Chaucer's "Franklyn's Tale" *Dorigen* goes
into her garden to try to divert herself in the absence
of her husband:

> And this was on the sixte morne of May,
> Which May had painted with his softe shoures.
> This gardeyn full of leves and of flowers:
> And craft of mannes hand so curiously
> Arrayed had this gardeyn of such pris,
> As if it were the verray paradis.

In the "Roman de Berte" *Charles Martel* dines in
the garden, when the rose is in bloom—*que la rose
est fleurie*—and in "La Mort de Garin" a big dinner-
party is given in the garden. Naturally the garden
was the place of all places for lovers. In "Blonde
of Oxford" *Blonde* and *Jean* meet in the garden
under a blossoming pear-tree, silvery in the blue

[1] Pear.
[2] Birds.

moonlight, and in the "Roman of Maugis et la Belle Oriande" the hero and heroine "met in a garden to make merry and amuse themselves after they had dined; and it was the time for taking a little repose. It was in the month of May, the season when the birds sing and when all true lovers are thinking of their love."

In many of the illuminated manuscripts of these delightful *romans* there are pictures of ladies gathering flowers in the garden, sitting on the sward, or on stone seats, weaving chaplets and garlands; and these little pictures are drawn and painted with such skill and beauty that we have no difficulty in visualizing what life was like in a garden six hundred years ago.

So valued were these gardens—not only for their flowers but even more for the potential drugs, salves, unguents, perfumes, and ointments they held in leaf and petal, seed and root, in those days when every castle had to be its own apothecary storehouse—that the owner kept them locked and guarded the key. Song, story, and legend are full of incidents of the heroine's trouble in gaining possession of the key of the postern gate in order to meet at midnight her lover who adventurously scaled the high garden wall. The garden was indeed the happiest and the most romantic spot in the precincts of the feudal castle and the baronial manor-house.

We do not have to depend entirely upon the *trouveres* and poets for a knowledge of Medieval flowers. A manuscript of the Fifteenth Century (British Museum) contains a list of plants considered necessary for a garden. Here it is: violets, mallows, dandelions, mint, sage, parsley, golds,[1] marjoram, fennel, caraway, red nettle, daisy, thyme, columbine, basil, rosemary, gyllofre,[2] rue, chives, endive, red rose, poppy, cowslips of Jerusalem, saffron, lilies, and Roman peony.

Herbs and flowers were classed together. Many were valued for culinary purposes and for medicinal purposes. The ladies of the castle and manor-house were learned in cookery and in the preparation of "simples"; and they guarded, tended, and gathered the herbs with perhaps even more care than they gave to the flowers. Medieval pictures of ladies, in tall peaked head dresses, fluttering veils, and graceful, flowing robes, gathering herbs in their gardens, are abundant in the old illustrated manuscripts.

[1] Marigolds.
[2] Gilliflower.

III

The Italian Renaissance Garden

It is but a step from this Medieval "Pleasance"
to the Shakespeare garden. But before we try to
picture what the Tudor gardens were like it will
be worth our while to pause for a moment to consider the Renaissance garden of Italy on which the
gardens that Shakespeare knew and loved were
modeled. No one is better qualified to speak of
these than Vernon Lee:

"One great charm of Renaissance gardens was
the skillful manner in which Nature and Art were
blended together. The formal design of the
Giardino segreto agreed with the straight lines of
the house, and the walls with their clipped hedges
led on to the wilder freer growth of woodland and
meadow, while the dense shade of the *bosco* supplied
an effective contrast to the sunny spaces of lawn and
flower-bed. The ancient practice of cutting box-
trees into fantastic shapes, known to the Romans
as the topiary art, was largely restored in the
Fifteenth Century and became an essential part of
Italian gardens. In that strange romance printed
at the Aldine Press in 1499, the *Hypernotomachia*

of Francesco Colonna, Polyphilus and his beloved are led through an enchanted garden where banquet-houses, temples and statues stand in the midst of myrtle groves and labyrinths on the banks of a shining stream. The pages of this curious book are adorned with a profusion of wood-cuts by some Venetian engraver, representing pergolas, fountains, sunk parterres, pillared *loggie*, clipped box and ilex-trees of every variety, which give a good idea of the garden artist then in vogue.

"Boccaccio and the Italians more usually employ the word *orto*, which has lost its Latin signification, and is a place, as we learn from the context, planted with fruit-trees and potherbs, the sage which brought misfortune on poor Simona and the sweet basil which Lisabetta watered, as it grew out of Lorenzo's head, only with rosewater, or that of orange-flowers, or with her own tears. A friend of mine has painted a picture of another of Boccaccio's ladies, Madonna Dianora, visiting the garden which the enamored Ansaldo has made to bloom in January by magic arts; a little picture full of the quaint lovely details of Dello's wedding-chests, the charm of roses and lilies, the flashing fountains and birds singing against a background of wintry trees, and snow-shrouded fields, dainty youths and damsels

LOVERS IN THE CASTLE GARDEN, FIFTEENTH CENTURY MS.

GARDEN OF DELIGHT, ROMAUNT OF THE ROSE, FIFTEENTH CENTURY

treading their way among the flowers, looking like tulips and ranunculus themselves in their fur and brocade. But although in this story Boccaccio employs the word *giardino* instead of *orto*, I think we must imagine that magic flower garden rather as a corner of orchard connected with fields of wheat and olive below by the long tunnels of vine-trellis and dying away into them with the great tufts of lavender and rosemary and fennel on the grassy bank under the cherry trees. This piece of terraced ground along which the water spurted from the dolphin's mouth, or the Siren's breasts—runs through walled channels, refreshing impartially violets and salads, lilies and tall, flowering onions under the branches of the peach-tree and the pomegranate, to where, in the shade of the great pink oleander tufts, it pours out below into the big tank for the maids to rinse their linen in the evening and the peasants to fill their cans to water the bedded out tomatoes and the potted clove-pinks in the shadow of the house.

"The Blessed Virgin's garden is like that where, as she prays in the cool of the evening, the gracious Gabriel flutters on to one knee (hushing the sound of his wings lest he startle her) through the pale green sky, the deep blue-green valley; and you may still see in the Tuscan fields clumps of cypress, clipped wheel shape, which might mark the very spot."

I may recall here that the early Italian and Flemish painters were fond of representing the Madonna and the Infant Jesus in a garden; and the garden that they pictured was always the familiar little enclosed garden of the period. The flowers that grew there were limited by the Church. Each flower had its significance: the rose and the pink both expressed divine love; the lily, purity; the violet, humility; the strawberry, fruit and blossom, for the fruit of the spirit and the good works of the righteous; the clover, or trefoil, for the Trinity; and the columbine for the Seven Gifts of the Holy Spirit, because of its dove-shaped petals.

The enclosed garden is ancient indeed.

O garden enclosed—a garden of living waters
And flowing streams from Lebanon:
Awake O North Wind; and come thou South;
Blow upon my garden that the spices may thereof flow out!

So sang the esthetic Solomon.

A garden enclosed, a garden of living waters, a garden of perfumes—these are the motives of the Indian gardens of the luxurious Mogul emperors, whose reigns coincide with Tudor times.

Symbolism played an important part in Indian gardens. The beautiful garden of Babar (near Kabul) was called the Bagh-i-vafa—"The Garden of Fidelity." This has many points in common with the illustration of the "Romaunt of the Rose," particularly the high walls.

There is also great similarity with the gardens of Elizabethan days. The "pleached allies" and "knots" of the English gardens of Shakespeare's time find equivalents in the vine pergolas and geometrical parterres of the Mogul emperors; and the central platform of the Mogul gardens answered the same purpose as the banqueting-hall on the mound, which decorated nearly every English nobleman's garden.

IV

Bagh-i-vafa

Babar's "Garden of Fidelity" was made in the year 1508. We see Babar personally superintending the laying out of the "four-field plot." Two gardeners hold the measuring line and the architect stands by with his plan. The square enclosure at the bottom of the garden (right) is the tank. The whole is bordered with orange and pomegranate trees. An embassy knocks at the gate, but

Babar is too absorbed in his gardening to pay any attention to the guests.

Fifteen years later Babar stole three days away from his campaign against the Afghans and visited his beautiful garden. "Next morning," he wrote in his "Memoirs," "I reached Bagh-i-vafa. It was the season when the garden was in all its glory. Its grass-plots were all covered with clover; its pomegranate trees were entirely of a beautiful yellow color. It was then the pomegranate season and pomegranates were hanging red on the trees. The orange-trees were green and cheerful, loaded with innumerable oranges; but the best oranges were not yet ripe. I never was so much pleased with the 'Garden of Fidelity' as on this occasion."

Several new ideas were introduced into English gardens in the first quarter of the Sixteenth Century. About 1525 the geometrical beds called "knots" came into fashion, also rails for beds, also mounds, or "mounts," and also arbors. Cardinal Wolsey had all these novelties in his garden at Hampton Court Palace. It was a marvelous garden, as any one who will read Cavendish may see for himself; but Henry VIII was not satisfied with it when he seized the haughty Cardinal's home in 1529. So four years later the King had an entirely new garden made at

BABAR'S "GARDEN OF FIDELITY"

Hampton Court (the Privy Garden is on the site now) with gravel paths, beds cut in the grass, and railed and raised mounds decorated with sun-dials. Over the rails roses clambered and bloomed and the center of each bed was adorned with a yew, juniper, or cypress-tree.   Along the walls fruit-trees were planted—apples, pears, and damsons—and beneath them blossomed violets, primroses, sweet williams, gilliflowers, and other old favorites.

Toward the end of his reign Henry VIII turned his attention to beautifying the grounds of Nonsuch Palace near Ewell in Surrey.   These gardens were worthy of the magnificent buildings.   A contemporary wrote: "The Palace itself is so encompassed with parks full of deer, delicious gardens, groves ornamented with trellis-work, cabinets of verdure and walks so embowered with trees that it seems to be a place pitched upon by Pleasure herself to dwell in along with health."

V

New Fad for Flowers

An example of a typical Tudor estate, Beaufort House, Chelsea, later Buckingham House, is said to have been built by Sir Thomas More in 1521 and rebuilt in 1586 by Sir Robert Cecil, Earl of Salisbury, who died in 1615. The flowers at this period were the same for palace and cottage. Tudor gardens bloomed with acanthus, asphodel, auricula, anemone, amaranth, bachelor's buttons, cornflowers or "bottles," cowslips, daffodils, daisies, French broom (genista), gilliflowers (three varieties), hollyhock, iris, jasmine, lavender, lilies, lily-of-the-valley, marigold, narcissus (yellow and white), pansies or heartsease, peony, periwinkle, poppy, primrose, rocket, roses, rosemary, snapdragon, stock gilliflowers, sweet william, wallflowers, winter cherry, violet, mint, marjoram, and other sweet-smelling herbs.

During "the great and spacious time" of Queen Elizabeth there was an enormous development in gardens. The Queen was extremely fond of flowers and she loved to wear them. It must have pleased her hugely when Spenser celebrated her as "Eliza, Queen of the Shepherds," and painted her portrait in one of the pretty enclosed gardens, seated among the fruit-trees, where the grass was sprinkled with flowers:

> See where she sits upon the grassy green,
>   O seemly sight!
> Yclad in scarlet, like a Maiden Queen,
>   And ermines white;

Upon her head a crimson coronet,
With daffodils and damask roses set;
   Bay leaves between,
   And primeroses green,
Embellish the sweet violet.

So fond was the Queen of gardens that Sir Philip Sidney could think of no better way to please her than to arrange his masque of the "May Lady" so that it would surprise her when she was walking in the garden at Wanstead in Essex. Then, too, in 1591, when visiting Cowdry, Elizabeth expressed a desire to dine in the garden. A table forty-eight yards long was accordingly laid.

The Tudor mansions were constantly growing in beauty. Changes and additions were made to some of them and many new palaces and manor-houses were erected. Architects—among them John Thorpe—and landscape gardeners now planned the pleasure-grounds to enhance the beauty of the mansion they had created, adapting the ideas of the Italian Renaissance to the English taste. The Elizabethan garden in their hands became a setting for the house and it was laid out according to a plan that harmonized with the architecture and continued the lines of the building. The form of the garden and the lay-out of the beds and walks were deemed of the greatest importance. Flowers, also, took a new place in general estimation. Adventurous mariners constantly brought home new plants and bulbs and seeds from the East and lately discovered America; merchants imported strange specimens from Turkey and Poland and far Cathay; and travelers on the Continent opened their eyes and secured unfamiliar curiosities and novelties. The cultivation of flowers became a regular fad. London merchants and wealthy noblemen considered it the proper thing to have a few "outlandish" flowers in their gardens; and they vied with one another to develop "sports" and new varieties and startling colors.

Listen to what an amateur gardener, William Harrison, wrote in 1593:

"If you look into our gardens annexed to our houses how wonderfully is their beauty increased, not only with flowers and variety of curious and costly workmanship, but also with rare and medicinable herbs sought up in the land within these forty years. How Art also helpeth Nature in the daily coloring, doubling and enlarging the proportion of one's flowers it is incredible to report, for so curious and cunning are our gardeners now in these days that they presume to do in manner what they list with Nature and moderate her course in things as if they were her superiors. It is a world also to see how many strange herbs, plants and annual fruits are daily brought unto us from the Indies, Americas, Taprobane, Canary Isles and all parts of the world.

"For mine own part, good reader, let me boast a little of my garden, which is but small, and the whole area thereof little above 300 foot of ground, and yet, such hath been my good luck in purchase of the variety of simples, that, notwithstanding my small ability, there are very near 300 of one sort and another contained therein, no one of them being common or usually to be had. If, therefore, my little plat void of all cost of keeping be so well furnished, what shall we think of those of Hampton Court, Nonesuch, Theobald's, Cobham Garden and sundrie others appertaining to divers citizens of London whom I could particularly name?"

VI

Tudor Gardens

Several men of the New Learning, who, like Shakespeare, lived into the reign of James I, advanced many steps beyond the botanists of the early days of Queen Elizabeth. The old Herbals—the

"Great Herbal," from the French (1516) and the
"Herbals" published by William Turner, Dean of
Wells, who had a garden of his own at Kew, treat
of flowers chiefly with regard to their properties and
medical uses.

The Renaissance did indeed "paint the lily" and
"throw a perfume on the violet";·for the New Age
brought recognition of their esthetic qualities and
taught scholastic minds that flowers had beauty and
perfume and character as well as utilitarian qualities. Elizabeth as Queen had very different gardens
to walk in than the little one in the Tower of London in which she took exercise as a young Princess
in 1564.

Let us look at some of them. First, that of Richmond Palace. Here the garden was surrounded by
a brick wall and in the center was "a round knot
divided into four quarters," with a yew-tree in the
center. Sixty-two fruit-trees were trained on the
wall.

This seems to have been of the old type—the
orchard-garden, where a few old favorite flowers
bloomed under the trees and in the central "knot,"
or bed. In the Queen's locked garden at Havering-
atte-Bower trees, grass, and sweet herbs seem to have
been more conspicuous than the flowers. The

Queen's gardens seem to have been overshadowed by those of her subjects. One of the most celebrated belonged to Lord Burleigh, and was known as Theobald's. Paul Hentzner, a German traveler who visited England in 1598, went to see this garden the very day that Burleigh was buried.

He described it as follows:

"We left London in a coach in order to see the remarkable places in its neighborhood. The first was Theobald's, belonging to Lord Burleigh, the Treasurer. In the Gallery was painted the genealogy of the Kings of England. From this place one goes into the garden, encompassed with a moat full of water, large enough for one to have the pleasure of going in a boat and rowing between the shrubs. Here are great variety of trees and plants, labyrinths made with a great deal of labor, a *jet d'eau* with its basin of white marble and columns and pyramids of wood and other materials up and down the garden. After seeing these, we were led by the gardener into the summer-house, in the lower part of which, built semicircularly, are the twelve Roman Emperors in white marble and a table of touchstone. The upper part of it is set round with cisterns of lead into which the water is conveyed through pipes so that fish may be kept in them and in summer time they are very convenient for bathing. In another room for entertainment near this, and joined to it by a little bridge, was an oval table of red marble."

Another and accurate picture of a stately Elizabethan garden is by a most competent authority, Sir Philip Sidney (1554-86), who had a superb garden of his own in Kent. In "Arcadia" we read:

"Kalander one afternoon led him abroad to a well-arrayed ground he had behind his house which he thought to show him before his going, as the place himself more than in any other, delighted in. The backside of the house was neither field, garden, nor orchard; or, rather, it was both field, garden and orchard: for as soon as the descending of the stairs had delivered they came into a place curiously set with trees of the most taste-pleasing fruits; but scarcely had they taken that into their consideration but that they were suddenly stept into a delicate green; on each side of the green a thicket, and behind the thickets again new beds of flowers which being under the trees, the trees were to them a pavilion, and they to the trees a mosaical floor, so that it seemed that Art therein would needs be delightful by counterfeiting his enemy, Error, and making order in confusion. In the midst of all the

ITALIAN RENAISSANCE GARDEN, VILLA GIUSTI, VERONA

place was a fair pond, whose shaking crystal was a perfect mirror to all the other beauties, so that it bare show of two gardens; one in deed and the other in shadows; and in one of the thickets was a fine fountain."

VII

Garden Pleasures

There were many such splendid gardens. Shakespeare was familiar, of course, with those of Warwickshire, including the superb examples at Kenilworth, and with those in the vicinity of London.

The Elizabethans used their gardens in many ways. They took recreation in them in winter and summer, and enjoyed the perfume and colors of their flowers with an intensity of delight and appreciation rarely found to-day. In their gardens the serious and the frivolous walked and talked, and here they were frequently served with refreshments.

It was also a fashion to use the garden as a setting for masques and surprises, such as those Leicester planned on a grand scale to please Queen Elizabeth at Kenilworth. Several of Ben Jonson's entertainments were arranged for performance on the terrace opening from house to garden.

By looking into that mirror of the period,

"Euphues and His England," by John Lyly (1554-1606), we can see two charming ladies in ruffs and farthingales and a gallant in rich doublet and plumed hat walking in a garden, and we gain an idea of the kind of "garden talk" that was *comme il faut:*

"One of the ladies, who delighted much in mirth, seeing Philautus behold Camilla so steadfastly, said unto him: 'Gentleman, what flower do you like best in all this border? Here be fair Roses, sweet Violets, fragrant Primroses; here be Gilliflowers, Carnations, Sops-in-Wine, Sweet Johns, and what may either please you for sight, or delight you with savor. Loth we are you should have a posie of all, yet willing to give you one, not that which shall look best but such a one as you shall like best.' "

What could *Philautus* do but bow gallantly and say: "Of all flowers, I love a fair woman."

"THE CURIOUS KNOTTED GARDEN"

I

Flower Lovers and Herbalists

THE Elizabethan flower garden as an independent garden came into existehce about 1595. It was largely the creation of John Parkinson (1567-1650), who seems to have been the first person to insist that flowers were worthy of cultivation for their beauty quite apart from their value as medicinal herbs. Parkinson was also the first to make of equal importance the four enclosures of the period: (1) the garden of pleasant flowers; (2) the kitchen garden (herbs and roots); (3) the simples (medicinal); and (4) the orchard.

One would hardly expect to find such esthetic appreciation of flowers from Parkinson, because he was an apothecary, with a professional attitude toward plants; and our ideas of an Elizabethan apothecary picture a dusty seller of narcotics and "drams of poison," like the old man to whom *Romeo* and *Juliet* repaired.

John Parkinson was of a different type. Our portrait illustration depicts him, wearing a stylish Genoa velvet doublet with lace ruff and cuffs, a man who could apparently hold his own in any company of courtiers and men of fashion. Parkinson knew a great many distinguished persons and entertained visitors at his nurseries, where he must have held them spellbound (if he talked as well as he wrote) while he explained the beauties of a new yellow gilliflower, the latest new scarlet martagon lily, or the flower that he so proudly holds in his hand—"the orange-color Nonesuch."

Parkinson's talents were recognized at court, for he was appointed "Apothecary to James I." He had a garden of his own at Long Acre, which he cultivated with enthusiasm, raising new varieties of well-known flowers and tending with care new specimens of foreign importations and exotics—"outlandish flowers" they were called in Shakespeare's day—and, finally, writing about his floral pets with great knowledge, keen observation, poetic insight, and quaint charm. His great book, "Paradisi in Sole; Paradisus Terrestris," appeared in London in 1629, the most original book of botany of the period and the most complete English treatise until Ray came.

Although published thirteen years after Shake-

JOHN GERARD

PARKINSON AND LOBEL

speare's death, Parkinson's book describes exactly the style of gardens and the variety of flowers that were familiar to Shakespeare; and to this book we may go with confidence to learn more intimately the aspect of what we may call the Shakespeare garden. In it we learn to our surprise that horticulture in the late Tudor and early Stuart days was not in the simple state that it is generally supposed to have been in. There were flower fanciers in and near London—and indeed throughout England—and there were expert gardeners and florists.

Parkinson was very friendly with the other London flower growers of whom he speaks cordially in his book and with never the least shadow of jealousy. He frequently mentions visiting the gardens of Gerard, Nicholas Leate, and Ralph Tuggy (or Tuggie).

Everybody has heard of Gerard's "Herbal or General Historie of Plants," published in 1597, for it is one of the most famous ancient books on flowers. A contemporary botanist said that "Gerard exceeded most, if not all of his time, in his care, industry and skill in raising, increasing, and preserving plants." For twenty years Gerard was superintendent of Lord Burleigh's famous gardens—one of which was in the Strand, London, and the other at Theobald's in Hertfordshire. Gerard also had a garden of his own at Holborn (then a suburb of London), where he raised many rare specimens and tried many experiments. He employed a collector, William Marshall, to travel in the Levant for new plants. Gerard (1545-1607) was a physician, as well as a practical gardener; but, although he possessed great knowledge, he does not appear to have had the esthetic appreciation of flowers that Parkinson had in such great measure. His name is also written Gerade. Gerard's "Herbal" was not the first. Horticulturists could consult the "Grete Herbal," first printed by Peter Treveris in 1516; Fitzherbert, "Husbandry" (1523); Walter Cary, "Herbal" (1525); a translation of Macer's "Herbal" (1530); the "Herbal" by Dodoens, published in Antwerp in 1544; William Turner's "The Names of Herbs in Greke, Latin, Englishe, Duche and Frenche," etc. (1548), reprinted by the English Dialect Society (1881); Thomas Tusser's "Five Pointes of Good Husbandry," etc. (1573), reprinted by the English Dialect Society (1878); Didymus Mountain's (Thomas Hill) "A Most Brief and Pleasant Treatise Teaching How to Sow and Set a Garden" (1563), "The Proffitable Art of Gardening" (1568), and "The Gardener's Labyrinth" (1577);

Barnaby Googe's "Four Books of Husbandry," collected by M. Conradus Heresbachius, "Newly Englished and increased by Barnaby Googe" (1577); William Lawson's "A New Orchard and Garden" (1618); Francis Bacon's "Essay on Gardening" (1625); and John Parkinson's "Paradisi in Sole, Paradisus Terrestris" (1629).

Ralph Tuggie, or Tuggy, so often spoken of by Parkinson, had a fine show garden at Westminster, where he specialized in carnations and gilliflowers. After his death his widow, "Mistress Tuggie," kept it up.

Another flower enthusiast was the Earl of Salisbury, who placed his splendid garden at Hatfield under the care of John Tradescant, the first of a noted family of horticulturists. John Tradescant also had a garden of his own in South Lambeth, "the finest in England" every one called it. Here Tradescant introduced the acacia; the lilac, called in those days the "Blue Pipe Flower"; and, if we may believe Parkinson, the pomegranate. Among other novelties that attracted visitors to this show garden he had the "Sable Flag," known also as the "Marvel of Peru."

Lord Zouche was another horticulturist of note. His fine garden at Hackney contained plants that he himself collected on his travels in Austria, Italy, and Spain. Lord Zouche gave his garden into the keeping of the distinguished Mathias de Lobel, a famous physician and botanist of Antwerp and Delft. Lobel was made botanist to James I and had a great influence upon flower culture in England. For him the Lobelia was named—an early instance of naming plants for a person and breaking away from the quaint descriptive names for flowers.

Elizabethan gardens owed much to Nicholas Leate, or Lete, a London merchant who about 1590 became a member of the Levant Company. As a leading merchant in the trade with Turkey and discharging in connection with commercial enterprise the duties of a semi-political character, Leate became wealthy and was thus able to indulge his taste for flowers and anything else he pleased. He had a superb garden and employed collectors to hunt for specimens in Turkey and Syria. His "servant at Aleppo" sent many new flowers to London, such as tulips, certain kinds of lilies,—the martagon, or Turk's Cap, for instance,—irises, the Crown-Imperial, and many new anemones, or windflowers. The latter became the rage, foreshadowing the tulip-mania of later years. Nicholas Leate also imported the yellow Sops-in-Wine, a famous carnation from

NICHOLAS LEATE

Poland, which had never been heard of before in England, and the beautiful double yellow rose from Constantinople. Leate was a member of the Worshipful Company of Ironmongers, London, and Master of it in 1616, 1626, and 1627, and his portrait, given here, said to be by Daniel Mytens, hung in Ironmongers' Hall in London until this famous building was destroyed by a German bomb in 1917. Leate died in 1630.

Leate, being a most enthusiastic flower fancier and garden lover, not only imported rare specimens but tried many experiments. Indeed we are surprised in going through old garden manuals of Shakespearean days to see how many and how varied were the attempts to produce "sports" and novelties. We read of grafting a rosebush and placing musk in the cleft in an effort to produce musk-roses; recipes for changing the color of flowers; methods for producing double flowers; and instructions for grafting and pruning plants, sowing seeds, and plucking flowers during the increase, or waning, of the moon.

These professional florists and gentlemen amateurs valued their rare specimens from foreign countries as they valued their emeralds from Peru, Oriental pearls from Ceylon and rubies from India. Parkinson says very earnestly:

"Our English gardeners are all, or most of them, ignorant in the ordering of their outlandish [1] flowers, as not being trained to know them. And I do wish all gentlemen and gentlewomen whom it may concern for their own good, to be as careful whom they trust with the planting and replanting of their fine flowers as they would be with so many jewels; for the roots of many of them, being small and of great value, may soon be conveyed away and a clean, fair tale told that such a root is rotten, or perished in the ground, if none be seen where it should be; or else that the flower hath changed in color when it had been taken away, or a counterfeit one had been put in the place thereof; and thus many have been deceived of their daintiest flowers, without remedy or knowledge of the defect."

The influence of the Italian Renaissance upon the Elizabethan garden has already been shown (see page 15), but the importance of this may be appropriately recalled here in the following extract from Bloom:

"The Wars of the Roses gave little time for gardening; and when matters were settled and the educational movements which marked the dawn of the Renaissance began, the gardens once again, after a

[1] Exotic.

break of more than a thousand years, went back to classical models, as interpreted by the Italian school of the time. Thus the gardens of the Palace of Nonesuch (1529) and Theobald's (1560) showed all the new ideas: flower-beds edged with low trellises, topiary work of cut box and yew, whereby the natural growth of the trees was trained into figures of birds and animals and especially of peacocks; while here and there mounts were thrown up against the orchard or garden wall, ascended by flights of steps and crowned with arbors, while sometimes the view obtained in this manner was deemed insufficient and trellised galleries extended the whole length of the garden. In 1573 the gardens of Kenilworth, which Shakespeare almost certainly visited, had a terrace walk twelve feet in width and raised ten feet above the garden, terminating at either end in arbors redolent with sweetbrier and flowers. Beneath these again was a garden of an acre or more in size divided into four quarters by sanded walks and having in the center of each plot an obelisk of red porphyry with a ball at the top. These were planted with apple, pear and cherry while in the center was a fountain of white marble."

II

The Elizabethan Garden

The Elizabethan garden was usually four-square, bordered all around by hedges and intersected by paths. There was an outer hedge that enclosed the entire garden and this was a tall and thick hedge made of privet, sweetbrier, and white thorn intermingled with roses. Sometimes, however, this outer hedge was of holly. Again some people preferred to enclose their garden by a wall of brick or stone. On the side facing the house the gate was placed. In stately gardens the gate was of elaborately wrought iron hung between stone or brick pillars on the top of which stone vases, or urns, held brightly blooming flowers and drooping vines. In simple gardens the entrance was a plain wooden door, painted and set into the wall or hedge like the quaint little doors we see in England to-day and represented in Kate Greenaway's pictures that show us how the style persists even to the present time.

Stately gardens were usually approached from a terrace running along the line of the house and commanding a view of the garden, to which broad flights of steps led. Thence extended the principal walks,

called "forthrights," in straight lines at right angles
to the terrace and intersected by other walks parallel
with the terrace. The lay-out of the garden, therefore, corresponded with the ground-plan of the mansion. The squares formed naturally by the intersection of the "forthrights" and other walks were filled
with curious beds of geometrical patterns that were
known as "knots"; mazes, or labyrinths; orchards;
or plain grass-plots. Sometimes all of the spaces or
squares were devoted to "knots." These ornamental
flower-beds were edged with box, thrift, or thyme
and were surrounded with tiny walks made of gravel
or colored sand, walks arranged around the beds so
that the garden lovers might view the flowers at
close range and pick them easily.

It will be remembered that in "Love's Labour's
Lost" Shakespeare speaks of "the curious knotted
garden." There are innumerable designs for these
"knots" in the old Elizabethan garden-books, representing the simple squares, triangles, and rhomboids
as well as the most intricate scrolls, and complicated
interlacings of Renaissance design that resemble the
motives on carved furniture, designs for textiles and
ornamental leather-work (known as strap-work, or
cuirs). Yet these many hundreds of designs were
not sufficient, for the amateur as well as the profes-

sional gardener often invented his own garden "knots."

Where the inner paths intersected, a fountain or a statue or some other ornament was frequently placed. Sometimes, too, vases, or urns, of stone or lead, were arranged about the garden in formal style inspired by the taste of Italy. Sometimes, also, large Oriental or stone jars were placed in conspicuous spots, and these were not only intended for decoration but served as receptacles for water.

There were four principles that were observed in all stately Elizabethan gardens. The first was to lay out the garden in accordance with the architecture of the house in long terraces and paths of right lines, or "forthrights," to harmonize with the rectangular lines of the Tudor buildings, yet at the same time to break up the monotony of the straight lines with beds of intricate patterns, just as in the case of architecture bay-windows, clustered and twisted chimneys, intricate tracery, mullioned windows, and ornamental gables relieved the straight lines of the building.

The second principle was to plant the beds with *mixed* flowers and to let the colors intermingle and blend in such a way as to produce a mosaic of rich, indeterminate color, ever new and ever varying as the flowers of the different seasons succeeded each other.

The third principle was to produce a garden of flowers and shrubs for all seasons, even winter, that would tempt the owner to take pleasure and exercise there, where he might find recreation, literally re-creation of mind and body, and become freshened in spirit and renewed in health.

The fourth principle was to produce a garden that would give delight to the sense of smell as well as to the sense of vision—an idea no longer sought for by gardeners.

Hence it was just as important, and infinitely more subtle, to mingle the perfumes of flowers while growing so that the air would be deliciously scented by a combination of harmonizing odors as to mingle the perfumes of flowers plucked for a nosegay, or Tussie-mussie, as the Elizabethans sometimes quaintly called it.

Like all cultivated Elizabethans, Shakespeare appreciated the delicious fragrance of flowers blooming in the garden when the soft breeze is stirring their leaves and petals. There was but one thing to which this subtle perfume might be compared and that was ethereal and mysterious music. For example, the elegant Duke in "Twelfth Night," reclining on his divan and listening to music, commands:

> That strain again! It had a dying fall.
> O it came o'er my ear like the sweet south
> That breathes upon a bank of violets
> Stealing and giving odor.

Lord Bacon also associated the scent of delicate flowers with music. He writes: "And because the breath of flowers is far sweeter in the air (whence it comes and goes like the warbling of music) than in the hand, therefore nothing is more fit for delight than to know what be the flowers and plants that do best perfume the air. Roses, damask, and red, are fast flowers of their smells, so that you may walk by a whole row of them and find nothing of their sweetness, yea though it be in a morning's dew. Bays, likewise, yield no smell as they grow, rosemary little, nor sweet marjoram. That which above all others yields the sweetest smell in the air is the violet, especially the white double violet, which comes twice a year—about the middle of April and about Bartholomew-tide. Next to that is the muskrose, then the strawberry leaves dying, which yield a most excellent cordial smell, then the flower of the vines, it is a little dust, like the dust of a bent,

THE KNOT-GARDEN, NEW PLACE, STRATFORD-UPON-AVON

which grows upon the cluster in the first coming forth; then sweetbrier, then wall-flowers, which are very delightful to be set under a parlor or lower chamber window; then pinks and gilliflowers; then the flowers of the lime-tree; then the honeysuckles, so they be somewhat afar off; of bean flowers, I speak not, because they are field flowers. But those which perfume the air most delightfully not passed by as the rest but being trodden upon and crushed are three: burnet, wild thyme and water-mints. Therefore, you are to set whole alleys of them to have the pleasure when you walk or tread."

Shakespeare very nearly follows Bacon's order of perfume values in his selection of flowers to adorn the beautiful spot in the wood where *Titania* sleeps. *Oberon* describes it:

> I know a bank where the wild thyme blows,
> Where oxlips and the nodding violet grows,
> Quite over-canopied with luscious woodbine,
> With sweet musk-roses and with eglantine.
> There sleeps Titania sometime of the night,
> Lulled in these flowers with dances and delight.

Fairies were thought to be particularly fond of thyme; and it is for this reason that Shakespeare carpeted the bank with this sweet herb. Moreover, as we have just seen, Bacon tells us that thyme is one of those plants which are particularly delightful if trodden upon and crushed. Shakespeare accordingly knew that the pressure of the Fairy Queen's little body upon the thyme would cause it to yield a delicious perfume.

The Elizabethans, much more sensitive to perfume than we are to-day, appreciated the scent of what we consider lowly flowers. They did not hesitate to place a sprig of rosemary in a nosegay of choice flowers. They loved thyme, lavender, marjoram, mints, balm, and camomile, thinking that these herbs refreshed the head, stimulated the memory, and were antidotes against the plague.

The flowers in the "knots" were perennials, planted so as to gain uniformity of height; and those that had affinity for one another were placed side by side. No attempt was made to group them; and no attempt was made to get *masses* of separate color, what Locker-Lampson calls "a mist of blue in the beds, a blaze of red in the celadon jars" and what we try for to-day. On the contrary, the Elizabethan gardener's idea was to mix and blend the flowers into a combination of varied hues that melted into one another as the hues of a rainbow blend and in such a way that at a distance no one could possibly tell what flowers produced this effect. This must have required much study on the part of the gardeners, who kept pace with the seasons and always had their beds in bloom. Sir Henry Wotton, Ambassador to Venice in the reign of James I, and author of the "Elements of Architecture," but far better known by his lovely verse to Elizabeth of Bohemia beginning, "You meaner beauties of the night," was an ardent flower lover. He was greatly impressed by what he called "a delicate curiosity in the way of color":

"Namely in the Garden of Sir Henry Fanshaw at his seat in Ware Park, where I well remember he did so precisely examine the *tinctures* and *seasons* of his *flowers* that in their *settings*, the *inwardest* of which that were to come up at the same time, should be always a little *darker* than the *outmost*, and so serve them for a kind of gentle *shadow*, like a piece not of *Nature* but of *Art*."

Browne also gives a splendid idea of the color effect of the garden beds of this period:

As in a rainbow's many color'd hue,
Here we see watchet deepen'd with a blue;
There a dark tawny, with a purple mix'd;
Yellow and flame, with streaks of green betwixt;
A bloody stream into a blushing run,
And ends still with the color which begun;
Drawing the deeper to a lighter strain,

Bringing the lightest to the deepest again;
With such rare art each mingled with his fellow,
The blue with watchet, green and red with yellow;
Like to the changes which we daily see
Around the dove's neck with variety;
Where none can say (though he it strict attends),
Here one begins and there another ends.
Using such cunning as they did dispose
The ruddy Piony with the lighter Rose,
The Monkshood with the Buglos, and entwine
The white, the blue, the flesh-like Columbine
With Pinks, Sweet-Williams; that, far off, the eye
Could not the manner of their mixture spy.

By the side of the showy and stately flowers, as well as in kitchen gardens, were grown the "herbs of grace" for culinary purposes and the medicinal herbs for "drams of poison." Rosemary —"the cheerful Rosemary," Spenser calls it—was trained over arbors and permitted to run over mounds and banks as it pleased. Sir Thomas More allowed it to run all over his garden because the bees loved it and because it was the herb sacred to remembrance and friendship.

In every garden the arbor was conspicuous. Sometimes it was a handsome little pavilion or summer-house; sometimes it was set into the hedge; sometimes it was cut out of the hedge in fantastic topiary work; sometimes it was made of lattice work; and sometimes it was formed of upright or horizontal poles, over which roses, honeysuckle, or clematis (named also Lady's Bower because of this use) were trained. Whatever the framework was, plain or ornate, mattered but little; it was the creeper that counted, the trailing vines that gave character to the arbor, that gave delight to those who sought the arbor to rest during their stroll through the gardens, or to indulge in a pleasant chat, or delightful flirtation. Shakespeare's arbor for *Titania*

> Quite over-canopied with luscious woodbine,
> With sweet musk-roses and with eglantine,

was not unusual. Nor was that retreat where saucy *Beatrice* was lured to hear the whisperings of *Hero* regarding *Benedick's* interest in her. It was a pavilion

> Where honeysuckles ripened by the sun
> Forbid the sun to enter.

Luxuriant and delicious was this bower with the flowers hot and sweet in the bright sunshine.

Eglantine was, perhaps, the favorite climber for arbors and bowers. Browne speaks of

> An arbor shadow'd with a vine
> Mixed with rosemary and with eglantine.

Barnfield, in "The Affectionate Shepherd," pleads:

I would make cabinets for thee, my love,
Sweet-smelling arbors made of eglantine.

And in Spenser's "Bower of Bliss":

Art, striving to compare
With Nature, did an arbor green dispread
Framed of wanton ivy, flow'ring fair,
Through which the fragrant eglantine did spread
His prickling arms, entrayl'd with roses red,
Which dainty odors round about them threw;
And all within with flowers was garnished,
That when Zephyrus amongst them blew
Did breathe out bounteous smells and painted odors
shew.

A beautiful method of obtaining shady walks was to make a kind of continuous arbor or arcade of trees, trellises, and vines. This arcade was called poetically the "pleached alley." [1] For the trees, willows, limes (lindens), and maples were used, and the vines were eglantine and other roses, honeysuckle (woodbine), clematis, rosemary, and grapevines.

Another feature of the garden was the maze, or

---

[1] *Pleaching* means trimming the small branches and foliage of trees, or bushes, to bring them to a regular shape. Certain trees only are submissive to this treatment—holly, box, yew privet, whitethorn, hornbeam, linden, etc., to make arbors, hedges, bowers, colonnades and all cut-work.

"*Plashing* is the half-cutting, or dividing of the quick growth almost to the outward bark and then laying it orderly in a slope manner as you see a cunning hedger lay a dead hedge and then with the smaller and more pliant branches to wreath and bind in the tops." Markham, "The County Farm" (London, 1616).

labyrinth. It was a favorite diversion for a visitor
to puzzle his way through the green walls, breast
high, to the center; and the owner took delight in
watching the mistakes of his friend and was always
ready to give him the clue. When James I on his
"Southern Progress" in 1603 visited the magnificent
garden known as Theobald's and belonging to Lord
Burleigh, where we have already seen [1] Gerard was
the horticulturist, the King went into the labyrinth
of the garden "where he re-created himself in the
meanders compact of bays, rosemary and the like,
overshadowing his walk."

The labyrinth, or maze, was a fad of the day. It
still exists in many English gardens that date from
Elizabethan times and is a feature of many more
recent gardens. Perhaps of all mazes the one at
Hampton Court Palace is the most famous.

The orchard was another feature of the Elizabethan garden. It was the custom for gentlemen
to retire after dinner (which took place at eleven
o'clock in the morning) to the garden arbor, or
to the orchard, to partake of the "banquet" or
dessert. Thus *Shallow* addressing *Falstaff* after
dinner exclaims:

"Nay, you shall see mine orchard, where, in an

[1] Page 33.

arbor, we will eat a last year's pippin of my own grafting with a dish of carraways and so forth." [1]

The uses of the Elizabethan garden were many: to walk in, to sit in, to dream in. Here the courtier, poet, merchant, or country squire found refreshment for his mind and recreation for his body. The garden was also intended to supply flowers for nosegays, house decoration, and the decoration of the church. Sweet-smelling herbs and rushes were strewn upon the floor as we know by *Grumio's* order for *Petruchio's* homecoming in "The Taming of the Shrew." One of Queen Elizabeth's Maids of Honor had a fixed salary for keeping fresh flowers always in readiness. The office of "herb-strewer to her Majesty the Queen" was continued as late as 1713, through the reign of Anne and almost into that of George I.

The houses were very fragrant with flowers in pots and vases as well as with the rushes on the floor. Flowers were therefore very important features in house decoration. A Dutch traveler, Dr. Leminius, who visited England in 1560, was much struck by this and wrote:

"Their chambers and parlors strewed over with sweet herbs refreshed me; their nosegays finely in-

[1] "King Henry IV"; Part II, Act V, Scene III.

termingled with sundry sorts of fragrant flowers in their bed-chambers and private rooms with comfortable smell cheered me up and entirely delighted all my senses."

We have only to look at contemporary portraits to see how essential flowers were in daily life. For instance, Holbein's "George Gisze," a London merchant, painted in 1523, has a vase of choice carnations beside him on the table filled with scales, weights, and business paraphernalia.

The Elizabethan lady was just as learned in the medicinal properties of flowers and herbs as her Medieval ancestor. She regarded her garden as a place of delight and at the same time as of the greatest importance in the economic management of the household.

"The housewife was the great ally of the doctor: in her still-room the lady with the ruff and farthingale was ever busy with the preparation of cordials, cooling waters, conserves of roses, spirits of herbs and juleps for calentures and fevers. All the herbs and flowers of the field and garden passed through her fair white hands. Poppy-water was good for weak stomachs; mint and rue-water was efficacious for the head and brain; and even walnuts yielded a cordial. Then there was cinnamon water and the

essence of cloves, gilliflower and lemon water, sweet
marjoram water and the spirit of ambergris.

"These were the Elizabethan lady's severer toils,
besides acres of tapestry she had always on hand.
Her more playful hours were devoted to the manu-
facture of casselettes, month pastilles, sweet waters,
odoriferant balls and scented gums for her husband's
pipe (God bless her!) and there were balsams and
electuaries for him to take to camp, if he were a
soldier fighting in Ireland or in the Low Countries,
and wound-drinks if he was a companion of
Frobisher and bound against the Spaniard, or the
Indian pearl-diver of the Pacific. She had a specific
which was of exceeding virtue in all swooning of
the head, decaying of the spirits, also in all pains
and numbness of joints and coming of cold.

"That wonderful still-room contains not only
dried herbs and drugs, but gums, spices, ambergris,
storax and cedar-bark, civet and dried flowers and
roots. In that bowl angelica, carduus benedictus
(Holy Thistle), betony, juniper-berries and wormwood are steeping to make a cordial-water for the
young son about to travel; and yonder is oil of
cloves, oil of nutmegs, oil of cinnamon, sugar, am-
begris and musk, all mingling to form a quart of

liquor as sweet as hypocras. Those scents and spices
are for perfumed balls to be worn round the ladies'
necks, there to move up and down to the music of
sighs and heart-beating, envied by lovers whose let-
ters will perhaps be perfumed by their contact.

"What pleasant bright London gardens we dream
of when we find that the remedy for a burning fever
is honeysuckle leaves steeped in water, and that a
cooling drink is composed of wood sorrel and Roman
sorrel bruised and mixed with orange juice and
barley-water. Mint is good for colic; conserves of
roses for the tickling rheum; plaintain for flux;
vervain for liver-complaint—all sound pleasanter
than those strong biting minerals which now kill or
cure and give nature no time to heal us in her own
quiet way." [1]

Bacon's "Essay on Gardening" is very detailed
and very practical, and it must be remembered that
he was addressing highly cultivated and skilfully
trained amateurs and professional gardeners when
he wrote:

"God almighty first planted a garden; and indeed
it is the purest of human pleasures; it is the greatest
refreshment to the spirit of man. And a man shall

[1] Thornbury.

ever see that when ages grow to civility and elegancy men come to build stately sooner than to garden finely, as if gardening were the greater perfection."

The Elizabethan Age, with its superlatively cultivated men and women, was certainly one of those ages of civility and elegancy of which Bacon speaks. The houses were stately and the gardens perfection, affording appropriate setting for the brilliant courtiers and accomplished ladies of both Tudor and early Stuart times.

We sometimes hear it said that Francis Bacon's garden was his *ideal* of what a garden should be and that his garden was never realized. This, however, is not the case. Old prints are numerous of gardens of wealthy persons in the reign of Elizabeth and James I. Then, too, we have Sir William Temple's description of Moor Park, and "this garden," says Horace Walpole, "seems to have been made after the plan laid down by Lord Bacon in his Forty-sixth Essay."

Sir William's account is as follows:

"The perfectest figure of a garden I ever saw, either at home or abroad, was that of Moor Park in Hertfordshire, when I knew it about thirty years ago. It was made by the Countess of Bedford, esteemed among the perfectest wits of her time and

TYPICAL GARDEN OF SHAKESPEARE'S TIME—CRISPIN DE PASSE (1614)

celebrated by Dr. Donne; and with very great care, excellent contrivance and much cost.

"Because I take the garden I have named to have been in all kinds the most beautiful and perfect, at least in the figure and disposition, that I have ever seen, I will describe it for a model to those that meet with such a situation and are above the regards of common expense.

"It lies on the side of a hill, upon which the house stands, but not very steep. The length of the house, where the best rooms and of most use or pleasure are, lies upon the breadth of the garden; the great parlor opens into the middle of a terrace gravel walk that lies even with it, and which may lie, as I remember, about three hundred paces long and broad in proportion; the border set with standard laurels and at large distances, which have the beauty of orange-trees out of flower and fruit. From this walk are three descents by many stone steps, in the middle and at each end, into a very large parterre. This is divided into quarters by gravel walks and adorned with two fountains and eight statues in the several quarters. At the end of a terrace walk are two summer-houses, and the sides of the parterre are ranged with two large cloisters open to the garden, upon arches of stone, and ending with two

other summer-houses even with the cloisters, which
are paved with stone, and designed for walks of
shade, there being none other in the whole parterre.
Over these two cloisters are two terraces covered
with lead and fenced with balustrades; and the
passage into these airy walks is out of the two summer-houses at the end of the first terrace walk. The
cloister facing the south is covered with vines and
would have been proper for an orange-house, and
the other for myrtles or other more common greens,
and had, I doubt not, been cast for that purpose, if
this piece of gardening had been then in as much
vogue as it is now.

"From the middle of this parterre is a descent by
many steps flying on each side of a grotto that lies
between them, covered with lead and flat, into the
lower garden, which is all fruit-trees ranged about
the several quarters of a wilderness which is very
shady; the walks here are all green, the grotto embellished with figures of shell rock-work, fountains
and water-works. If the hill had not ended with the
lower garden, and the wall were not bounded by a
common way that goes through the park, they might
have added a third quarter of all greens; but this
want is supplied by a garden on the other side of

the house, which is all of that sort, very wild, shady,
and adorned with rough rock work and fountains."

To write of Elizabethan gardens without giving
Bacon's beautifully worked out theories would be
like performing "Hamlet" without the character of
Hamlet. Bacon's Essay is too long to quote in its
entirety, but the specific instructions are as follows:

"For gardens (speaking of those which are indeed prince-like), the contents ought not well to
be under thirty acres of ground; and to be divided
into three parts: a green in the entrance; a heath or
desert in the going forth; and the main garden in
the midst, besides alleys on both sides. And I like
well that four acres of ground be assigned to the
green, six to the heath, four and a half to either
side and twelve to the main garden. The green hath
two pleasures: the one because nothing is more
pleasant to the eye than green grass kept finely
shorn; the other because it will give you a fair alley
in the midst, by which you may go in front upon
a stately hedge, which is to enclose this garden.
But because the alley will be long, and in great heat
of the year or day, you ought not to buy the shade
in the garden by going in the sun through the green;
therefore, you are of either side the green to plant

a covert alley upon carpenter's work, about twelve foot in height, by which you may go in shade into the garden.

"The garden is best to be square, encompassed on all the four sides with a stately arched hedge. The arches to be upon pillars of carpenter's work, of some ten foot high and six foot broad, and the spaces between of the same dimension with the breadth of the arch; over the arches let there be an entire hedge of some four foot high, framed also upon carpenter's work; and upon the upper hedge, over every arch, a little turret with a belly, enough to receive a cage of birds; and over every space, between the arches, some other little figure, with broad plates of round colored glass, gilt, for the sun to play upon. But this hedge I intend to be raised upon a bank, not steep, but gentle slope, of some six foot, set all with flowers. Also I understand that this square of the garden should not be the whole breadth of the ground, but to leave on either side ground enough for diversity of side alleys, into which the two covert alleys of the green may deliver you. But there must be no alleys with hedges at either end of this great enclosure.

"For the main garden I do not deny there should be some fair alleys, ranged on both sides with fruit-trees, and arbors with seats set in some decent order; but these to be by no means set too thick, but to leave the main garden so as it be not close, but the air open and free. For, as for shade, I would have you rest upon the alleys of the side grounds, there to walk, if you be disposed, in the heat of the year, or day, but to make account that the main garden is for the more temperate parts of the year and in the heat of the summer for the morning and the evening, or overcast days.

"For the side grounds you are to fill them with variety of alleys, private, to give a full shade, some of them wheresoever the sun be. You are to frame some of them likewise for shelter, that when the wind blows sharp you may walk as in a gallery. And these alleys must be, likewise, hedged at both ends to keep out the wind, and these closer alleys must be ever finely graveled and no grass, because of going wet. In many of these alleys, likewise, you are to set fruit-trees of all sorts, as well upon the walls as in ranges. And this would be generally observed that the borders wherein you plant your fruit-trees be fair and large and low (and not steep) and set with fine flowers, but thin and sparingly lest they deceive the trees. At the end of both the side grounds I would have a mount of some pretty

height, leaving the wall of the enclosure breast high,
to look abroad into the fields.

"For the heath, which was the third part of our
plot, I wish it to be framed, as much as may be, to
a natural wildness. Trees, I would have none in it;
but some thickets made only of sweetbrier and
honeysuckle and some wild vine amongst; and the
ground set with violets, strawberries and primroses;
for these are sweet and prosper in the shade; and
these to be in the heath, here and there, not in any
order. I also like little heaps in the nature of mole-
hills (such as are in wild heaths) to be set, some
with wild thyme, some with pinks, some with
germander that gives a good flower to the eye; some
with periwinkle, some with violets, some with strawberries, some with cowslips, some with daisies, some
with red roses, some with *lilium convallium*,[1] some
with sweet williams, red, some with bear's foot [2] and
the like low flowers, being withal sweet and sightly.
Part of which heaps to be with standards of little
bushes pricked upon their top and put without. The
standards to be roses, juniper, holly, barberries (but
here and there, because of the smell of their blossom), red currants, gooseberries, rosemary, bays,

[1] Lily-of-the-valley.
[2] *Auricula.*

sweetbrier and the like. But these standards to be kept with cutting that they grow not out of course.

"For the ordering of the ground within the great hedge, I leave it to variety of device; advising, nevertheless, that whatsoever form you cast it into, first it be not too busy or full of work. Wherein I, for my part, do not like images cut out in juniper, or cther garden stuff—they be for children. Little low hedges, round like welts, with some pretty pyramids, I like well, and in some places fair columns upon frames of carpenter's work. I would also have the alleys spacious and fair. You may have closer alleys upon the side grounds, but none in the main garden. I wish also in the very middle a fair mount with three ascents and alleys, enough for four to walk abreast, which I would have to be perfect circles without any bulwarks or embossments, and the whole mount to be thirty foot high; and some fine banqueting-house with some chimneys neatly cast and without too much glass.

"As for the making of knots, or figures, with divers colored earths that they may lie under the windows of the house, on that side which the garden stands, they be but toys. You may see as good sights many times in tarts."

Fountains Bacon considered "a great beauty and

refreshment," but he did not care for pools, nor did he favor aviaries "unless they were large enough to have living plants and bushes set in them and supply natural nesting for the birds."

We have already seen that Bacon was very choice regarding "the flowers that best perfume the air"; and he felt it was very essential that people should know what to plant for the different seasons. So he tells us:

"There ought to be gardens for all months of the year, in which, severally, things of beauty may be in season. For December and January and the latter part of November, you must take such things as are green all winter: holly, ivy, bays, juniper, cypress-trees, yew, pine, apple-trees, fir-trees, rosemary, lavender, periwinkle, the white, the purple, and the blue; germander, flags; orange-trees, lemontrees and myrtle, if they be stoved; and sweet marjoram warm set. There followeth for the latter part of January and February, the mezerion tree which then blossoms; crocus vernus, both the yellow and the gray; primroses, anemones, the early tulip, hyacinthus orientalis, *chamaires fritellaria.* For March there come violets, especially the single blue, which are the earliest, the yellow daffodil, the daisy, the almond-tree in blossom, the peach-tree in

LABYRINTH, VREDEMAN DE VRIES

"A CURIOUS-KNOTTED GARDEN"—CRISPIN DE PASSE (1614)

blossom, the cornelian tree in blossom, sweetbrier. In April follow the double white violet, the wall-flower, the stock gilliflower, the cowslip, flower-de-luces, and lilies of all natures, rosemary flowers, the tulip, the double peony, the pale daffodil, the French honeysuckle, the cherry-tree in blossom, the damson and plum-trees in blossom, the white thorn in leaf, the lilac tree. In May and June come pinks of all sorts, roses of all kinds except the musk, which comes later, honeysuckles, strawberries, bugloss, columbine, the French marigold (*Flos Africanus*), cherry-tree in fruit, ribes, figs in fruit, rasps, vine-flowers, lavender in flowers, the sweet satyrian, with the white flower, *herba muscaria, lilium convallium*, the apple-tree in blossom. In July come gilliflowers of all varieties, musk-roses, the lime tree in blossom, early pears and plums in fruit, gennitings, quodlins. In August come plums of all sorts in fruit, pears, apricots, barberries, filberts, musk-melons, monks-hood of all colors. In September come grapes, apples, poppies of all colors, peaches, melocotones, nectarines, cornelians, wardens, quinces. In Octo-ber and the beginning of November come services, medlars, bullaces, roses cut, or removed to come late, hollyhocks and such like. These particulars are for the climate of London; but my meaning is perceived that you may have *ver perpetuum*, as the place affords."

Gardening was a serious business. The duties of gardeners were not light. We are told that "Gardeners should not only be diligent and painful, but also experienced and skilful; at the least, one of them to have seen the fine gardens about London and in Kent; to be able to cast out the Quarters of the garden as may be most convenient that the Walks and the Alleys be long and large; to cast up Mounts, to tread out Knots in the Quarters of arms and fine devices, to set and sow in them sweet smelling flowers and strewing herbs; to have in the finest parts of the garden Artichokes, Pompions, Melons, Cucumbers and such-like; in other places convenient Radishes, Keritts, Carrats and other roots with store of all kind of herbs for the Kitchen and Apothecary; to know what Flowers and Herbs will best endure the Sun and which need most to be shaded: in like sort, for the East and North winds, not only to be skilful in planting and grafting of all kinds of fruit-trees, but also how to place them in best order; and to be able to judge of the best times and seasons to plant and graft all fruits and to set and sow all flowers, herbs and roots; and also the best time when to cut and gather all herbs and seeds and fruits, and in what sort to keep and preserve them; to make fair Bowling Alleys well banked and sealed, which, being well kept, in many houses are very profitable to the gardeners."

The instructions in the Elizabethan manuals for grafting, pleaching, and plashing (see page 50) are most explicit and elaborate. There are rules for the care of every flower and herb. Nothing is too small for attention. The old authors even say what flowers should be picked often and what flowers prefer to be let alone. One old gardener gives the following details with regard to the sowing of seeds:

"If you will [he writes], you may sow your seeds in rows, or trails, either round about the edges of your beds to keep them in fashion, and plant either herbs or flowers in the body of your beds, or you may furnish your beds all over, making three, four, or five rows, or trails, according to the bigness of your bed; the order, or manner, is to make each trail of like distance and range your line and by it, either with your finger or a small stick, to make your trail about an inch thick, or thereabout; and therein to sow your seed, not over-thick. If you put your seeds in a white paper, you may (if the seeds are small) very easily and equally sow them by shaking the lower end of your paper with the forefinger of that hand you sow with. The paper must not be much open at the end. Then with your hand, or a trowel, to smooth the earth into each trail."

III

Old Garden Authors

The books from which both professional and amateur gardeners gained their instruction are full of delightful information, and to us are quaintly expressed. Many of them were standard authorities for several generations and went through various editions, which, as time went on, were touched up by a more recent authority. One of these well-known garden authors was Thomas Hill, who wrote under the peculiar name of Didymus Mountain; another was Gervase Markham whose "Country Farm," published in London in 1616 (the year of Shakespeare's death), often passes for an original work. "The Country Farm," however, was an earlier book, and a French one at that, called "La Maison Rustique," published in Paris in 1600 by Charles Stevens and John Liébault, "doctors of physicke." This was translated into English very soon after its appearance by Richard Surflet and published under the title of "The Country Farm."

It became an extremely popular book before Gervase Markham took hold of it. Markham became a great authority on all garden topics and wrote and adapted many books on the subject. From his edition of "The Country Farm" we learn that

"It is a commendable and seemly thing to behold out at a window many acres of ground well-tilled and husbanded; but yet it is much more to behold fair and comely proportions, handsome and pleasant arbors, and, as it were, closets, delightful borders of lavender, rosemary, box and other suchlike; to hear the ravishing music of an infinite number of pretty, small birds, which continually, day and night, do chatter and chant their proper and natural branch-songs upon the hedges and trees of the garden; and to smell so sweet a nosegay so near at hand, seeing that this so fragrant a smell cannot but refresh the lord of the farm exceedingly when going out of his bedchamber in the morning after sunrise; and while as yet the clear and pearl-like dew doth perch on to the grass he giveth himself to hear the melodious music of the bees which do fill the air with a most acceptable sweet and pleasant harmony.

"Now for the general proportion of gardens. They may at your pleasure carry any of these four shapes: that is to say, either square, round, oval, or diamond. This is but the outward proportion, or the verge and girdle of your garden. As for the inward proportions and shapes of the Quarters, Beds, Banks, Mounts and such-like, they are to be divided by Alleys, Hedges, Borders, Rails, Pillars and such-like; and by these you may draw your garden unto what form you please, not respecting whatsoever shape the outward verge carrieth. For you may make that garden which is square without to be round within, and that which is round, either square, or oval; that which is oval, either of the former, and that which is diamond any shape at all,—and yet all exceedingly comely. You may also, if your ground be naturally so situated, or if your industry please so to bring it to pass, make your garden rise and mount by several degrees, one level ascending above another, in such sort as if you had divers gardens one above another, which is exceedingly beautiful to the eye and very beneficial to your flowers and fruit-trees, especially if such ascents have the benefit of the Sun rising upon them; and thus, if you please, you may have in one level a square plot; in another, a round; in a third a diamond; and in a fourth, an oval; then amongst the ascending banks, which are on either side the stairs, you mount into your several gardens, you shall make your physic garden or places to plant your physic herbs."

We also learn from "The Country Farm" that

"The Garden of Pleasure shall be set about and compassed with arbors made of jessamin, rosemarie, box, juniper, cypress-trees, savin, cedars, rose-trees and other dainties first planted and pruned according as the nature of every one doth require, but after brought into some form and order with willow or juniper poles, such as may serve for the making of arbors. The ways and alleys must be covered and sown with fine sand well beat, or with the powder of the sawing of marble, or else paved handsomely with good pit stone.

"This garden, by means of a large path of the breadth of six feet, shall be divided into two equal parts; the one shall contain the herbs and flowers used to make nosegays and garlands of, as March violets, Provence gilliflowers, purple gilliflowers, Indian gilliflowers, small pansies, daisies, yellow and white gilliflowers, marigolds, lily connally,[1] daffodils, Canterbury bells, purple velvet flowers, anemones, corn-flag,[2] mugwort, lilies and other suchlike; and it may be indeed the Nosegay Garden.

[1] Lily-of-the-valley.
[2] Gladiolus.

"The other part shall have all other sweet-smelling herbs whether they be such as bear no flowers, or, if they bear any, yet they are not put in nosegays alone, but the whole herb be with them, as Southernwood, wormwood, pellitory, rosemary, jessamine, marierom, balm-mints, pennyroyal, costmarie, hyssop, lavender, basil, sage, savory, rue, tansy, thyme, camomile, mugwort, bastard marierum, nept, sweet balm, all-good, anis, horehound and others such-like; and this may be called the garden for herbs and good smell.

"These sweet herbs and flowers for nosegays shall be set in order upon beds and quarters of such-like length and breadth as those of the kitchen garden; others in mazes made for the pleasing and recreating of the sight, and other some are set in proportions made of beds interlaced and drawn one within another or broken off with borders, or without borders."

This arrangement is interesting as not only showing the division of flower-beds but that certain herbs were used in nosegays. It did not, therefore, strike Shakespeare's audiences as strange that *Perdita* offered to her guests rosemary and rue on an equality with marigolds, violets, the crown-imperial (then so rare), daffodils, and lilies of all kinds.

In William Lawson's "A New Orchard and Gar-

THE KNOT-GARDEN, NEW PLACE, STRATFORD-UPON-AVON

den," which also appeared about the time of Shakespeare's death, the gardens of the period are perfectly described. Lawson was a practical gardener and had a poetic appreciation of flowers and trees. His book was long an authority. Every one had it. Lawson writes quaintly and delightfully:

"The Rose, red, damask, velvet and double-double, Provence rose, the sweet musk Rose double and single, the double and single white Rose, the fair and sweet-scenting Woodbine double and single and double-double, purple Cowslips and double-double Cowslips, Primrose double and single, the Violet nothing behind the best for smelling sweetly and a thousand more will provoke your content.

"And all these by the skill of your gardener, so comely and orderly placed in your borders and squares and so intermingled that none looking thereon cannot but wonder to see what Nature corrected by Art can do.

"When you behold in divers corners of your Orchard Mounts of stone, or wood, curiously wrought within and without, or of earth covered with fruit-trees: Kentish cherry, damsons, plums, etc., with stairs of precious workmanship; and in some corner a true Dial or Clock and some antique works and especially silver-sounding music—mixt

Instruments and Voices—gracing all the rest—how will you be rapt with delight!

"Large walks, broad and long, close and open, like the Tempe groves in Thessaly, raised with gravel and sand, having seats and banks of Camomile,—all this delights the mind and brings health to the body. Your borders on every side hanging and drooping with Raspberries, Barberries and Currants and the roots of your trees powdered with strawberries—red, white and green,—what a pleasure is this!

"Your gardener can frame your lesser wood (shrubs) to the shape of men armed in the field ready to give battle, or swift-running greyhounds, or of well-scented and true running hounds to chase the deer or hunt the hare. This kind of hunting shall not waste your corn nor much your coin.

"Mazes, well formed, a man's height, may, perhaps, make your friend wander in gathering of berries till he cannot recover himself without your help.

"To have occasion to exercise within your Orchard, it shall be a pleasure to have a Bowling-Alley.

"Rosemary and sweet Eglantine are seemly ornaments about a door, or window; so is Woodbine.

"One chief grace that adorns an Orchard I cannot let slip. A brood of nightingales, who with their
several notes and tunes with a strong, delightsome
voice out of a weak body, will bear you company,
night and day. She will help you cleanse your trees
of caterpillars and all noisome worms and flies. The
gentle Robin Redbreast will help her and in Winter
in the coldest storms will keep a part. Neither will
the silly Wren be behind in summer with her distinct whistle (like a sweet Recorder) [1] to cheer your
spirits. The Blackbird and Throstle (for I take it
the Thrush sings not but devours) sing loudly on a
May morning and delight the ear much (and you
need not want their company if you have ripe Cherries or Berries) and would gladly, as the rest, do you
pleasure. But I had rather want their company than
my fruit.

"What shall I say? A thousand of delights are
in an Orchard."

Parkinson endeavors in the kindliest way to help
the amateur. He is genuinely desirous to encour-
age gardening and offers his knowledge and experience with bounteous generosity. He has no preference regarding site. He says:

"According to the situations of men's dwellings,

[1] A kind of flute. See "Hamlet"; Act II, Scene II.

so are the situations of their gardens. And, although divers do diversely prefer their own several places which they have chosen, or wherein they dwell; as some those places that are near unto a river or brook to be best for the pleasantness of the water, the ease of transportation of themselves, their friends and goods, as also for the fertility of the soil, which is seldom near unto a river's side; and others extol the side or top of an hill, be it small or great, for the prospect's sake. And again, some the plain or champian ground for the even level thereof. Yet to show you for every of these situations which is the fittest place to plant your garden in and how to defend it from the injuries of the cold winds and frosts that may annoy it, I hope be well accepted.

"To prescribe one form for every man to follow were too great presumption and folly; for every man will please his own fancy, be it orbicular or round, triangular or three-square, quadrangular or four-square, or more long than broad. Let every man choose which him liketh best. The four-square form is the most usually accepted with all and doth best agree to any man's dwelling. To form it therefore with walks cross the middle both ways and round about it also with hedges, knots or trayles, or any other work within the four-square parts is according to every man's conceit. For there may be therein walls either open or close, either public or private, a maze or wilderness, a rock or mount with a fountain in the midst to convey water to every part of the garden either in pipes under the ground, or brought by hand and emptied into large cisterns or great Turkey jars placed in convenient places. Arbors also being both graceful and necessary may be appointed in such convenient places as the corners, or elsewhere, as may be most fit to serve both for shadow and rest after walking.

"To border the whole square to serve as a hedge thereunto everyone taketh what liketh him best, as either privet alone, or sweetbriar and whitethorn enlaced together and roses of one, or two, or more sorts, placed here and there amongst them. Some also take lavender, rosemary, sage, southernwood, lavender-cotton, or some such thing. Some again plant Cornell trees and plash them, or keep them low to form into a hedge. And some again take a low prickly shrub that abideth always green called in Latin *Pyracantha*, which in time will make an evergreen hedging, or border, and when it beareth fruit, which are red berries like unto hawthorn berries, make a glorious show among the green leaves in winter time when no other shrubs have fruit, or leaves."

For the borders of the knots, Parkinson recommends thrift, hyssop and germander, but "chiefly above all herbs the small low, or dwarf French or Dutch box, because it is evergreen, thick and easily cut and formed."

Roses, he says, should be planted in "the outer borders of the quarters, or in the middle of the long beds"; and lilies should be placed in a "small, round or square in a knot without any tall flowers growing about them."

IV

"Outlandish" and English Flowers

The flowers for the knots, or beds, Parkinson divides into two classes: the "Outlandish flowers" and the "English flowers."

Of the outlandish flowers first of all he mentions daffodils, of which there were "almost a hundred sorts, some either white, or yellow, or mixed, or else being small or great, single or double, and some having but one flower on a stalk; others, many." Other daffodils were so exceedingly sweet that a very few were sufficient to perfume a whole chamber: the "single English Bastard daffodil, which groweth wild in many woods, groves and orchards in England; the double English Bastard, the French single white, the French double yellow, the Spanish yellow Bastard, the great or little Spanish white, and the Turkie single white Daffodil are some of the varieties Parkinson mentions. Then of the *Fritillaria* or the "checkerd Daffodil" Parkinson gives "half a score, several sorts, both white and red, both yellow and black, which are a wonderful grace and ornament in a garden in regard of the checker-like spots in the flower."

Hyacinths in Parkinson's book are about "half a hundred sorts: some like unto little bells or stars, others like unto little bottles or pearls, both white and blue, sky colored and blush, and some star-like of many pretty various forms and all to give delight to them that will be curious to observe them."

Shakespeare does not mention hyacinths.

Of crocus, or saffron flowers, there were twenty sorts, some flowering in the spring, others in the autumn, but all of "glorious beauty."

Of lilies there were "twenty several sorts and colors," among which the Crown Imperial, "for her stately form deserveth some special place in the garden, as also the Martagons, both white and red, both blush and yellow, that require to be set by themselves apart."

Tulips (which are never mentioned by Shakespeare) were so many and various that Parkinson considered it beyond his ability to describe them all "for there is such a wonderful variety and mixture of colors that it is almost impossible for the wit of man to decipher them and to give names," and he added that "for every one that he might name ten others would probably spring up somewhere" and "besides this glory of variety in colors that these flowers have, they carry so stately and delightful a form and do abide so long in their bravery, there is no lady or gentlewoman of any worth that is not caught with this delight, or not delighted with these flowers."

Then the anemones, or windflowers, "so full of variety, so dainty, so pleasant and so delightsome, so plentiful in bearing and durable," he tells us were great favorites.

Then the bear's-ears,[1] or French cowslips, each one "seeming to be a nosegay of itself alone" and of so many colors as "white, yellow, blush, purple, red, tawny, murray, hair color and so on" and "not

[1] *Auriculas.*

unfurnished with a pretty sweet scent, which doth add an increase of pleasure in those that make them an ornament for wearing."

Flower-de-luces also of many sorts, one kind "being the Orris roots that are sold at the Apothecaries whereof sweet powders are made to lie among garments" and "the greater Flag kind frequent enough in this land" and which "well doth serve to deck up both garden and house with Nature's beauties."

Chief of all was "Your Sable Flower, so fit for a mourning habit that I think in the whole compass of Nature's store there is not a more pathetical."

The hepatica, or noble liverwort, white, red, blue, or purple, somewhat resembling violets; the cyclamen, or sow-bread, a "flower of rare receipt with flowers like unto red, or blush-colored violets and leaves having no small delight in their pleasant color, being spotted and circled white upon green"; the *Leucoinum*, or bulbous violet; *Muscari*, or musk grape flower; star-flowers of different sorts; *Phalangium*, or spiderwort; winter crowfoot, or wolfsbane; the Christmas flower, "like unto a single white rose"; bell-flowers of many kinds; yellow larkspur,[1]

[1] Nasturtium.

"the prettiest flower of a score in the garden; flower gentle, or Floramour; Flower-of-the-Sun;[1] the Marvel of Peru, or of the World; double marsh marigold, or double yellow buttons; double French marigolds; and the double red *Ranunculus*, or crowfoot, "for exceeding the most glorious double anemone," completes Parkinson's list for flowers to be planted in the beds. The jasmine, white and yellow; the double honeysuckle and the lady's-bower (clematis), both white, and red and purple, single and double are "the fittest of Outlandish plants to set by arbors and banqueting-houses[2] that are open both before and above, to help to cover them and to give sight, smell and delight."

Parkinson has not quite finished, however, with the outlandish flowers for he calls attention to the cherry bay, or *Laurocerasus*, saying that "the Rose Bay, or Oleander, and the white and blue Syringa, or Pipe Tree,[3] are all graceful and delightful to set at several distances in the borders of knots, for some of them give beautiful and sweet flowers."

Furthermore Parkinson writes that "the Pyra-

[1] Sunflower.
[2] The banqueting-house does not signify a place for great entertainments. It was a simple summer-house, or arbor, to which people repaired after dinner to eat the dessert, then called "banquet."
[3] Lilac-tree.

cantha, or Prickly Coral Tree, doth remain with green leaves all the year and may be plashed, or laid down, or tyed to make up a fine hedge to border the whole knot" and that "the Dwarf Bay, or Mezereon, is most commonly either placed in the middle of a knot, or at the corners thereof, and sometimes all along a walk for the more grace."

So much for the "outlandish" flowers!

Turning now to the "English flowers," we find that Parkinson includes primroses and cowslips, single rose campions, white, red, and blush and the double red campion and the Flower of Bristow, or Nonesuch, "a kind of Campion, white and blush as well as orange-color." And here Parkinson stops a moment to talk about this Nonesuch, for he was so fond of it that he holds it in his hand in the portrait that appears as a frontispiece to his "Paradisus" and from which our reproduction is made. Of it he writes: "The orange color Nonesuch with double flowers as is rare and not common so for his bravery doth well deserve a Master of account that will take care to keep and preserve it."

Then he continues: Bachelors'-buttons, both white and red; wall-flowers, double and single; stock-gilliflowers, queen's gilliflowers (which some call dame's violets and some winter gilliflowers, a kind of stock-gilliflower); violets, "the spring's chief flowers for beauty, smell and use," both single and double; snap-dragons, "flowers of much more delight"; columbines, "single and double, of many sorts, fashions and colors, very variable, both speckled and parti-colored—no garden would willingly be without them." Next "Larks' heels, or spurs, or toes, as they are called, single and double"; pansies, or heartsease, of divers colors, "although without scent yet not without some respect and delight"; double poppies "adorning a garden with their variable colors to the delight of the beholders"; double daisies, "white and red, blush and speckled and parti-colored, besides that which is called Jack-an-Apes-on-Horseback," double marigolds; French marigolds "that have a strong, heady scent, both single and double, whose glorious show for color would cause any to believe there were some rare goodness or virtue in them; and carnations and gilliflowers."

Here again Parkinson's enthusiasm causes him to pause, for he exclaims:

"But what shall I say to the Queen of Delight and of Flowers, Carnations and Gilliflowers, whose bravery, variety and sweet smell joined together tieth every one's affection with great earnestness both to like and to have them?"

Of the overwhelming number he singles out the red and gray Hulo, the old carnation, the Grand Père; the Cambersive, the Savadge, the Chrystal, the Prince, the white carnation or delicate, the ground carnation, the French carnation, the Dover, the Oxford, the Bristow, the Westminster, the Daintie, the Granado, and the orange tawny gilliflower and its derivatives, the Infanta, the striped tawny, the speckled tawny, the flaked tawny, the Grifeld tawny, and many others.

Many sweet pinks are included, "all very sweet coming near the Gilliflowers, Sweet Williams and Sweet Johns," both single and double, red and spotted, "and a kind of wild pinks, which for their beauty and grace help to furnish a garden." Then, too, we have peonies, double and single; hollyhocks, single and double; and roses.

The Elizabethan gardens, therefore, presented a magnificent array of flowers; and it was not only in the grand gardens of castles and manor-houses, but in the estates of London merchants along the Strand and of the florists in Holborn, Westminster, and elsewhere that fine flower shows were to be enjoyed during every month of the year. In the country before the simple dwellings and the half-timbered and thatched cottages bright flowers blossomed in the same beauty and profusion as to-day.

The charming cottage garden has changed little.

Finally, in summing up, if we imagine as a background a group of Tudor buildings in the Perpendicular style of architecture of red brick broken with bay-windows and groups of quaint chimneys variously ornamented with zigzag and other curious lines, gables here and there—the whole façade rising above a terrace with broad flights of steps—one at the middle and one at each end—and from the terrace "forthrights" and paths intersecting and in the squares formed by them bright beds of flowers so arranged that the colors intermingle and blend so as to produce the effect of a rich mosaic and redolent with the sweetest perfumes all mingled with particular and peculiar care and art, we shall have a mental picture of the kind of garden that lay before *Olivia's* house in "Twelfth Night," where *Malvolio* parades up and down the "forthrights," as Shakespeare distinctly tells us, in his yellow cross-garters, to pick up the letter dropped on the path by *Maria* while the rollicking *Sir Toby Belch*, witless *Sir Andrew Aguecheek*, and merry *Maria* watch his antics from their hiding-place in the box-tree, or hedge.

Such also was the garden at Belmont, *Portia's* stately home, in which *Lorenzo* and *Jessica*, while waiting for their mistress on that moonlight night "when the sweet wind did gently kiss the trees and they did make no noise," voiced their ravishing duet, "On Such a Night."

Such also was the garden into which *Romeo* leaped over the high wall to sing before *Juliet's* window a song that in her opinion was far sweeter than that of the nightingale that nightly sang in the pomegranate-tree by her balcony.

If, on the other hand, we wish to visualize *Perdita's* garden—that of a simple shepherdess—we must imagine a tiny cottage enclosure gay and bright with blooms of many hues, arranged in simple beds neatly bordered with box or thrift, but where there are no terraces, forthrights, or ornamental vases, urns or fountains. This little cottage garden is the kind that brightened the approach to Anne Hathaway's house at Shottery and Shakespeare's own dwelling at Stratford.

This is a descendant, as we have seen, of the little Garden of Delight, the Pleasance of the Medieval castle. The simple cottage garden is the easier of the two to reproduce to-day. Although it only occupies a small corner in the garden proper, yet *all* the flowers mentioned by Shakespeare can be grown in it.

In rural England it is not rare to come across old gardens that owed their existence to disciples of Didymus Mountain, Markham, Lawson, and Parkinson—gardens that have been tended for three hundred years and more with loving care, where the blossoms are descendants of "outlandish" importations of Nicholas Leate and Lord Burleigh, and of simple English flowers. These gladden the eyes of their owners to-day as the original flowers gladdened the eyes of those who planted them. Generations of people in the house and generations of flowers in the garden thus flourished and faded side by side while the old stock put forth new blossoms in both house and garden to continue the family traditions of both the human and the floral world.

A typical garden dating from Shakespearean times was thus described a few years ago in "The Gentleman's Magazine":

"In all England one could, perhaps, find no lovelier garden than that of T——, an old manorhouse, sheltered by hill and bounded by the moat, which is the only relic of the former feudal castle.

HERBACEOUS BORDER, NEW PLACE, STRATFORD-UPON-AVON

The tiled roof, the gables inlaid with oaken beams, are almost hidden by fragrant roses and jasmine flowers that shine like stars against their darker foliage. A sun-dial stands in the square of lawn before the porch, and the windows to your right open upon a yew-hedged bowling-green. Beyond, the smooth lawn slopes down to a little stream, thick with water-loving reeds and yellow flags; and lime-trees, whose fragrance the breeze wafts to us, sweep the greensward in magnificent curves. If you turn to the left, along yonder grassy path you will find yourself between borders gorgeous with poppies and sweet william and hollyhocks and lilies that frame distances of blue hills and clear sky.

"The kitchen-garden lies through that gate in the wall of mellowed brick—an old-fashioned kitchen-garden, with mingled fruit and vegetables and flowers. There are pear and plum-trees against the wall and strawberry beds next the feathery asparagus and gooseberry bushes hidden by hedges of sweet peas. Another turn will bring you into a labyrinth of yew hedges and so back to the bowling-green, across which the long shadows lie, and the sun-dial which marks the approach of evening. The light is golden on the house and on the tangled borders; the air is fragrant with many scents."

PART TWO

THE FLOWERS OF SHAKESPEARE

Spring

"THE SWEET O' THE YEAR"

I

Primroses, Cowslips, and Oxlips

PRIMROSE (*Primula vulgaris*). **English** poets have always regarded the primrose as the first flower of spring—the true *Flor di prima vera.* This name calls to mind Botticelli's enchanting *Primevera* that hangs in the Uffizi, in which the sward is dotted with spring flowers that seem to have burst into blossom beneath the footsteps of Venus and her three Graces—those lovely ladies of the Italian Renaissance, clad in light, fluttering draperies. This decorative picture expresses not only the joy and beauty of newly-awakened spring, but something much deeper, something that the painter did not realize himself; and this was what the Italian Renaissance was destined to mean to all the world: a New Birth of beauty in the arts and a new era of human sympathy for mankind.

Sandro Botticelli, whom we may appropriately call *Flor di prima vera* among painters, was as unaware of his mission in art as the primroses that come into being at the call of a new day of spring sunshine from a long dark winter's sleep in a soil of frozen stiffness. Something of the tender and wistful beauty of early spring—her faint dreams and soft twilights, her languid afternoons and her veiled nights, when pale stars tremble through gray mists and when warm rains softly kiss the drowsy earth—Botticelli has put into his enchanting spring idyl; and this same wistful, half-drowsy, and evanescent beauty is characteristic of the primrose.

> Primrose, first born child of Ver,
> Merry Springtime's harbinger,
> With her bells dim

is a perfect and sympathetic description of the flower in "The Two Noble Kinsmen." [1]

Observe that the bells of the primrose are "dim" —pale in hue—because the earth is not sufficiently awake for bright colors or for joyful chimes—so the color is faint and the sound is delicate. Trees are now timidly putting forth tender leaves, buds

[1] Act I, Scene I.

peer cautiously from the soil, and few birds sing;
for leaves, buds, and birds know full well that winter is lurking in the distance and that rough winds
occasionally issue from the bag of Boreas. The
time has not yet come for "lisp of leaves and ripple
of rain" and for choirs of feathered songsters. Yet
all the more, because of its bold daring and its
modest demeanor, the primrose deserves the enthusiastic welcome it has always received from poets
and flower lovers.

"The primrose," writes Dr. Forbes Watson,
"seems the very flower of delicacy and refinement;
not that it shrinks from our notice, for few plants are
more easily seen, coming as it does when there is a
dearth of flowers, when the first birds are singing
and the first bees humming and the earliest green
putting forth in the March and April woods. And
it is one of those plants which dislikes to be looking
cheerless, but keeps up a smouldering fire of blossom
from the very opening of the year, if the weather
will permit.

"The flower is of a most unusual color, a pale,
delicate yellow, slightly tinged with green. And the
better flowers impress us by a peculiar paleness, not
dependent upon any feebleness of hue, which we
always find unpleasing, but rather upon the *exquisite*

softness of their tone. And we must not overlook
the little round stigma, that green and translucent
gem, which forms the pupil of the eye, and is surrounded by a deeper circle of orange which helps it
to shine forth more clearly. Many flowers have a
somewhat pensive look; but in the pensiveness of
the primrose there is a shade of melancholy—a
melancholy which awakens no thought of sadness
and does but give interest to the pale, sweet, inquir-
ing faces which the plant upturns towards us.

"In the primrose, as a whole, we cannot help
being struck by an exceeding softness and delicacy;
there is nothing sharp, strong, or incisive; the smell
is 'the faintest and most ethereal perfume,' as Mrs.
Stowe has called it in her 'Sunny Memories,' though
she was mistaken in saying that it disappears when
we pluck the flower. It is meant to impress us as
altogether soft and yielding. One of the most beautiful points in the primrose is the manner in which
the paleness of the flowers is taken up by the herbage.
This paleness seems to hang about the plant like a
mystery, for though the leaves of the primrose may
at times show a trace of the steady paleness of the
cowslip, it is more usually confined to their undersurfaces and the white flower-stalks with their clothing of down. And when we are looking at the prim-

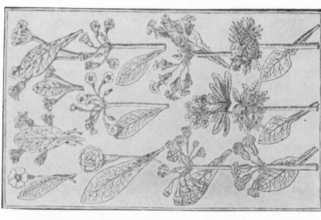

CARNATIONS AND GILLIFLOWERS; PRIMROSES AND COWSLIPS; AND DAFFODILS: FROM PARKINSON

rose one or other of these downy, changeful portions is continually coming into view, so that we get a feeling as if there hung about the whole plant a clothing of soft, evanescent mist, thickening about the center of the plant and the undersurfaces of the leaves which are less exposed to the sun. And then we reach one of the main expressions of the primrose. When we look at the pale, sweet flowers, and the soft-toned green of the herbage, softened further here and there by that uncertain mist of down, the dryness of the leaf and fur enters forcibly into our impression of the plant, giving a sense of extreme delicacy and need of shelter, as if it were some gentle creature which shrinks from exposure to the weather."

The Greeks associated the idea of melancholy with this flower. They had a story of a handsome youth, son of Flora and Priapus, whose betrothed bride died. His grief was so excessive that he died, too, and the gods than changed his body into a primrose.

In Shakespeare's time, the primrose was also associated with early death; and it is one of the flowers thrown upon the corse of *Fidele*, whose lovely, wistful face is compared to the "pale primrose." Thus *Arviragus* exclaims as he gazes on the beautiful youth, *Fidele*, the assumed name of *Imogen* in disguise:

> I 'll sweeten thy sad grave: thou shalt not lack
> The flower that 's like thy face, pale primrose.[1]

Perdita, in "The Winter's Tale," [2] mentions

> Pale primroses that die unmarried
> Ere they can behold bright Phœbus in his strength.

Shakespeare appreciated the delicate hue and perfume of this flower. He seems to be alluding to both qualities when he makes *Hermia* touch *Helena's* memory by the following words:

> And in the wood, where often you and I
> Upon faint primrose beds were wont to lie.[3]

Other English poets speak of the flower as "the pale," or "the dim." Milton writes:

> Now the bright star, day's harbinger
> Comes dancing from the East and leads with her
> The flow'ry May, who, from her green lap, throws
> The yellow cowslip and the pale primrose.

And again, Thomas Carew:

> Ask me why I send you here
> The firstling of the infant year?

[1] "Cymbeline"; Act IV, Scene II.
[2] Act IV, Scene III.
[3] "A Midsummer Night's Dream"; Act I, Scene I.

Ask me why I send to you
This Primrose, all bepearled with dew?
I straight whisper in your ears:
The sweets of Love are wash'd with tears

Ask me why this flower doth show
So yellow, green and sickly, too?
Ask me why the stalk is weak
And, bending, yet it doth not break?
I will answer: these discover
What doubts and fears are in a lover.

The English primrose is one of a large family of more than fifty species, represented by the primrose, the cowslip, and the oxlip. All members of this family are noted for their simple beauty and their peculiar charm.

Parkinson writes:

"We have so great variety of Primroses and Cowslips in our country breeding that strangers, being much delighted with them, have often furnished into divers countries to their good content.

"All Primroses bear their long and large, broad yellowish-green leaves without stalks most usually, and all the Cowslips have small stalks under the leaves, which are smaller and of a darker green. The name of *Primula veris*, or Primrose, is indifferently conferred on those that I distinguish for *Paralyses*, or Cowslips. All these plants are called most usually in Latin *Primulæ veris*, *Primulæ pretenses* and *Primulæ silvarum*, because they shew by their flowering the new Spring to be coming on, they being, as it were, the first Embassadors thereof. They have also divers other names, as *Herba Paralysis*, *Arthritica*, *Herba Sancti Petri*, *Claues Sancti Petri*, *Verbasculum odoratum*, *Lunaria arthritica*, *Phlomis*, *Alisma silvarum* and *Alismatis alterum genus*. Some have distinguished them by calling the Cowslips *Primula Veris Elatior*, that is the Taller Primrose, and the other *Humilis*, Low, or Dwarf, Primrose.

"Primroses and Cowslips are in a manner wholly used in Cephalicall diseases to ease pains in the head. They are profitable both for the Palsy and pains of the joints, even as the Bears' Ears[1] are, which hath caused the names of *Arthritica Paralysis* and *Paralytica* to be given them."

Tusser in his "Husbandry" includes the primrose among the seeds and herbs of the kitchen; and Lyte says that "the cowslips, primroses and oxlips are now used daily amongst other pot-herbs, but in physic there is no great account made of them." "The old name was Primerolles," Dr. Prior notes in his quaint book on flowers. "Primerole as an

[1] Auriculas.

outlandish, unintelligible word was soon familiar-
ized into Primerolles and this into Primrose." The
name was also written primrolles and finally settled
down into primrose. Chaucer wrote primerole, a
name derived from the French *Primeverole*, meaning, like the Italian *Flor di prima vera*, the first
spring flower.

COWSLIP (*Paralysis vulgaris pratensis*). The
cowslip is an ingratiating little flower, not so aloof
as its cousin the primrose, and not at all melancholy.
In the popular lore of Shakespeare's time the cowslip was associated with fairies. In many places it
was known as "fairy cups." For this reason Shakespeare makes *Ariel* lie in a cowslip's bell when the
fay is frightened by the hooting of owls, or tired of
swinging merrily in "the blossom that hangs on the
bough." One of the duties of *Titania's* little maid
of honor was "to hang a pearl in every cowslip's
ear"; and this gay little fairy informs *Puck* of the
important place cowslips hold in the court of the
tiny *Queen Titania:*

> The cowslips tall her pensioners be,
> In their gold coats spots you see:
> These be rubies, fairy favors,
> In these freckles live their savors.[1]

[1] "A Midsummer Night's Dream"; Act II, Scene I.

To appreciate the meaning of this comparison, it must be remembered that the "pensioners" of Queen Elizabeth's court were a guard of the tallest and handsomest men to be found in the whole kingdom, men, moreover, who were in the pride of youth, and scions of the most distinguished families. Their dress was of extraordinary elegance and enriched heavily with gold embroidery. Hence, "gold coats" for the cowslips. Here and there jewels sparkled and glistened on the pensioners' coats. Hence rubies—fairy favors—favors from the Queen! The pensioners also wore pearls in their ears, like Raleigh and Leicester and other noblemen. Hence the fairy had to "hang a pearl in every cowslip's ear." An idea, too, of the size of *Titania* and her elves is given when the cowslips are considered "tall," and tall enough to be the body-guard of *Queen Titania*. This was a pretty little allusion to Queen Elizabeth and her court, which the audience that gathered to see the first representation of "A Midsummer Night's Dream" did not fail to catch.

We get a sidelight on the importance of the pensioners in "The Merry Wives of Windsor" [1] when *Dame Quickly* tells *Falstaff* a great cock-and-bull story about the visitors who have called on *Mistress.*

[1] Act II, Scene II.

Ford. "There have been knights and lords and gentlemen with their coaches, letter after letter, gift after gift; smelling so sweetly (all musk) and so rushling, I warrant you in silk and gold; and yet there has been earls, and, what is more, *pensioners!*" Shakespeare also speaks of "the freckled cowslip" in "Henry V," [1] when the *Duke of Burgundy* refers to

> The even mead, that erst brought sweetly forth
> The freckled cowslip.

All poets love the flower.

> In the language wherewith spring
> Letters cowslips on the hill,

writes Tennyson—a charming fancy!

Sydney Dobell has a quaint flower song containing this verse:

> Then came the cowslip
> Like a dancer in the fair,
> She spread her little mat of green
> And on it dancèd she,
> With a fillet bound about her brow,
> A fillet round her happy brow,
> A golden fillet round her brow,
> And rubies in her hair.

Never mind if country dancers rarely wear rubies; the idea is pretty and on Shakespeare's authority

[1] Act V, Scene II.

we know that rubies do gleam in the cup of the cowslip, as he has told us through the lips of the fairy.

With great appreciation of the beauty of the
flower he has *Jachimo's* description:

> Cinque-spotted like the crimson drops
> In the bottom of a cowslip.[1]

Most sympathetically did Dr. Forbes Watson,
when lying on a bed of fatal illness, put into words
what many persons have felt regarding this flower:
"Few of our wild flowers give intenser pleasure
than the cowslip, yet perhaps there is scarcely any
whose peculiar beauty depends so much upon locality
and surroundings. There is a homely simplicity
about the cowslip, much like that of the daisy,
though more pensive,—the quiet, sober look of an
unpretending country girl, not strikingly beautiful
in feature or attire, but clean and fresh as if new
bathed in milk and carrying us away to thoughts of
daisies, flocks and pasturage and the manners of a
simple, primitive time, some golden age of shepherd-
life long since gone by. And more; in looking at
the cowslip we are always most forcibly struck by
its apparent wholesomeness and health. This wholesomeness is quite unmistakable. It belongs even to

[1] "Cymbeline"; Act II, Scene II.

the smell so widely different from the often oppres-
sive perfume of other plants, as lilies, narcissuses,
or violets. Now just such a healthy milk-fed look,
just such a sweet, healthy odor is what we find in
cows—an odor which breathes around them as they
sit at rest in the pasture. The 'lips,' of course, is
but a general resemblance to the shape of the petals
and suggests the source of the fragrance. The cowslip, as we have said, is a singularly healthy-looking
plant, indeed, nothing about it is more remarkable.
It has none of the delicacy and timidity of the primrose. All its characters are well and healthily pro-
nounced. The paleness is uniform, steady, and
rather impresses us as whiteness; and the yellow of
the cup is as rich as gold. The odor is not faint, but
saccharine and luscious. It does not shrink into the
sheltered covert, but courts the free air and sunshine of the open fields; and instead of its flowers
peeping timidly from behind surrounding leaves, it
raises them boldly on a stout, sufficient stalk, the
most conspicuous object in the meadow. Its poetry
is the poetry of common life, but of the most delicious common life that can exist. The plant is in
some respects careless to the verge of disorder; and
you should note that carelessness well, till you feel
the force of it, as especially in the lame imperfec-

tion of the flower buds, only, perhaps half of them well developed and the rest dangling all of unequal lengths.   Essentially the cowslip and the primrose are only the same plant in two different forms, the one being convertible into the other.   The primrose is the cowslip of the woods and sheltered lanes; the cowslip is the primrose of the fields."

The name cowslip is not derived from the lips of the cow, but, according to Skeat, the great Anglo-Saxon authority, it comes from an Anglo-Saxon word meaning dung and was given to the plant because it springs up in meadows where cows are pastured.

"The common field Cowslip," says Parkinson, "I might well forbear to set down, being so plentiful in the fields; but because many take delight in it and plant it in their gardens, I will give you the description of it here.   It hath divers green leaves, very like unto the wild Primrose, but shorter, rounder, stiffer, rougher, more crumpled about the edges and of a sadder green color, every one standing upon his stalk which is an inch or two long Among the leaves rise up divers long stalks, a foot or more high, bearing at the top many fair, yellow, single flowers with spots of a deep yellow at the bottom of each leaf, smelling very sweet.

"In England they have divers names according

to several countries, as Primroses, Cowslips, Oxlips, Palsieworts and Petty Mullins. The Frantic Fantastic, or Foolish, Cowslip in some places is called by country people Jack-an-Apes-on-Horseback, which is a usual name given by them to many other plants, as Daisies, Marigolds, etc., if they be strange or fantastical, differing in form from the ordinary kind of the single ones. The smallest are usually called through all the North Country Birds' Eyen, because of the small yellow circle in the bottoms of the flowers resembling the eye of a bird."

OXLIP (*Primula eliator*). The oxlip combines the qualities of primrose and cowslip. "These two plants," writes a botanist, "appear as divergent expressions of a simple type, the cowslip being a contracted form of primrose, the sulphur yellow and the fine tawny, watery rays of the latter brightened into well defined orange spots. In the oxlip these characters anastomose."

Thus, partaking of the character of primrose and cowslip, the oxlip is considered by some authorities a hybrid. "The oxlip and the polyanthus," says Dr. Forbes Watson, "with its tortoiseshell blossoms, are two of the immediate forms; the polyanthus being a great triumph of the gardener's art, a delightful flower, quite a new creation and originally

produced by cultivation of the primrose." In England the oxlip is found in woods, fields, meadows,
and under hedges. Though a spring flower it lingers
into summer and is found in company with the nodding violet, wild thyme, and luscious eglantine on
the bank where *Titania* loved to sleep lulled to rest
by song.[1] *Perdita* speaks of "bold oxlips" ("The
Winter's Tale," Act iv, Scene iii); and compared
with the primrose and cowslip the flower deserves
the adjective.

"Oxlips in their cradles growing," in the song in
"The Two Noble Kinsmen," [2] which Shakespeare
wrote with John Fletcher, shows great knowledge
of the plant, for the root-leaves of the oxlip are
shaped like a cradle.

Parkinson writes: "Those are usually called oxlips whose flowers are naked, or bare, without husks
to contain them, being not so sweet as the cowslip,
yet have they some little scent, although the Latin
name doth make them to have none."

[1] "A Midsummer Night's Dream"; Act II, Scene II.
[2] Act I, Scene I.

II

"Daffodils that Come Before the Swallow Dares"

DAFFODIL (*Narcissus pseudo-narcissus*).

> When daffodils begin to peer,
>> With heigh! the doxy over the dale,
> Why then comes in the sweet o' the year;
>> For the red blood reigns in the winter's pale.

Is the opening verse that *Autolycus* sings so gaily in "The Winter's Tale." [1] The daffodil was "carefully nourished up" in Elizabethan gardens, as the saying went. Before Shakespeare's time a great number of daffodils had been introduced into England from various parts of the Continent. Gerard describes twenty-four different species, "all and every one of them in great abundance in our London gardens."

There were many varieties both rare and ordinary. Parkinson particularly distinguishes the true daffodils, or *narcissus*, from the "Bastard Daffodils," or *pseudo narcissus;* and he gives their differences as follows:

"It consisteth only in the flower and chiefly in the middle cup, or chalice; for that we do, in a

[1] Act IV, Scene II.

manner only, account those to be *Pseudo Narcissus*, Bastard Daffodils, whose middle cup is altogether as long, and sometimes a little longer than, the outer leaves that do encompass it, so that it seemeth rather like a trunk, or a long nose, than a cup or chalice, such as almost all the *Narcissi*, or true Daffodils, have. Of the Bastard tribe Parkinson gives the great yellow Spanish Daffodil; the Mountain Bastard of divers kinds; the early straw-colored; the great white Spanish; the greatest Spanish white; the two lesser white Spanish; our common English wild Bastard Daffodil; the six-cornered; the great double yellow, or John Tradescant's great Rose Daffodil; Mr. Wilmer's great double Daffodil; the great double yellow Spanish, or Parkinson's Daffodil; the great double French Bastard; the double English Bastard, or Gerard's double Daffodil; the great white Bastard Rush Daffodil, or Junquilia; the greater yellow Junquilia; and many others."

Then he adds:

"The *Pseudo narcissus Angliens vulgaris* is so common in all England, both in copses, woods and orchards, that I might well forbear the description thereof. It hath three, or four, grayish leaves, long and somewhat narrow, among which riseth up the stalk about a span high, or little higher, bearing at the top, out of a skinny husk (as all other Daffodils have), one flower, somewhat large, having the six leaves that stand like wings, of a pale yellow color, and the long trunk in the middle of a faire yellow with the edges, or brims, a little crumpled, or uneven. After the flower is past, it beareth a round head, seeming three square, containing round black seed."

Shakespeare knew all of these varieties very well and had many of them in mind when he wrote the beautiful lines for *Perdita*, who exclaims:

> O Proserpina!
> For the flowers now that, frighted, thou lettst fall
> From Dis's wagon. Daffodils
> That come before the swallow dares, and take
> The winds of March with beauty.[1]

Much has been written about this description of the daffodils; and it is generally thought that "to take the winds of March with beauty" means to charm, or captivate, the wild winds with their loveliness. I do not agree with this idea, and venture to suggest that as the daffodils sway and swing in the boisterous March winds with such infinite grace and beauty, bending this way and that, they "take the winds with beauty," just as a graceful dancer

[1] "The Winter's Tale"; Act IV, Scene III.

is said to take the rhythmic steps of the dance with charming manner.

We get a hint for this also in Wordsworth's poem:

I wandered lonely as a cloud
    That floats on high o'er vales and hills,
When all at once I saw a crowd,
    A host of yellow daffodils;
Beside the lake, beneath the trees,
Fluttering and dancing in the breeze.

Continuous as the stars that shine
    And twinkle on the Milky-Way
They stretched in never-ending line
    Along the margin of the bay:
Ten thousand saw I at a glance,
Tossing their heads in sprightly dance.

The waves beside them danced, but they
    Outdid the sparkling waves in glee;
A poet would not be but gay
    In such a jocund company:
I gazed—and gazed—but little thought
What wealth the show to me had brought

For oft when on my couch I lie
    In vacant, or in pensive, mood,
They flash upon that inward eye
    Which is the bliss of solitude;
And then my heart with pleasure fills
And dances with the daffodils.

No one can read this poem without feeling that the dancing daffodils "take the winds of March with

GARDENERS AT WORK, SIXTEENTH CENTURY

GARDEN PLEASURES, SIXTEENTH CENTURY

beauty." The very name of the daffodil touches our imagination. It carries us to the Elysian Fields, for the ancient Greeks pictured the meads of the blessed as beautifully golden and deliciously fragrant with asphodels. The changes ring through asphodel, affodile, affodyl, finally reaching daffodil. Then there is one more quaint and familiar name and personification,

> Daffy-down-dilly that came up to town
> In a white petticoat and a green gown.

The idea of daffodil as a rustic maiden was popular in folk-lore and poetry. The feeling is so well expressed in Michael Drayton's sprightly eclogue called "Daffodil" that it forms a natural complement to the happy song of care-free *Autolycus* just quoted. This Pastoral captured popular fancy; and it is just as fresh and buoyant as it was when it was written three hundred years ago. Two shepherds, *Batte* and *Gorbo*, meet:

> ### BATTE
> Gorbo, as thou camst this way,
> By yonder little hill,
> Or, as thou through the fields didst stray,
> Sawst thou my Daffodil?
>
> She's in a frock of Lincoln green,
> Which color likes the sight;

And never hath her beauty seen
  But through a veil of white.

GORBO

Thou well describst the daffodil;
  It is not full an hour
Since by the spring, near yonder hill,
  I saw that lovely flower.

BATTE

Yet my fair flower thou didst not meet,
  No news of her didst bring;
And yet my Daffodil's more sweet
  Than that by yonder spring.

GORBO

I saw a shepherd that doth keep
  In yonder field of lilies
Was making (as he fed his sheep)
  A wreath of daffodillies.

BATTE

Yet, Gorbo, thou deludst me still,
  My flower thou didst not see;
For know my pretty Daffodil
  Is worn of none but me.

To show itself but near her feet
  No lily is so bold,
Except to shade her from the heat,
  Or keep her from the cold.

GORBO

Through yonder vale as I did pass
  Descending from the hill,

I met a smirking bonny lass;
    They call her Daffodil,

Whose presence as along she went
    The pretty flowers did greet,
As though their heads they downward bent
    With homage to her feet,

And all the shepherds that were nigh
    From top of every hill
Unto the valleys loud did cry:
    There goes sweet Daffodil!

BATTE

Ay, gentle shepherd, now with joy
    Thou see my flocks doth fill;
That's she alone, kind shepherd boy,
    Let's us to Daffodil!

The flower was also called jonquil, saffron lily, Lent lily and narcissus. It was the large yellow narcissus, known as the Rose of Sharon, so common in Palestine, of which Mohammed said: "He that hath two cakes of bread, let him sell one of them for a flower of the narcissus; for bread is the food of the body, but narcissus is the food of the soul."

Narcissus, the most beautiful youth of Bœotia, was told that he would live happily until he saw his own face. Loved by the nymphs, and particularly Echo, he rejected their advances for he was immune to love and admiration. One day, however, he beheld himself in a stream and became so fascinated with his reflection that he pined to death gazing at his own image.

> For him the Naiads and the Dryads mourn,
> Whom the sad Echo answers in her turn,
> And now the sister nymphs prepare his urn;
> When looking for his corpse, they only found
> A rising stalk with yellow blossoms crowned.

In the center of the cup are to be found the tears of Narcissus!

Because the flower was consecrated to Ceres and to the Underworld and to the Elysian Fields, the daffodil was one of the flowers that Proserpine was gathering when "dusky Dis" carried her off—and the myth also hints that the Earth purposely brought the asphodel forth from the Underworld to entice the unsuspecting daughter of Ceres. Sophocles associates the daffodil with the garlands of great goddesses: "And ever, day by day, the narcissus with its beauteous clusters, the ancient coronet of the mighty goddesses, bursts into bloom by heaven's dew." [1]

The delightful Dr. Forbes Watson writes of the daffodil like a painter, with accurate observation and bright palette:

[1] *Œdipus Coloneus.*

GARDEN IN MACBETH'S CASTLE OF CAWDOR

"In the daffodil the leaves and stems are of a full glaucous green, a color not only cool and refreshing in itself, but strongly suggestive of water, the most apparent source of freshness and constituting a most delicious groundwork for the bright, lively yellow of the blossoms. Now what sort of spathe would be likely to contribute best to this remarkable effect of the flower? Should the colors be unusually striking or the size increased, or what? Strange to say, in both Daffodil and Pheasant's Eye (Poet's Narcissus) we find the spathe dry and withered, shrivelled up like a bit of thin brown paper and clinging round the base of the flowers. We cannot overlook it, and most assuredly we were never meant to do so. Nothing could have been more beautifully ordered than this contrast, there being just sufficient to make us appreciate more fully that abounding freshness of life.

"It is a plant which affords a most beautiful contrast, a cool, watery sheet of leaves with bright, warm flowers, yellow and orange, dancing over the leaves like meteors over a marsh. The leaves look full of watery sap, which is the life blood of plants and prime source of all their freshness, just as the tissues of a healthy child look plump and rosy from the warm blood circulating within.

"In its general expression the Poet's Narcissus seems a type of maiden purity and beauty, yet warmed by a love-breathing fragrance; and yet what innocence in the large soft eye which few can rival among the whole tribe of flowers. The narrow, yet vivid fringe of red so clearly seen amidst the whiteness suggests again the idea of purity and gushing passion—purity with a heart which can kindle into fire."

III

"Daisies Pied and Violets Blue"

DAISY (*Bellis perennis*). Shakespeare often mentions the daisy. With "violets blue" "ladysmocks all silver-white," and "cuckoo-buds of every hue," it "paints the meadows with delight" in that delightful spring-song in "Love's Labour 's Lost." [1] Shakespeare also uses this flower as a beautiful comparison for the delicate hand of *Lucrece* in "The Rape of Lucrece": [2]

> Without the bed her other fair hand was
> On the green coverlet; whose perfect white
> Showed like an April daisy on the grass.

[1] Act V, Scene II.
[2] Stanza 57.

The daisy is among the flowers in the fantastic garlands that poor *Ophelia* wove before her death.[1]

The botanical name *Bellis* shows the origin of the flower. Belides, a beautiful Dryad, trying to escape the pursuit of Vertumnus, god of gardens and orchards, prayed to the gods for help; and they changed her into the tiny flower. In allusion to this Rapin wrote:

> When the bright Ram, bedecked with stars of gold,
> Displays his fleece the Daisy will unfold,
> To nymphs a chaplet and to beds a grace,
> Who once herself had borne a virgin's face.

The daisy was under the care of Venus. It has been beloved by English poets ever since Chaucer sang the praises of the day's eye—daisy. Chaucer tells us, in what is perhaps the most worshipful poem ever addressed to a flower, that he always rose early and went out to the fields, or meadows, to pay his devotions to this "flower of flowers," whose praises he intended to sing while ever his life lasted, and he bemoaned the fact, moreover, that he had not words at his command to do it proper reverence.

Next to Chaucer in paying homage to the daisy comes Wordworth with his

[1] "Hamlet"; Act IV, Scene VII.

A nun demure, of lowly port;
Or sprightly maiden, of Love's court;
In thy simplicity the sport
    Of all temptations;
Queen in crown of rubies drest,
A starveling in a scanty vest,
Are all, as seems to suit the best
    My appellations.

A little cyclops with one eye
Staring to threaten and defy
That thought comes next—and instantly
    The freak is over,
The shape will vanish—and behold,
A silver shield with boss of gold
That spreads itself some fairy bold
    In fight to cover.

Bright flower! for by that name at last
When all my reveries are past
I call thee, and to that cleave fast,
    Sweet, silent creature
That breathst with me the sun and air,
Do thou as thou art wont repair
My heart with gladness and a share
    Of thy meek nature.

"Daisies smell-less yet most quaint" is a line from
the flower-song in "The Two Noble Kinsmen," written by John Fletcher and Shakespeare.[1]

Milton speaks of

    Meadows trim with daisies pied

[1] Act I, Scene I.

and Dryden pays a tribute to which even Chaucer
would approve:

> And then a band of flutes began to play,
> To which a lady sang a tirelay;
> And still at every close she would repeat
> The burden of the song—"The Daisy is so sweet!
> The Daisy is so sweet!"—when she began
> The troops of Knights and dames continued on.

The English daisy is "The wee, modest crimson-
tipped flower," as Burns has described it, and must
not be confused with the daisy that powders the
fields and meadows in our Southern States with a
snow of white blossoms supported on tall stems.
This daisy, called sometimes the moon-daisy (*Chrysanthemum Leucanthemum*), is known in England
as the midsummer daisy and ox-eye. In France it is
called marguerite and paquerette. Being a midsummer flower, it is dedicated to St. John the Baptist. It is also associated with St. Margaret and
Mary Magdalen, and from the latter it derives the
names of maudlin and maudelyne. As *Ophelia*
drowned herself in midsummer the daisies that are
described in her wreath are most probably marguerites and not the "day's eye" of Chaucer.

Parkinson does not separate daisies very particularly. "They are usually called in Latin," he tells

us, "*Bellides* and in English Daisies. Some of them
Herba Margarita and *Primula veris*, as is likely
after the Italian names of Marguerita and *Flor di
prima vera gentile*. The French call them
Paquerettes and *Marguerites;* and the fruitful sort,
or those that have small flowers about the middle
one, *Margueritons*. Our English women call them
Jack-an-Apes-on-Horseback."

The daisy that an Elizabethan poet quaintly describes as a Tudor princess resembles the midsummer daisy rather than the "wee, modest, crimson-
tipped flower" of Burns:

> About her neck she wears a rich wrought ruff
> With double sets most brave and broad bespread
> Resembling lovely lawn, or cambric stuff
> Pinned up and prickt upon her yellow head.

Also Browne in his "Pastorals" seems to be thinking
of this flower:

> The Daisy scattered on each mead and down,
> A golden tuft within a silver crown.

VIOLET (*Viola odorata*). The violet was considered "a choice flower of delight" in English gardens. Shakespeare speaks of the violet on many
occasions and always with tenderness and deep appreciation of its qualities. Violets are among the

flowers that the frightened Proserpine dropped from
Pluto's ebon car—

> Violets dim
> And sweeter than the lids of Juno's eyes,
> Or Cytherea's breath.[1]

Thus in Shakespeare's opinion the violet out-
sweetened both Juno, majestic queen of heaven, and
Venus, goddess of love and beauty.

How could he praise the violet more?

> To throw a perfume on the violet
> Is wasteful and ridiculous excess.

Shakespeare informs us in "King John." [2] With
the utmost delicacy of perfection he describes
Titania's favorite haunt as

> a bank where the wild thyme blows,
> Where oxlips and the nodding violet grows.[3]

In truth, the tiny flower seems to nod among its
leaves.

Shakespeare makes the elegant *Duke* in "Twelfth
Night," who is lounging nonchalantly on his divan,
compare the music he hears to the breeze blowing
upon a bank of violets [4] (see page 44).

---

[1] "The Winter's Tale"; Act IV, Scene III.
[2] Act IV, Scene II.
[3] "A Midsummer Night's Dream"; Act II, Scene II.
[4] Act I, Scene I.

Shelley held the same idea that the delicious perfume of flowers is like the softest melody:

> The snowdrop and then the violet
> Arose from the ground with warm rain wet;
> And there was mixed with fresh color, sent
> From the turf like the voice and the instrument.
>
> And the hyacinth, purple and white and blue,
> Which flung from its bells a sweet peal anew
> Of music, so delicate, soft and intense
> It was felt like an odor within the sense.

Ophelia laments that she has no violets to give to the court ladies and lords, for "they withered" when her father died, she tells us. Shakespeare also associates violets with melancholy occasions. *Marina* enters in "Pericles" with a basket of flowers on her arm, saying: [1]

> The yellows, blues,
> The purple violets and marigolds
> Shall as a carpet hang upon thy grave
> While summer days do last.

On another occasion, with a broad sweeping gesture, Shakespeare mentions

> The violets that strew
> The green lap of the new-come Spring.

[1] Act IV, Scene II.

In "Sonnet XCIX" he writes:

The forward violet thus did I chide:
Sweet thief, whence didst thou steal the sweet that smells
If not from my love's breath?   The purple pride
Which on thy soft cheek for complexion dwells
In my love's veins thou hast too grossly dyed.

Bacon deemed it most necessary "to know what flowers and plants do best perfume the air," and he thought "that which above all others yields the sweetest smell is the violet, and next to that the musk-rose."   (See page 44.)

"Perhaps of all Warwickshire flowers," writes a native of Shakespeare's country, "none are so plentiful as violets; our own little churchyard of Whitechurch is sheeted with them.   They grow in every hedgebank until the whole air is filled with their fragrance.   The wastes near Stratford are sometimes purple as far as the eyes can see with the flowers of *viola canina*.   Our English violets are twelve in number.   The plant is still used in medicine and acquired of late a notoriety as a suggested cancer cure; and in Shakespeare's time was eaten raw with onions and lettuces and also mingled in broth and used to garnish dishes, while crystallized violets are not unknown in the present day."

For the beauty of its form, for the depth and richness of its color, for the graceful drooping of its stalk and the nodding of its head, for its lovely heart-shaped leaf and above all for its delicious perfume, the violet is admired.   Then when we gaze into its tiny face and note the delicacy of its veins, which Shakespeare so often mentions, we gain a sense of its deeper beauty and significance.

Dr. Forbes Watson observed:

"I give one instance of Nature's care for the look of the stamens and pistils of a flower.   In the blossom of the Scented Violet the stamens form, by their convergence, a little orange beak.   At the end of this beak is the summit of the pistil, a tiny speck of green, but barely visible to the naked eye.   Yet small as it is, it completes the color of the flower, by softening the orange, and we can distinctly see that if this mere point were removed, there would be imperfection for the want of it."

St. Francis de Sales, a contemporary of Shakespeare, gave a lovely description of the flower when he said:

"A true widow is in the Church as a March Violet, shedding around an exquisite perfume by the fragrance of her devotion and always hidden under the ample leaves of her lowliness and by her subdued coloring, showing the spirit of her mortification. She seeks untrodden and solitary places."

The violet's qualities of lowliness, humility, and sweetness have always appealed to poets. The violet is also beloved because it is one of the earliest spring flowers. Violets are, like primroses and cowslips,

> The first to rise
> And smile beneath Spring's wakening skies,
> The courier of a band of coming flowers.

The violet was also an emblem of constancy. At the floral games, instituted by Clemence Isaure at Toulouse in the Fourteenth Century, the prize was a golden violet, because the poetess had once sent a violet to her Knight as a token of faithfulness. With the Troubadours the violet was a symbol of constancy. In "A Handful of Pleasant Delights," a popular song-book published in Elizabeth's reign in 1566, there is a poem called "A Nosegay always Sweet for Lovers to send Tokens of Love at New Year's tide, or for Fairings, as they in their minds shall be disposed to write." This poem contains a verse to the violet:

> Violet is for faithfulness
>   Which in me shall abide;
> Hoping likewise that from your heart
>   You will not let it slide,

> And will continue in the same,
>   As you have now begun;
> And then forever to abide
>   Then you my heart have won.

The violet has always held a loved place in the English garden. Gerard writes quaintly in his "Herbal":

"The Black, or Purple Violets, or March Violets, of the garden have a great prerogative above all others, not only because the mind conceiveth a certain pleasure and recreation by smelling and handling of those most odoriferous flowers, but also for the very many by these Violets receive ornament and comely grace; for there be made of them garlands for the head, nosegays and poesies, which are delightful to look on and pleasant to smell to, speaking nothing of their appropriate virtues; yea, gardens themselves receive by these the greatest ornament of all chiefest beauty and most gallant grace; and the recreation of the mind, which is taken thereby, cannot but be very good and honest; for they admonish and stir up a man to that which is comely and honest; for flowers through their beauty, variety of color and exquisite form do bring to a liberal and great mind the remembrance of honesty, comeliness and all kinds of virtue."

Proserpine was gathering violets among other flowers in the fields of Enna in Sicily when Pluto carried her off. Shakespeare touched upon the story most exquisitely, through the lips of *Perdita*, as quoted above.

Another Greek myth accounts for the Greek word for the violet, which is *ion*. It seems when, in order to protect her from the persecutions of Juno, Jove transformed lovely Europa into a white heifer whom he named Io, he caused sweet violets to spring up from the earth wherever the white cow placed her lips; and from her name, Io, the flower acquired the name *ion*.

The Athenians adored the flower. Tablets were engraved with the word *ion* and set up everywhere in Athens; and of all sobriquets the citizens preferred that of "Athenian crowned with violets."

The Persians also loved the violet and made a delicious wine from it. A sherbet flavored with violet blossoms is served in Persia and Arabia to-day at feasts; and Mohammedans say: "The excellence of the violet is as the excellence of El Islam above all other religions."

IV

"Lady-smocks all Silver White" and "Cuckoo Buds of Yellow Hue"

LADY-SMOCK (*Cardamine pratensis*). The lovely little spring song in "Love's Labour's Lost" [1] with the line,

Lady-smocks all silver white,

has immortalized this little flower of the English meadows, but little known in our country. The lady-smock is very common in England in early spring. Properly speaking it should be Our Lady's-smock, as it is one of the many plants dedicated to the Virgin Mary and bearing her name. The list is a long one, including Lady's-slippers, Lady's-bower, Lady's-cushion, Lady's-mantle, Lady's-laces, Lady's-looking-glass, Lady's-garters, Lady's-thimble, Lady's-hair (maidenhair fern), Lady's-seal, Lady's-thistle, Lady's-bedstraw, Lady's-fingers, Lady's-gloves, and so on. These flowers, originally dedicated to Venus, Juno, and Diana in Greek and Roman mythology and to Freya and Bertha in Northern lore and legend, were gradually trans-

[1] Act V, Scene II.

ferred to the Virgin with the spread of Christianity. The Lady's-smock takes its name from the fancied, but far-fetched, resemblance to a smock. It is said, by way of explanation, that when these flowers are seen in great quantity they suggest the comparison of linen smocks bleaching on the green meadow. Other names for the plant are Cuckooflower, Meadow-cress, Spinks, and Mayflower; and in Norfolk the *Cardamine pratensis* is called Canterbury-bells. The petals have a peculiarly soft and translucent quality with a faint lilac tinge. Shakespeare describes the flower as "silver white," an epithet that has puzzled many persons. However, one ardent Shakespeare lover has made a discovery:

"Gather a lady-smock as you tread the rising grass in fragrant May, and although in individuals the petals are sometimes cream color, as a rule the flower viewed in the hand is lilac—pale, but purely and indisputably lilac. Where then is the silver-whiteness? It is the meadows, remember, that are painted, when, as often happens, the flower is so plentiful as to hide the turf, and most particularly, if the ground be a slope and the sun be shining from behind us, all is changed; the flowers are lilac no longer; the meadow is literally 'silver-white.' So it is always—Shakespeare's epithets are like prisms. Let them tremble in the sunshine and we discover that it is he who knows best."

The beautiful song begins:

> When daisies pied and violets blue,
>   And lady-smocks all silver white,
> And cuckoo buds of yellow hue,
>   Do paint the meadows with delight,
> The cuckoo then, on every tree,
>   Mocks married men, for thus sings he:
>   Cuckoo,
> Cuckoo, Cuckoo—or word of fear,
> Unpleasing to a married ear.

CUCKOO BUDS (*Ranunculus*). It is quite possible that in "cuckoo buds of yellow hue" Shakespeare meant the blossoms of the buttercup or king-cup (called by the country people of Warwickshire horse-blobs). Some authorities claim that cuckoo-buds is intended to represent the lesser celandine, of which Wordsworth was so fond that he wrote three poems to it. Others call cuckoo-buds *carmine pratensis;* but that could hardly be possible because Shakespeare speaks of "lady-smocks all silver white" in one line and "cuckoo buds of yellow hue" in the succeeding line.

There is much confusion in the identification of

lady-smocks, cuckoo-buds, cuckoo-flowers, and crow-flowers, for they are more or less related.

Gerard says: "Our Lady-Smock is also called the cuckoo-flower because it flowers in April and May when the cuckoo doth begin to sing her pleasant notes without stammering."

V

Anemones and "Azured Harebells"

ANEMONE (*Anemone purpurea striata stellata*). The anemone is described in "Venus and Adonis" very minutely: [1]

> By this, the boy that by her side lay kill'd,
> Was melted like a vapor from her sight,
> And in his blood that on the ground lay spill'd,
> A purple flower sprung up chequer'd with white.
> Resembling well his pale cheeks, and the blood,
> Which in round drops upon their whiteness stood.

Adonis, the beautiful youth, beloved of Venus, was wounded by a boar, to which he had given chase. Venus found him as he lay dying on the grass. To make him immortal she changed him into an anemone, or windflower. Naturally the flower was dedicated to Venus.

[1] Verse 195.

Bion sang:

Alas! the Paphian! fair Adonis slain!
Tears plenteous as his blood she pours amain,
But gentle flowers are born and bloom around
From every drop that falls upon the ground.
Where streams his blood, there blushing springs a **Rose**
And where a tear has dropped a windflower blows.

Pliny asserted the anemone only blooms when the wind blows.

The flower was associated with illness in the days of the Egyptians and also during the Middle Ages, when there was also a superstition that the first anemone gathered would prove a charm against disease. The first spring blossom was, therefore, eagerly searched for, delightedly plucked, and carefully guarded. No token of affection was more prized by a loved one going off on a journey than the gift of an anemone. An old ballad has the lines:

The first Spring-blown Anemone she in his doublet wove,
To keep him safe from pestilence wherever he should rove.

Anemones were greatly valued in Elizabethan gardens. Indeed it was a fad to grow them. Parkinson distinguishes the family of anemones as "the wild and the tame, or manured, both of them nourished up in gardens." He classifies them still further as "those that have broader leaves and those that have thinner, or more jagged, leaves"; and then again into those "that bear single flowers and those that bear double flowers." The wild kinds included "all the Pulsatillas, or Pasque (Easter) flowers." Parkinson mentions many varieties. He describes the "tame" anemones as white, yellow, purple, crimson, scarlet, blush gredeline (between peach color and violet), orange-tawny, apple-blossom, rose-color, and many others. From his list we can have no doubt that Shakespeare's flower was one of the purple star anemones—the *Anemone purpurea striata stellata*, "whose flowers have many white lines and stripes through the leaves." Parkinson's name is "the purple-striped Anemone."

Of recent years anemones have again become the fashion.

"How gorgeous are these flowers to behold," exclaims Ryder Haggard, "with their hues of vivid scarlet and purple! To be really appreciated, however, they should, I think, be seen in their native home, the East. In the neighborhood of Mount Tabor in Palestine, I have met with them in such millions that for miles the whole plain is stained red, blue and white, growing so thickly indeed that to walk across it without setting foot on a flower at every step would be difficult. I believe, and I think that this view is very generally accepted, that these are the same lilies of the field that 'toil not neither do they spin,' which Our Lord used to illustrate His immortal lesson. Truly Solomon in all his glory was not arrayed like one of these."

The Adonis flower (*Flos Adonis*) spoken of by Ben Jonson and others has nothing to do with the anemone. It is a kind of camomile. "Some have taken the red kind to be a kind of Anemone," says Parkinson. "The most usual name now with us is *Flos Adonis*. In English it is also called the Mayweed and Rosarubie and Adonis Flower."

HAREBELL (*Scilla nutans*).[1] The "azured harebell," which Shakespeare uses in "Cymbeline" for comparison with the delicate veins of *Fidele* (*Imogen*), has been identified as the English jacinth, blue harebell, or hare's-bell. Browne's "Pastorals" show that this flower was only worn by faithful lovers; and, therefore, the flower is most appropriately selected for association with *Imogen*. Browne says:

> The Harebell, for her stainless, azured hue
> Claims to be worn of none but who are true.

This flower is also called the "wild hyacinth." Blossoming in May and June, it is one of the precious

[1] See p. 207.

AN ELIZABETHAN MANOR HOUSE ; HADDON HALL

ornaments of English woods. "Dust of sapphire," its
jewel-like flowers have been called.

"Our English jacinth, or harebells," writes
Parkinson, "is so common everywhere that it scarce
needeth any description. It beareth divers long narrow green leaves, not standing upright, not yet fully
lying on the ground, among which springeth up the
stalk, bearing at the top many long and hollow
flowers, hanging down their heads, all forwards, for
the most part, parted at the brims into six parts,
turning up their points a little again, of a sweetish,
but heady, scent, like unto the Grapeflower. The
heads for seed are long and square, wherein is much
black seed. The color of the flowers is in some of
a deep blue tending to purple, in others of a paler
blue, or of a bleak blue tending to an ash color.
Some are pure white and some are parti-colored blue
and white; and some are of a fine delayed purplish
red, or bluish color, which some call a pearl color."

VI

Columbine and Broom-flower

COLUMBINE (*Aquilegia vulgaris*). "There's
fennel for you, and columbines," says *Ophelia*, as
she hands the flowers to the courtiers.[1] Shakespeare

[1] "Hamlet"; Act IV, Scene V.

also mentions the columbine in "Love's Labour 's Lost" [1] where *Don Armado*, the "fantastical Spaniard" (a caricature of a real person at Queen Elizabeth's court), exclaims, "I am that flower," to which *Dumain* and *Longueville* reply in derision, "That mint! That columbine!" Of the columbine of Shakespeare's time, Parkinson says:

"There be many sorts of Columbines as well differing in form as color of the flowers, and of them, both single and double, carefully nursed up in our gardens for the delight both of their forms and colors. The variety of the colors of these flowers are very much, for some are wholly white, some of a blue, or violet, color, others of a bluish, or flesh, color, or deep, or pale, red, or of a dead purple, or dead murrey color, as Nature listeth to show."

The generic name is derived from the word *aquila*, an eagle, because of the fancied resemblance of some parts of the flower to the talons of an eagle. The English name comes from the Latin *columba*, a dove, from the likeness of its nectaries to the heads of doves in a ring around a dish, or to the figure of a dove hovering with expanded wings discovered by pulling off one petal with its detached sepals. Hence this was called the dove plant. From the belief that

[1] Act V, Scene II.

it was the favorite plant of the lion it was called *Herba leonis.*

The columbine was valued for many medicinal virtues.

"The scarlet and yellow columbine," writes Matthew, "is one of our most beautiful wild flowers. It is my experience that certain flowers have certain favorite haunts, which are exclusively held by them year after year. This flower is in its prime about the first of June, and is nearly always found beside some lichen-covered rock."

The English and American flowers differ, although the early colonists brought the English flower with them. Grant Allen tells us:

"The English columbine is a more developed type than the American scarlet, is never yellow in the wild state, but often purple, and, sometimes, blue. Larkspur, ranking still higher in the floral scale, in virtue of its singular bilateral blossoms, is usually blue, though it sometimes reverts to reddish-purple, or white; while monkshood, the very top of the tree on this line of development, is usually deep ultramarine, only a few species being prettily variegated with pale blue and white. As a rule, blue flowers are the very highest; and the reason seems to lie in the strange fact, first discovered by Sir John Lubbock, that bees are fonder of blue than of any other color. Still, they are fond enough even of red; and one may be sure that the change from yellow to scarlet in the petals of the American columbine is due in one way or another to the selective tastes and preferences of the higher insects."

The colors of the American columbine are dark opaque blues, smoky purples, dull pinks, pale blues, lavenders, reds and yellows—an infinite variety!

"The flowering of the 'Columbine Commendable,' as Skelton called it four hundred years ago," says Harriet L. Keeler, "marks the beginning of summer. The reign of the bulbs is over;

> The windflower and the violet
> They perished long ago;

the petals of the early roses are falling; the elder-blossoms show white along the fence rows; and the season waxes to its prime.

"A wild flower of English fields, the columbine was early transferred into English gardens and has held its place securely there for at least five hundred years. Its seeds were among the treasures borne over the sea to the New World and it early bloomed in Pilgrim gardens. This primitive stock still persists in cultivation.

"The flower of the columbine is a unique and interesting form. The sepals look like petals and the petals are veritable horns of plenty filled with nectar at the closed ends for the swarms of bees which gather about. The sweets are produced by the blossoms on a generous scale, and to a columbine bed in full bloom the bees come, big and little, noisy and silent—all giddy with the feast. There is no use trying to drive them away for they will not go. Clumsy bumble bees with tongues long enough to reach the honey by the open door, wise honey bees who have learned to take the short road to the nectar by biting through the spur, quiet brown bees, little green carpenters—all are there, 'vehement, voluble, velvety,' in a glorious riot of happiness and honey.

"The doubling occurs chiefly with the petals; the sepals, as a rule, hold true to the five, but the petals sometimes double in number, becoming ten spurs in place of five, and each spur becomes a nest of spurs like a set of Chinese cups, though the innermost are frequently imperfect."

The columbine frequently appears in the paintings of the Great Masters. Luini has immortalized it in his picture of this title now in the gallery of the Hermitage at Petrograd. A fascinating woman with a smile as enchanting—if not so famous—as Leonardo da Vinci's "Mona Lisa" holds an exquisitely painted columbine in her left hand and gazes at it with tender, loving emotion.

The early Italian and Flemish painters include the columbine with the rose, lily, pink, violet, strawberry, and clover in the gardens where the Madonna sits with the Holy Child. The reason that the columbine was chosen as a flower of religious symbolism was because of the little doves formed by the five petals. The columbine signified the "Seven Gifts of the Holy Spirit," and the Flemish painters in their zeal for accuracy corrected the number of petals to seven to make the flower agree with the teaching of the Church.

Yet although the columbine has these religious associations, we always think of it as an airy, piquant flower, the gay and irresponsible dancer of the rocks and dells, clad, as it were, in fantastic and parti-colored dress. Graceful in form and charming in color, put together with extreme delicacy on slender, flexible, fragile stems and adorned with a leaf approaching that of the fern in delicacy and lace-like beauty, the columbine is one of the most delightful of flowers. Always associated with folly, we love it none the less for that, for there are times when we enjoy *Harlequin* and *Columbine* among our flowers,—and these fantastic and frivolous columbines dancing so gaily in the breeze always fill us with delight.

BROOM (*Cytisus scoparius*). Although the broom was a popular plant in Elizabethan days it is only mentioned once by Shakespeare. In "The Tempest," [1] where *Iris* in the mask in her apostrophe to "Ceres, most bounteous lady," speaks of

> thy broom-groves
> Whose shadow the dismissed bachelor loves,
> Being lass-lorn . . .
> . . . the queen o' the sky . . .
> Bids thee leave these.

When in blossom the broom is lovely to look upon. The large yellow flowers are gracefully arranged on the branches, and its perfume is delightful.

"Sweet is the Broome-flower!" exclaims Spenser. The broom is the *Planta genesta*, from which the Plantagenets took their name. The flower, having become heraldic during that dynasty, was embroidered on the clothes of the Plantagenet family and imitated in their jewels. When they died it was carved on their monuments. The story goes that Geoffrey, Earl of Anjou, father of Henry II of   •

[1] Act IV, Scene I.

England, once on his way to a field of battle, had to climb a rocky path, and he noticed as he went along the bushes of yellow broom clinging to the rocks. Breaking off a branch he placed it in his helmet with the words: "This golden plant shall be my emblem henceforth. Rooted firmly among rocks and upholding that which is ready to fall." His son, Henry, was called "the royal sprig of Genesta." The golden plume of broom-flowers was ·worn by the Plantagenets until the last one of the line, Richard III, lost the Crown of England to Henry VII, the first of the Tudors.

In 1264 the *Planta genesta* was honored by St. Louis, who instituted the Order of Genest on his marriage with Marguerite. The Knights of the Genest wore chains made of the broom-flower alternating with the fleur-de-lis. Shakespeare speaks of a "broom-staff" and sends *Puck*

> with broom before
> To sweep the dust behind the door.

Whether *Puck's* broom was made from the *Genesta* or not we do not know; but we do know that the broom, in common with other briars, was used to make besoms for sweeping and also for staffs to walk with and to lean upon.

ROSE ARBOR, WARLEY, ENGLAND

𝔖𝔲𝔪𝔪𝔢𝔯

"SWEET SUMMER BUDS"

I

"Morning Roses Newly Washed with Dew"

THE ROSE (*Rosa*). Shakespeare speaks of the rose more frequently than any other flower. Sixty references to the rose are scattered through his works. Sometimes he talks of the rose itself and sometimes he uses the word to make a striking comparison, or analogy. With magical touch he gives us the bold picture of a

> Red rose on triumphant briar,

then he brings before us a delicious whiff of the

> Perfumèd tincture of the roses,

or the luscious fragrance of

> Morning roses newly washed with dew.

With equal delicacy of perception he tells us

> So sweet a kiss the golden sun gives not
> To those fresh morning drops upon the rose.[1]

[1] "Love's Labour 's Lost"; Act IV, Scene III.

145

Shakespeare's special roses are the Red, the White, the Musk, the Eglantine (sweetbrier), the Provençal, or Provins, the Damask, the Canker, and the Variegated.

THE RED ROSE (*Rose Anglica rubra*), the English red, is thus described by Parkinson:

"The Red Rose, which I call English because this rose is more frequent and used in England than in other places, never groweth so high as the Damask Rose-bush, but more usually abideth low and shooteth forth many branches from the Rose-bush (and is but seldom suffered to grow up as the Damask Rose into standards) with a green bark thinner set with prickles and longer and greener leaves on the upper side than in the white, yet with an eye of white upon them, five likewise most usually set upon a stalk and grayish, or whitish, underneath. The Roses, or flowers, do very much vary according to their site and abiding, for some are of an orient red, or deep crimson, color and very double (although never so double as the White), which, when it is full blown, hath the largest leaves of any other Rose; some of them again are paler, tending somewhat to a Damask; and some are of so pale a red as that it is rather of the color of a Canker Rose, yet all for the most part with larger leaves than the Damask, and with many more yellow threads in the middle. The scent hereof is much better than in the White, but not comparable to the excellency of the Damask Rose, yet this Rose, being well dried and well kept, will hold both color and scent longer than the Damask."

THE WHITE ROSE (*Rosa Anglica alba*).

"The White Rose is of two kinds," says Parkinson, "the one more thick and double than the other. The one riseth up in some shadowy places unto eight or ten foot high, with a stock of great bigness for a rose. The other growing seldom higher than a Damask Rose. Both these Roses have somewhat smaller and whiter green leaves than in many other Roses, five most usually set on a stock and more white underneath, as also a whiter green bark, armed with sharp thorns, or prickles. The flowers in the one are whitish with an eye, or shew, of a blush, especially towards the ground, or bottom, of the flower, very thick, double and close set together; and, for the most part, not opening itself so largely and fully as either the Red, or Damask Rose. The other more white, less thick and double and opening itself more, and some so little double (as but of two or three rows) that they might be held to be single, yet all of little or no smell at all."

From this *Rosa alba*, Pliny says, the isle of Albion derived its name—a happy thought when we remember that the rose is still the national emblem of England.

MUSK-ROSE (*Rosa moschata*). Musk-roses and eglantine mingled with honeysuckle formed the canopy beneath which *Titania* slumbered on a bank made soft and lovely with wild thyme, oxlips and nodding violets. And in the "coronet of fresh and fragrant flowers" that the dainty little fairy queen placed upon the hairy temples of *Bottom* the Weaver, musk-roses were conspicuous; and the sweetness of these was intensified by "the round and Orient pearls of dew" that swelled upon the petals, as the "pretty flowerets bewailed their own disgrace."

It is this delicious rose which Keats, when listening to the nightingale, sensed rather than visualized in the twilight dimness:

> The coming musk-rose full of dewy wine,
> The murmurous haunt of flies on summer eves.

The musk-rose was adored by the Elizabethans. Lord Bacon considered its scent to come next to that of the violet, and before all other flowers.

"You remember the great bush at the corner of

the south wall just by the Blue Drawing-room window?" writes Mrs. Gaskell in "My Lady Ludlow."
"That is the old musk-rose, Shakespeare's musk-rose,
which is dying out through the kingdom now. The
scent is unlike the scent of any other rose, or of any
other flower."

The musk-rose is a native of North Africa, Spain,
and India (Nepal). Hakluyt in 1582 gave the date
of its introduction into England. "The turkey-cocks
and hens," he says, "were brought in about fifty
years past; the Artichoke in the time of Henry the
Eighth; and of later times was procured out of Italy
the Musk Rose plant and the Plum called Perdig-
wena."

Turning now to Parkinson and opening his big
volume at the page "*Rosa Moschata*, simple and
multiplex," we read:

"The Musk Rose, both single and double, rises
up oftentimes to a very great height that it over-
groweth any arbor in a Garden, or being set by a
house side to be ten or twelve foot high, or more,
but especially the single kind with many green far
spread branches armed with a few sharp great
thorns, as the wilder sorts of Roses are, whereof
these are accounted to be kinds, having small dark
green leaves on them, not much bigger than the

leaves of Eglantines. The Flowers come forth at the tops of the branches, many together as it were in an umbel, or tuft, which, for the most part, do flower all at a time, or not long one after another, every one standing on a pretty long stalk and are of a pale whitish, or cream color, both the single and the double, the single being small flowers consisting of five leaves with many yellow threads in the middle; and the double bearing more double flowers, as if they were once or twice more double than the single, with yellow thrums also in the middle, both of them of a very sweet and pleasing smell, resembling musk. Some there be that have avouched that the chief scent of these Roses consisteth not in the leaves but in the threads of the Flowers."

The color of the musk-rose is white, slightly tinged with pink.

EGLANTINE; ALSO SWEETBRIER (*Rosa eglanteria*). This is a conspicuous adornment of *Titania's* bower, and is as remarkable for its beauty as for its scent. The pink flowers with their golden threads in the center are familiar to every one.

"The Sweet Briar, or Eglantine," Parkinson writes, "is not only planted in Gardens for the sweetness of its leaves, but growing wild in many woods and hedges, hath exceeding long green shoots armed with the cruellest sharp and strong thorns and thicker set than is in any Rose, either wild or tame. The leaves are smaller than in most of those that are nourished up in Gardens, seven or nine, most usually set together on a rib, or stalk, very green and sweeter in smell about the leaves of any other kind of Rose. The flowers are small, single, blush Roses."

PROVENÇAL, or PROVINS (*Centifolia*). This old-fashioned cabbage-rose of globular flowers, massive foliage, hard knob of leaves in the center, and sweet perfume is affectionately known as the "Hundred Leaf," or *rose à cent feuilles*. Parkinson gives two varieties: the incarnate, or flesh-color; and the red.

In our country the light pink, or incarnate, is the more familiar. What associations does it not conjure up? To many of us Dean Hole's words make a touching appeal:

"The blushing, fresh, fragrant Provence! It was to many of us *the* Rose of our childhood and its delicious perfume passes through the outer sense into our hearts gladdening them with bright and happy dreams, saddening them with love and child awakenings. It brings more to us than the fairness and sweet smell of a Rose. We passed in our play to gaze on it with the touch of a vanished hand in ours, with a father's blessing on our heads and a mother's prayer that we might never lose our love of the beautiful. Happy they who return, or regain, that love."

THE DAMASK ROSE (*Rosa damascena*) is a native of Syria, whence it was brought to Europe about 1270 by Thibault IV, Comte de Brie, returning from the Holy Land. We know exactly when it was introduced into England because Hakluyt, writing in 1582, says: "In time of memory many things have been brought in that were not here before, as the Damask Rose by Doctor Liniker, King Henry the Seventh and King Henry the Eighth's physician."

"Gloves as sweet as Damask Roses" *Autolycus* carries in his peddler's pack for "lads to give their dears," along with masks for their faces, perfume, necklace-amber, pins, quoifs, and "lawn as white as driven snow." [1]

Parkinson informs us:

"The Damask Rose-bush is more usually nourished up to a competent height to stand alone (which we call Standards), than any other Rose. The bark, both of the stock and branches, is not fully so green as the Red or White Rose. The leaves are green

---

[1] "The Winter's Tale"; Act IV, Scene III.

with an eye of white upon them. The flowers are of a fine deep blush color, as all know, with some pale yellow threads in the middle, and are not so thick and double as the White, not being blown with so large and great leaves as the Red, but of the most excellent sweet pleasant scent, far surpassing all other Roses or Flowers, being neither heady, nor too strong, nor stuffing or unpleasant sweet, as many other flowers.

"The Rose is of exceeding great use with us, for the Damask Rose (besides the superexcellent sweet water it yieldeth, being distilled, or the perfume of its leaves, being dried, serving to fill sweet bags) serveth to cause solubleness of the body, made into a syrup, or preserved with sugar, moist or candied." The name is obviously from Damascus.

CANKER (*Rosa canina*). This is the wild dog-rose common to many countries. The name dog-rose was given to it by the Romans, because the root was said to cure the bite of a mad dog. Pliny says the remedy was discovered in a dream by the mother of a soldier who had been bitten by a mad dog. *Don Juan's* remark in "Much Ado About Nothing." [1]

> I had rather be a canker in the hedge
> Than a rose in his garden,

[1] Act I, Scene III.

refers, of course, to the canker-rose. According to legend, the Crown of Thorns was made from the briers of this variety of rose.

VARIEGATED ROSE (*Rosa versicolor*) of Shakespeare's plays is the curious bush which produces at the same time red roses, white roses, and roses of red mottled with white and of white mottled with red. The growth of the tree is stiff and erect and the flowers have a sweet scent. The rose is often called the "York and Lancaster." Parkinson says:

"This Rose in the form and order of the growing is nearest unto the ordinary Damask Rose both for stem, branch, leaf and flower, the difference consisting in this—that the flower (being of the same largeness and doubleness as the Damask Rose) hath the one half of it sometimes of a pale whitish color and the other half of a paler damask color than the ordinary. This happeneth so many times, and sometimes also the flower hath divers stripes and marks on it, one leaf white, or striped with white, and the other half blush, or striped with blush, sometimes all striped, or spotted over, and at other times little or no stripes, or marks, at all, as Nature listeth to play with varieties in this as in other flowers. Yet this I have observed, that the longer it abideth blown open to the sun, the paler and the fewer stripes, marks, or spots will be seen in it. The smell is of a weak Damask Rose scent."

This rose recalls the old song of a "Lover to His Lancastrian Mistress," on handing her a white rose:

> If this fair rose offend thy sight,
>   Placed in thy bosom bare,
> 'T will blush to find itself less white,
>   And turn Lancastrian there,
>
> But if thy ruby lip it spy,
>   As kiss it thou mayst deign,
> With envy pale 't will lose its dye,
>   And Yorkish turn again.

In his play of "King Henry VI," which passes during the Wars of the Roses, Shakespeare introduces the noted scene in the Temple Garden, London, where the emblem of the Yorkists (a white rose) and that of the Lancastrians (a red rose) is chosen. Richard Plantagenet plucks a white rose and the Earl of Somerset a red rose from rose-bushes that are still growing and blooming in the same spot, as they did when Shakespeare imagined the scene in "King Henry VI." [1]

In Shakespeare's day the rose was enormously cultivated. In the gardens of Ely Place, the home of Queen Elizabeth's dashing lord chancellor,

[1] Part I, Act II, Scene IV.

twenty bushels of roses were gathered annually—a good deal for the time.

"About thirty species of roses," writes Edmund Gosse, "were known to the Elizabethan gardeners, and most of them did particularly well in London until in the reign of James I, when the increasing smoke of coal-fires exterminated the most lovely and the most delicate species, the double yellow rose. Things grew rapidly worse in this respect, until Parkinson in despair, cried out: 'Neither herb, nor tree, will prosper since the use of sea-coal.' Up to that time in London, and afterwards in country-places, the rose preserved its vogue. It was not usually grown for pleasure, since the petals had a great commercial value; there was a brisk trade in dried roses and a precious sweet water was distilled from the damask rose. The red varieties of the rose were considered the best medicinally, and they produced that rose syrup which was so widely used both as a cordial and as an aperient. The fashion for keeping *potpourri* in dwelling-rooms became so prevalent that the native gardens could not supply enough, and dried yellow roses became a recognized import from Constantinople. We must think of the parlors of the ladies who saw Shakespeare's plays

performed for the first time as all redolent with the
perfume of dried, spiced and powdered rose-leaves."
In "Sonnet LIV" Shakespeare says:

> The rose looks fair, but fairer it we deem
> For that sweet odor which doth in it live.
> The canker-blooms have full as deep a dye
> As the perfumèd tincture of the roses,
> Hang on such thorns and play as wantonly
> When summer's breath their maskèd buds discloses.
> But, for their virtue only is their show,
> They live unwoo'd, and unrespected fade;
> Die to themselves. Sweet roses do not so;
> Of their sweet deaths are sweetest odors made.

For twenty-seven centuries—and more—the rose
has been considered queen of flowers. Her perfume,
her color, her elegance, and her mystic fascination
have won all hearts. Shakespeare says: "A rose by
any other name would smell as sweet." In one sense
that is true; but we would not be willing to try another title, for the very word rose is a beautiful one
and conjures up a particular and very special vision
of sweetness and beauty.

Thousands and thousands of poems have been
written in praise of this flower, ever since Sappho
sang to her lyre the words "Ho! the rose! Ho! the
rose!"

Sir Henry Wotton wrote:

> You Violets that first appear,
> By your pure purple mantles known,
> Like the proud virgins of the year,
> As if the Spring were all your own,
> What are you when the Rose is blown?

And Hood sang:

> The Cowslip is a country wench;
>   The Violet is a nun;
> But I will woo the dainty Rose
>   The queen of every one.

And Shelley:

> And the rose, like a nymph to the bath addrest,
> Which unveiled the depths of her glowing breast,
> Till, fold after fold, to the fainting air,
> The soul of her beauty and love laid bare.

Shelley's "fold after fold" reminds us that Ruskin points out that one of the rose's beauties is that her petals make shadows over and over again of their own loveliness.

Dr. Forbes Watson has, perhaps, been the most successful of all writers in putting into words the reasons why the rose has such power over mankind:

"The flower has something almost human about it—warm, breathing, soft as the fairest cheek; of white, no longer snowy like the narcissus, but flushed with hues of animating pink; either flower, white or red, being alike symbolical of glowing, youthful passion."

In the East the rose gardens have been famed for centuries. The flower is said to burst into bloom at the voice of the nightingale. The poet Jami says: "You may place a handful of fragrant herbs of flowers before the nightingale, yet he wishes not in his constant heart for more than the sweet breath of his beloved rose." It is said that an Arabian doctor discovered the recipe for rose-water in the Tenth Century; but the perfume may be older than that. The *Rosa centifolia* is the blossom used. The Indians and Persians have known how to make their attar of rose for centuries.

A large volume would be required to chronicle the romance of the rose, for it is the flower of love, beauty, and poetry. It is dedicated to Venus, and Venus is frequently represented as wearing a crown of roses. Her son, Eros or Cupid, is also wreathed and garlanded with roses. Cupid gave a rose to Harpocrates, god of silence—hence the rose is also the symbol of silence. "Under the rose," a saying that expresses silence and secrecy, is derived from this legend. A siren holding a rose stands among the sculptured ruins of Pæstum. Roses and myrtle adorned the brides of Greece and Rome. The profusion of roses used for decorations at feasts astounds us even to-day. No epicure was satisfied with the cup of Falernian wine unless it were perfumed with roses; and the Spartan soldiers at the Battle of Cirrha actually refused wine because it was not perfumed with roses. This makes us wonder if those Spartan mothers, of whom we hear so much, were really as severe as they are reputed to have been. Red roses were dedicated to Jupiter; damask roses to Venus; and white roses to Diana or the moon. The rose was given to the Virgin Mary as her particular flower; and many Italian painters as well as Flemish, Spanish, and German, have painted the Madonna of the Rose, the Madonna of the Rose-hedge, the Madonna of the Rose-bush, and the Madonna of the Rose-garden. The rosary, introduced by St. Dominick in commemoration of his having been shown a chaplet of roses by the Virgin, originally consisted of rose-leaves pressed into balls.

II

"Lilies of All Kinds"

THE LILY (*Lilium candidum*). The fact that *Perdita* calls for "lilies of all kinds" shows that

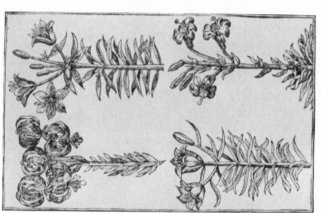

RED, WHITE DAMASK AND MUSK-ROSES; LILIES; AND EGLANTINES AND DOG-ROSES: FROM PARKINSON

Shakespeare loved one of the most beautiful families of flowers that grace the earth, and knew the many varieties that grew in the English gardens of his day, which include the Lily-of-the-Valley (in his time called Lily Conally); the splendid yellow lilies; the red martagon and spotted martagon (tiger-lilies); as well as the pure white lily. Parkinson, who writes so beautifully of plants and blossoms, did not neglect the lily. He says: "The lily is the most stately flower among many," and he directs attention "to the wonderful variety of lilies known to us in these days, much more so than in former times."

First on the list comes the white lily, which has always been regarded from time immemorial as the most beautiful member of this most beautiful family, a picture of purity with its white silken petals exquisitely set off by the yellow anthers and breathing such delicious fragrance. This is the lily of which Shelley sings:

> And the wand-like lily, which lifteth up
> As a Mænad, its moonlight colored cup,
> Till the fiery star which is its eye
> Gazed through clear dew on the tender sky.

"The ordinary White Lily, *Lilium candidum*," writes Parkinson, "scarce needeth any description,

it is so well known and so frequent in every garden.
The stalk is of a blackish green color, having many
fair broad and long green leaves. The flower stands
upon long green footstalks, of a fair white color,
with a long pointell in the middle and white chives
tipt with yellow pendants about it. The smell is
something heady and strong. It is called *Lilium
album*, the White Lily, by most writers; but by
poets, *Rosa Junonis*, Juno's Rose."

How perfect is this flower! Texture, form, hue,
sheen, perfume—all express exquisite loveliness.
The lily refreshes us with its cool beauty and its
purity and lifts our thoughts upward to heaven.

Gerard describes eight lilies in his "Herbal"
(1597), all of which were known to Shakespeare.
Certainly among *Perdita's* flowers was the martagon,
which takes its name from the Italian *martagone*,
meaning a Turk's turban. This lily is also called
"Chalcedonian" and "Scarlet martagon" and
"Turk's Cap," by Parkinson, who tells us that the
*"Lilium rubrum Byzantinum Martagon Constan-
tinopolitanum*, or the red martagon of Constantinople, is become so common everywhere and so well
known to all lovers of these delights that I shall
seem unto them to lose time to bestow many lines
upon it; yet because it is so fair a flower and was

at the first so highly esteemed, it deserveth its place and commendations. It riseth out of the ground bearing a round, brownish stalk, beset with many fair green leaves confusedly thereon, but not so broad as the common White Lily, upon the top whereof stand one, two, or three, or more, flowers upon long footstalks, which hang down their heads and turn up their leaves again, of an excellent red crimson color and sometimes paler, having a long pointel in the middle compassed with whitish chives, tipt with loose yellow pendants, of a reasonable good scent, but somewhat faint. We have another of this kind, the Red Spotted Martagon of Constantinople, that groweth somewhat greater and higher with a larger flower, and of a deeper color, spotted with divers black spots, or streaks, and lines, as is to be seen in Mountain Lilies."

The martagon belongs to the tiger-lily class, whose characteristics have been so imaginatively brought out by Thomas Bailey Aldrich:

> I like the chaliced lilies,
> The heavy Eastern lilies,
> The gorgeous tiger-lilies,
> That in our garden grow.
>
> For they are tall and slender;
> Their mouths are dashed with carmine,

And when the wind sweeps by them,
On their emerald stalks
They bend so proud and graceful,—
They are Circassian women,
The favorites of the Sultan,
Adown our garden walks.

And when the rain is falling,
I sit beside the window
And watch them glow and glisten,—
How they burn and glow!
O for the burning lilies,
The tender Eastern lilies
The gorgeous tiger-lilies,
That in our garden grow.

Shakespeare has many beautiful passages concerning the lily. He often refers to its whiteness. He considers it as impossible a task "to paint the lily" as it is "to gild refined gold," or "to throw a perfume on the violet."

How the lily was loved by the ancients! The Egyptians adored it; the Persians named cities for it; the Hebrews worshiped it. The Greeks and Romans called the lily Juno's flower, and fancied that the flower owed its very existence to drops of milk spilled on earth from Juno's white breast when she was nursing the infant Hercules.

The church consecrated the lily to the Virgin Mary. It was her flower as Queen of Heaven. In many old religious paintings of the Annunciation, the Angel Gabriel, appearing before the Virgin, usually holds the "Annunciation Lily," or "Madonna Lily" in his hand. Joseph's staff was said to have blossomed into lilies, and it is the white lily that is usually represented in this connection.

Wonderful family this lily tribe, flowers of the grand style and haughty demeanor! Ruskin enlightens us as to why it is every one loves them and why they are entwined with many of our thoughts of art and life:

"Under the name of *Drosidæ* come plants delighting in interrupted moisture—moisture which comes either partially, or at certain seasons—into dry ground. They are not water-plants, but the signs of water resting among dry places. In the *Drosidæ* the floral spirit passes into the calix also, and the entire flower becomes a six-rayed star, bursting out of the stem laterally, as if it were the first of flowers and had made its way to the light by force through the unwilling green. They are often required to retain moisture, or nourishment, for the future blossom through long times of drought; and this they do in bulbs underground, of which some become a rude and simple, but most wholesome food for man.

"Then the *Drosidæ* are divided into five great

orders—lilies, asphodels, amaryllis, irids and rushes. No tribes of flowers have had so great, so varied, or so healthy an influence on man as this great group of *Drosidæ*, depending not so much on the whiteness of some of their blossoms, or the radiance of others, as on the strength and delicacy of the substance of their petals; enabling them to take forms of faultless, elastic curvature, either in cups, as the Crocus, or expanding bells, as the true Lily, or heathlike bells, as the Hyacinth, or bright and perfect stars, like the Star of Bethlehem, or, when they are affected by the strange reflex of the serpent nature which forms the labiate group of all flowers, closing into forms of exquisitely fantastic symmetry as the Gladiolus.   Put by their side their Nereid sisters the Water-lilies, and you have in them the origin of the loveliest forms of ornamental design and the most powerful floral myths yet recognized among human spirits, born by the streams of the Ganges, Nile, Arno and Avon.

"For consider a little what each of those five tribes has been to the spirit of man.   First, in their nobleness; the Lilies gave the Lily of the Annunciation; the Asphodels, the flower of the Elysian Fields; the Irids, the fleur-de-lys of chivalry; and the Amaryllis, Christ's lily of the fields; while the

Rush, trodden always under foot, became the emblem of humility. Then take each of the tribes and consider the extent of their lower influence. *Perdita's* 'the Crown Imperial, lilies of all kinds,' are the first tribe, which, giving the type of perfect purity in the Madonna's Lily, have, by their lovely form, influenced the entire decorative design of Italian sacred art; while ornament of war was continually enriched by the curves of the triple petals of the Florentine *'giglio'* and the French fleur-de-lys; so that it is impossible to count their influence for good in the Middle Ages, partly as a symbol of womanly character and partly of the utmost brightness and refinement in the city which was the 'flower of cities.' "

Astrologers placed the lily under the moon; and the flower is certainly dreamy enough and celestial enough to be under the rule of Diana, or Astarte.

III

Crown-Imperial and Flower-de-luce

THE CROWN-IMPERIAL (*Fritillaria imperalis*) is mentioned by *Perdita*. A native of Persia, Afghanistan, and Kashmir, it was taken to Constantinople, and thence to Vienna in 1576.

Finally it came to England with other luxuries of the Renaissance. Gerard had it in his garden, and describes it as follows:

"Out of a tuft of narrow leaves the stem rises and terminates in a second tuft immediately below which is a ring of large tulip-like flowers, pendulous and golden yellow. Looking into the bells at the base of every petal is a white and concave nectary from which hangs a drop of honey that shines like a pearl. In the bottom of each of the bells there is placed six drops of most clear shining water, in taste like sugar resembling in shew fair Orient pearls, the which drops if you take away there do immediately appear the like. Notwithstanding if they may be suffered to stand still in the flower according to his own nature, they will never fall away, no, not if you strike the plant until it be broken."

The Crown-Imperial was, perhaps, of all choice "outlandish flowers" the choicest. Parkinson gives it the first place in the Garden of Delight, opening his great book, "Paradisus Terrestris," with an account of it:

"The Crown Imperial," he writes, "for his stately beautifulness deserveth the first place in this our Garden of Delight. The stalk riseth up three, or four, foot high, being great, round and of a

MARTAGON LILIES, WARLEY, ENGLAND

purplish color at the bottom, but green above, beset
from thence to the middle thereof with many long
and broad green leaves of our ordinary white lily,
but somewhat shorter and narrower, confusedly
without order, and from the middle is bare, or naked,
without leaves for a certain space upwards, and then
beareth four, six, or ten flowers, more or less, according to the age of the plant and the fertility of the
soil where it groweth.   The buds at the first appearing are whitish, standing upright among a bush, or
tuft, of green leaves, smaller than those below and
standing above the flowers.   After a while they turn
themselves and hang downward every one upon his
own footstalk, round about the great stem, or stalk,
sometimes of an even depth and other while one
lower, or higher, than another, which flowers are
near the form of an ordinary Lily, yet somewhat
lesser and closer, consisting of six leaves of an
orange-color striped with purplish lines and veins,
which add a great grace to the flowers.   At the bottom of the flower, next unto the stalk, every leaf
thereof hath on the outside a certain bunch, or
eminence, of a dark purplish color, and on the inside
there lieth in those hollow bunched places certain
clear drops of water like unto pearls, of a very sweet
taste, almost like sugar.   In the midst of each flower

is a long white stile, or pointell, forked, or divided, at the end and six white chives, tipt with yellowish pendants, standing close above it. After the flowers are past, appear six square seed vessels, standing upright, winged as it were, or weltered on the edges, yet seeming but three-square, because each couple of those welted edges are joined closer together, wherein are contained broad, flat and thin seeds of a pale brownish color, like unto other lilies, but much greater and thicker also.

"This plant was first brought from Constantinople into these Christian countries, and, by relation of some that sent it, groweth naturally in Persia. It flowereth most commonly in the end of March, if the weather be mild, and springeth not out of the ground until the end of February, or beginning of March, so quick it is in the springing. The head with seeds are ripe in the end of May. It is of some called *Lilium Perticum*, or Persian Lily; but because we have another, which is more usually called by that name, I had rather, with Alphonsus Pancius, the Duke of Florence, his physician (who first sent the figure thereof unto Mr. John de Brancion) call it *Corona Imperialis*, the Crown Imperial."

There is a legend that the Crown-Imperial grew in the garden of Gethsemane, where it was often admired by Jesus Christ. At that time, according to the story, the flowers were *white* and erect on the stalk. During the night of the agony when Our Lord passed through the garden, this flower was the only one that did not bow its head. Later the proud flower bent its head and tears of sorrow filled its cup. Ever since that time the plant has continued to bow in sorrow and its tears flow forever.

Dr. Forbes Watson loves the flower with its "bold, decided outlines." His description is all too short. "The tall stem," he says, "rises like a mast through the lower leaves, is thence for a short space bare till it is topped by the crowning sheaf of leaf-swords, out of which droop so gracefully the large yellow wax-like bells. Here every line seems to pierce like an arrow, the composition is so clear and masterly."

The Crown-Imperial appears in the celebrated book called "Guirlande de Julie," which the Duc de Montausier gave on New Year's Day, 1634, to his bride, Julie de Rambouillet. This was a magnificent album: every leaf bore a beautifully painted flower and a verse descriptive of it or in praise of it contributed by different artists and poets. Chapelain chose the Crown-Imperial for his theme, pretending that it sprang from the blood of Gustavus Adolphus of Sweden, who, not being able to offer his hand to Julie, came to her in the guise of this flower.

FLOWER-DE-LUCE (*Iris pseudacorus*). *Perdita's* mention of "lilies of all kinds, the flower-de-luce being one," shows that Shakespeare classed this flower among the lilies. So did the botanists of his time. Symbol of eloquence and power, the Egyptians placed the purple iris upon the brow of the Sphinx. The scepter of their monarchs was adorned with this flower, its three petals representing faith, wisdom, and valor. The kings of Babylon and Assyria also bore it on their scepters. The Greeks laid the iris on the tombs of women because they believed that Iris guided dead women to the Elysian Fields. Although the iris was also dedicated to Juno, it is more particularly the flower of Iris, lovely Iris, one of the beautiful Oceanides, daughters of Ocean, and messenger of the gods, who whenever she wished to descend upon the earth threw her rainbow scarf across the sky and with all its prismatic colors glistening in her perfumed wings descended from heaven to earth upon the graceful bow that joins the seen and the unseen worlds. The purple, yellow, orange, and blue tints of the rainbow live again in the petals and drooping lips called "falls." What a flower of charm, mystery, and majesty! Sphinx of the flower world! The iris was extremely popular in Shakespeare's day. Parkinson gives a great many "Flower-de-luces, or Iris" in his monumental work. We find "the Purple, the Blue, the Purple-striped, the Peach-colored, the White, the White-striped, the Parti-colored, the Milk-White, the Silver color, the White with Yellow Falls, the Straw color, the Spanish Yellow, the Purple and Yellow, the Purple or Murrey, the Great Turkie, the Common Purple, the Great Dalmatian, the Yellow of Tripoli, the Double Blew, the Double Purple, the Purple Dwarf," and many others which prove how popular this flower was in Tudor and Stuart gardens, and what splendid specimens were known to the people of Shakespearian times. Parkinson also adds: "The dried root called Orris is of much use to make sweet powders, or other things, to perfume apparel or linen."

The fleur-de-lis early became the symbol of France. At the proclamation of a new king the Franks always placed a living flower, or flag, as it was called, in his hand as the symbol of power. Because his wife, St. Clotilde, had a vision of the iris, Clovis erased the three frogs on his shield and substituted the iris.   In consequence also of a dream, Louis VII took the iris for his device in 1137, from which it became known as the fleur de Louis, later contracted into fleur-de-lys and fleur-de-lis.   When Edward III claimed the crown of France in 1340, he quartered the old French shield bearing the fleur-de-lis with his English lion.   The iris, or flower-de-luce (as the English wrote it), did not disappear from the English coat of arms until 1801.

Shakespeare speaks of the fleur-de-lis in the *Messenger's* speech in "King Henry VI": [1]

> Awake, awake, English nobility!
> Let not sloth dim your honors new begot:
> Cropp'd are the flower-de-luces in your arms;
> Of England's coat one half is cut away.

And again in the same play: [2]

LA PUCELLE.   I am prepared: here is my keen-edged sword,
    Deck'd with fine flower-de-luces on each side.

In "The Merry Wives of Windsor" [3] there is a humorous play upon words regarding the heraldic use of "the flower-de-luce."

[1] Part I, Act I, Scene I.
[2] Part I, Act I, Scene II.
[3] Act I, Scene I.

IV

Fern and Honeysuckle

THE FERN (*Pteris aquilina*), with its graceful and beautifully indented leaves and its peculiar acrid scent, delicious to many persons, would be admitted into the Shakespeare garden because of its fantastic qualities, even if its beauty did not sue for recognition. The fern is a fairy plant. According to folk-lore it always blossomed at twelve o'clock on St. John's eve (June 21), Midsummer night. The flower is described as a wonderful globe of sapphire blue (according to other stories a ruby red); and in a few moments after its blossoming the seed appeared. *Oberon*, the fairy king, was supposed to watch for the precious seed so that he might prevent mortals from obtaining it; but any one fortunate enough to gather fern-seed would be under the protection of spirits, and would be enabled to realize all his fondest desires. Furthermore, any one who wore the fern-seed about him would be invisible. Shakespeare was familiar with this superstition, for he makes *Gadshill* exclaim in "King Henry IV": [1] "We steal as in a castle, cock-sure:

[1] Part I, Act II, Scene I.

we have the receipt of fern-seed, we walk invisible."

An old account tells us:

The fern flowers on Midsummer night at twelve o'clock,
and drives away all unclean spirits. First of all it puts
forth buds, which afterwards expand, then open, and
finally change into flowers of a dark red hue. At midnight
the flower opens to its fullest extent and illuminates everything around. But at that precise moment a demon plucks
it from its stalk. Whoever wishes to procure this flower
must be in the forest before midnight, locate himself near
the fern and trace a circle around it. When the Devil
approaches and calls, feigning the voice of a parent, sweet-
heart, etc., no attention must be paid, nor must the head be
turned; for if it is, it will remain so. Whoever becomes the
happy possessor of the flower has nothing to fear; by its
means he can recover lost treasure, become invisible, rule on
earth and under water and defy the Devil.

Because the fern was so powerful against evil
and because it was sacred to St. John the Baptist,
witches detested it.

Pliny stated that the fern had neither flower nor
seed; and some of the old English writers believed
this. William Turner, however, went to work to
investigate matters. In his famous "Herbal," published in 1562,[1] he says:

"Not only the common people say that the fern

[1] See p. 34.

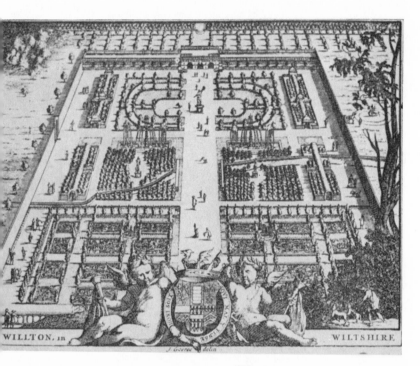

WILTON, FROM DE CAUX

WILTON GARDENS TO-DAY

hath seed, but that was also the opinion of a Christian physician named Hieronymus Tragus, who doth not only say that the fern hath seed, but writeth that he found upon Midsummer Even seed upon brakes.[1] Although all they that have written of herbs have affirmed and holden that the brake doth neither seed nor fruit, yet have I divers times proved the contrary, which thing I will testify here in this place for their sakes that be students of herbs. I have, four years together, one after another, upon the Vigil of St. John the Baptist, which we call in English Midsummer Even, sought for this seed of brakes upon the night; and, indeed, I found it early in the morning before day-break. The seed was small, black, and like unto poppy. I went about this business all figures, conjurings, saunters, charms, witchcraft, sorceries, taking with me two or three honest men. When I sought this seed all the village about did shine with bonfires that the people made there; and sometime when I sought the seed I found it, and sometimes I found it not. Sometime I found much and sometime I found little; but what should be the cause of this diversitie, or what Nature meaneth in this thing, surely I cannot tell."

HONEYSUCKLE (*Lonicera perfolium*). De-

[1] Brake, or bracken, fern.

licious name—honeysuckle! And truly this is one of "the sweetest flowers for scent that blows." It takes its name because of the honey dew found on it, so old writers say. Romantic is its other name, "woodbine," suggesting sylvan spots and mossy beds, where cool-rooted flowers grow, such as the "nodding violet." Shakespeare knew what he was about when he enwreathed and entwined *Titania's* canopy with "luscious woodbine" in loving union with the equally delicious eglantine. The honeysuckle is a flower that belongs particularly to moonlight and to fairy-time.

In "Much Ado About Nothing" *Hero* gives the command: [1]

Good Margaret, run into the parlor and whisper to Beatrice
And bid her steal into the pleachèd bower,
Where honeysuckles ripened by the sun,
Forbid the sun to enter.

A bower covered with the intense, yet subtle, perfume of the honeysuckle, doubly sweet in the hot sun that had ripened the blossoms and drawn out their inmost sweetness, was just the place to send "saucy Beatrice" for the purpose of lighting the flame of love for *Benedick*, and just the place to send, a little later, the cynical *Benedick* for the pur-

[1] Act III, Scene I.

pose of awakening his interest in the "Lady Disdain." Shakespeare evidently knew that the honeysuckle is the flower of ardent lovers, and so he framed his pleachèd bower with these sweet-scented blossoms. The French have a tender name for the flower, *cher feu* (dear flame), because it is given by lovers to one another. The other French name, *chèvre feuille*, is derived from the Latin *caprifolium* (goat-leaf), which may have been given to it because the plant leaps over high rocks and precipices, where only goats and others of the cloven-footed tribe dare venture. The honeysuckle in Shakespeare's day was a favorite remedy for wounds in the head. Witches also valued it for their sorcery. According to sorcerers and astrologers this plant was under the rule of Mercury.

It is hard to decide when the honeysuckle is at its best. Whether at hot noontide when the clusters of pale buff and white horns of plenty tipped with their long, feathery threads pour their incense into the golden sunlight, or when the less pungent, but equally intoxicating, perfume floats upon the silvery blue air of a moonlit night.

"How sweetly smells the Honeysuckle, in the hush'd night as if the world were one of utter peace and love and gentleness."

Landor has thus expressed what the delicious honeysuckle makes us feel.

"The monthly honeysuckle," writes Celia Thaxter, "is most divine.   Such vigor of growth I have never seen in any other plant.   It climbs the trellis on my piazza and spreads its superb clusters of flowers from time to time all summer.   Each cluster is a triumph of beauty, flat in the center and curving out to the blossoming edge in joyous lines of loveliness, most like a wreath of heavenly trumpets breathing melodies of perfume to the air.   Each trumpet of lustrous white deepens to a yellower tint in the center where the small ends meet; each blossom where it opens at the lips is tipped with fresh pink; each sends out a group of long stamens from its slender throat like rays of light; and the whole circle of radiant flowers has an effect of gladness and glory indescribable: the very sight of it lifts and refreshes the human heart.   And for its odor, it is like the spirit of romance, sweet as youth's tender dreams.   It is summer's very soul."

Enchanting season of fern and honeysuckle, perfumed stars that shine through green leaves and bells that send forth peals of incense instead of sound!

She show'd me her ferns and woodbine sprays
  Fox-glove and jasmine stars,
A mist of blue in the beds, a blaze
  Of red in the celadon jars,
And velvety bees in convolvulus beds
  And roses of bountiful June—
Oh, who would think that the summer spells
  Could die so soon? [1]

V

Carnations and Gilliflowers

CARNATIONS (*Dianthus caryophyllus*). *Per-dita* calls carnations and streak'd gilliflowers "the fairest flowers o' the season." Carnation was originally spelled coronation, because the flower was used to make crowns, garlands, and wreaths. In the days of Pliny it was called *dianthus*, or flower of Jove, and was also worn in wreaths and crowns. From Chaucer we know that it was cultivated as the "Clove Gilliflower" in English gardens; and because it was used to add a spicy flavor to wine and ale, it acquired the popular name of "sops in wine." Hence Spenser in his "Shepherd's Calendar" sings:

Bring hither the pink and purple Columbine
  With Gillyflowers;

[1] Locker-Lampson.

> Bring Coronations and Sops-in-wine
>   Worn of paramours.

And again:

> Youth's folk now flocken everywhere
> To gather May baskets and smelling Brere,[1]
> And home they hasten the posts to dight
> And all the kirk pillars in daylight
> With Hawthorn budes and sweet Eglantine
> And garlands of Roses and Sops-in-wine.

"Its second specific name," writes Ellacombe, "*Caryophyllus*, i. e., nut-leaved, seems at first very inappropriate for a grassy-leaved plant; but the name was first given to the Indian Clove tree and from it transferred to the Carnation on account of its fine clove scent. Its popularity as an English plant is shown by its many names—Pink, Carnation, Gilliflower (an easily-traced and well-ascertained corruption from *Caryophyllus*), Clove Picotee[2] and Sops-in-wine from the flowers being used to flavor wine and beer.

"There is an historical interest also in the flowers. All our Carnations, Picotees and Cloves came originally from the single *Dianthus caryophyllus*. This is not a true British plant; but it holds a place in

[1] Brier.

[2] From the French *picot*, a pinked edge. We still use the word "pinked" for a cut edge, and "pinking-iron" is the word for that with which the edge is cut.

the English flora, being naturalized on Rochester and other castles. It is abundant in Normandy; and I found it in 1874 covering the old castle of Falaise, in which William the Conqueror was born. I have found that it grows on the old castles of Dover, Deal and Cardiff, all of them of Norman construction, as was Rochester, which was built by Gandulf, the special friend of William. Its occurrence on these several Norman castles makes it very possible that it was introduced by the Norman builders, perhaps as a pleasant memory of their Norman homes, though it may have been incidentally introduced with the Norman (Caen) stone, of which parts of the castles are built. How soon it became a florist's flower we do not know; but it must have been early, for in Shakespeare's time the sorts of Cloves, Carnations and Pinks were so many that Gerard says: 'A great and large volume would not suffice to write of every one at large in particular, considering how infinite they are, and how every year, every climate and country bringeth forth new sorts and such as have not heretofore been written of.' "

Parkinson speaks of "Carnations, Pinks and Gilloflowers." "The number of them is so great," he says, "that to give several descriptions to them were end-

less." He therefore mentions a few favorites.
Among the Carnations we find the Great Harwich,
or old English Carnation; the Red, or Clove Gilloflower; the Yellow, or Orange Tawny Gilloflower;
the Gray Hulo; the Red Hulo; the Blue Hulo; the
Grimelo, or Prince; the White Carnation, or Delicate; the French Carnation; the Crystal, or Chrys-
talline; the Fragrant; the Striped Savage; the Oxford Carnation; the King's Carnation; the Granado;
the Grand Père; and the Great Lombard. His Gilliflowers include the Lustie Gallant, or Westminster;
the Bristow Blue; the Bristow Blush; the Red
Dover; the Fair Maid of Kent, or Ruffling Robin;
the Queen's Gilloflower; the Dainty; the Brassill
Gilloflower; the Turkie Gilloflower; the Pale
Pageant; the Sad Pageant; Master Bradshawe his
Dainty Lady; John Witte his great Tawny Gilloflower; the Striped Tawny; the Marbled Tawny;
Master Tuggie his Princess; the Feathered Tawny;
and Master Tuggie his Rose Gilloflower. The
Tuggies had a superb garden at Westminster in
which they made a specialty of Carnations, Gilliflowers, and Pinks. The flower upon which Parkinson spends his most loving description is the Great
Harwich. The enthusiasm of this old flower-
fancier, who writes so delightfully, makes us feel

A GARDEN OF DELIGHT

that the Great Harwich is an English institution, just as important as the Roast Beef of Old England or the English Plum Pudding.

"I take this goodly great old English Carnation," he writes, "as a precedent for the description of all the rest, which for his beauty and stateliness is worthy of a prime place. It riseth up with a great thick, round stalk divided into several branches somewhat thickly set with joints, and at every joint two long green (rather than whitish) leaves, turning, or winding, two or three times round. The flowers stand at the tops of the stalks in long great and round green husks, which are divided into five points, out of which rise many long and broad pointed leaves, deeply jagged at the ends, set in order, round and comely, making a gallant, great double Flower of a deep Carnation color, almost red, spotted with many blush spots and streaks, some greater and some lesser, of an excellent soft, sweet scent, neither too quick, as many others of these kinds are, nor yet too dull; and with two whitish crooked threads, like horns, in the middle. This kind never beareth many flowers; but as it is slow in growing, so in bearing, not to be often handled, which showeth a kind of stateliness fit to preserve the opinion of magnificence."

What a delightful idea Parkinson gives of the conscious dignity of the flower! How vividly he brings the Great Harwich before us and makes us love its green husk, its mottled leaves, its rich scent, and its curling horns!

"Gilloflowers," Parkinson continues, "grow like unto Carnations, but not so thick set with joints and leaves. The stalks are more, the leaves are narrower and whiter, for the most part, and in some, do as well a little turn.[1] The flowers are smaller, yet very thick and double in most; and the green husks in which they stand are smaller likewise. The ends of the leaves are dented and jagged. Some also have two small white threads, crooked at the ends like horns in the middle of the flower; others have none.

"Most of our later writers do call them by one general name, *Caryophyllus sativus* and *Flos Caryophyllus*, adding thereto *maximus* when we mean Carnations, and *major* when we would express Gilloflowers, which name is taken from Cloves in that the scent of the ordinary red Gilloflower especially doth resemble them. Divers other several names have been formerly given them, as *Vetonica*, or *Betonia altera* or *Vetonica altibus* and *coronaria*, *Herba Tunica*, *Viola Damascena*, *Ocellus Damas-*

---

[1] "Do a little turn" is charming, suggesting a quaint little waltz.

cenus and *Barbarieus*. Of some *Cantabrica Pliny*. Some think they were unknown to the Ancients and some would have them be *Iphium* of Theophrastus, whereof he maketh mention in his sixth and seventh chapters of his sixth book among garland and summer flowers; others to be his *Dios anthos* or *Louis flos*. We call them in English, the greatest kinds, Carnations, and the other Gilloflowers (quasi July Flowers). The Red, or Clove, Gilloflower is most used in physic in our apothecaries' shops (none of the others being accepted, or used) and is accounted to be a very cordial."

Some writers say that the gilliflower was a cure for pestilential fevers. Gerard writes: "Conserve made of the flowers of the Clove Gilloflower and sugar is exceeding cordial and wonderfully above measure, doth comfort the heart, being eaten now and then."

The Italian painter, Benvenuto Tisio, always painted a gilliflower in the corner of his pictures as his emblem, from which he is always called *Il Garofalo*.

The word "pink" is derived from the Dutch word *Pinkster* (Whitsuntide), the season a certain "Whitsuntide Gilliflower" was in bloom. The pink was regarded as an antidote for epilepsy; and a vinegar made of pinks was used as a valued remedy for the plague. The Elizabethans also thought "if a conserve be composed of it, it is the life and delight of the human race."

Our old friend Parkinson describes Pinks as "wild, or small, Gilloflowers, some bearing single and some double flowers, some smooth, almost without any deep dents on the edges, and some jagged, or, as it were, feathered. Some growing upright, like unto Gilloflowers, others creeping, or spreading, some of one color, some of another, and many of divers colors."

He gives Double and Single Pinks, Feathered or Jagged Pinks, Star Pinks, Great Sea Gilloflower, or Great Thrift, "often used in gardens to empale or border a knot, because it abideth green in Winter and Summer and that by cutting it may grow thick and be kept in what form one list." We also find Single Red Sweet John, Single White Sweet John; Double Sweet John; Single Red Sweet William; Double Red Sweet William; Speckled Sweet William, or London Pride; Deep Red, or Murrey Color, Sweet William; and Single White Sweet William.

"These," he adds, "are all generally called *Armerius* or *Armeria*, yet some have called them *Vetonica agrestis* and others *Herba Tunica, Scar-*

latea and *Carophyllus silvestris.* We do in English, in most places call the first, or narrower-leaved kinds, Sweet Johns and all the rest Sweet Williams; yet in some places they call the broader-leaved kinds that are not spotted *Tolmeiners* and London Tufts; but the speckled kind is termed by our English Gentlewomen, for the most part, London Pride. We have not known of any of these used in physic."

These spicy pinks and luscious July flowers and the simple Sweet-Johns and Sweet-Williams as well recall the lovely lines of Matthew Arnold:

Soon will the high midsummer pomp come on.
Soon will the musk carnations break and swell,
Soon shall we have gold-dusted Snapdragon,
    Sweet-william with his homely cottage smell,
And stocks in fragrant blow;
Roses that down the alleys shine afar,
    And open jasmine in muffled lattices
    And groups under the dreaming garden trees
And the pale moon and the white dreaming star.

VI

Marigold and Larkspur

MARIGOLD (*Calendula officinalis*). Shakespeare was devoted to the marigold. He always speaks of it with poetic rapture.

>The marigold that goes to bed with the sun
>And with him rises, weeping,

is *Perdita's* idea of the shining flower, which in these few words she tells us closes its petals in the evening and at dawn awakens wet with dew.[1]

Then in the beautiful dawn-song in "Cymbeline" [2] "winking Mary-buds" remind us that the gold-flower is consecrated to the Virgin Mary. This song, so full of the freshness of early morning and the sweet perfume of flowers holding in their deep cups sufficient dew to water the horses of the sun just appearing above the horizon, is one of the loveliest of lyrics:

>Hark! Hark! the lark at heaven's gate sings,
>   And Phœbus 'gins arise,
>His steeds to water at those springs
>   On chaliced flowers that lies;
>And winking Mary-buds begin to ope their golden eyes;
>With everything that pretty is—My lady, sweet, arise:
>   Arise, arise.

"The Marygold," says Lyte, "hath pleasant, bright and shining yellow flowers, the which do close at the setting down of the Sun and do spread and open again at the Sun rising."

And Lupton writes: "Some do call it *Spousa*

---

[1] "The Winter's Tale"; Act IV, Scene III.
[2] Act II, Scene III.

Solis, the Spowse of the Sun, because it sleeps and is awakened with him."

In "The Rape of Lucrece" Shakespeare also mentions the flower:

> Her eyes, like marigolds, hath sheathed their light
> And canopied in darkness sweetly lay
> Till they might open to adorn the day.

Very prettily the flower is introduced in Middleton and Rowley's "Spanish Gipsy":

> You the Sun to her must play,
> She to you the Marigold,
> To none but you her leaves unfold.

Another old English name for the marigold was ruddes and a prettier one was the gold-flower, often called simply the gold or goold. Chaucer talks of "yellow Goldes." The name was still used in Elizabeth's day. "Colin Clout" has:

> But if I her like ought on earth might read,
> I would her liken to a crown of lilies,
> Upon a Virgin bride's adorned head,
> With roses dight and goolds and daffodillies.

In Medieval times the monks gave to the gold-flower the prefix Mary, with the legend that the Virgin Mary loved to wear the flower in her bosom. Hence Shakespeare calls it "Mary-buds." Of Shakespeare's Marigolds Parkinson writes:

"They are called *Caltha* of divers and taken to be that *Caltha* whereof both Virgil and Columella have written. Others do call them *Calendula of the Kalends*, that is the first day of the months, wherein they are thought chiefly to flower. And thereupon the Italians call them *Fiori di ogni mese*, that is the Flowers of Every Month. We call them in English generally Golds, or Marigolds.

"The herb and flowers are of great use with us among other pot-herbs, and the flowers, either green or dyed, are often used in possets, broths and drinks; as a comforter of the heart and spirits; and to expel any malignant, or pestilential quality, gathered near thereunto. The Syrup and Conserve made of the fresh flowers are used for the same·purpose to good effect."

Parkinson divides marigolds unto two classes: single and double.

"The garden Marigold," he says, "hath round green stalks, branching out from the ground into many parts, whereon are set long, flat green leaves, broader and rounder at the point than anywhere else. The flowers are sometimes very thick and double (breaking out of a scaly, clammy green head), composed of many rows of leaves, set so close together, one within another, that no middle thrum

The House at Chelsey in the County of Midlesex one of the Seats
Marques[...] of Worcester Baron H[...] of Chepstow Ragla[...] G[...]

The West Neole, a Potent[...] orange Henry Duke of Beaufort
and Temple of the Mo[...]noble order of the Garter

can be seen; and sometimes less double, having a small brown spot of a thrum in the middle; and sometimes but of two or three rows of leaves with a large brown thrum in the middle: every one whereof is somewhat broader at the point and nicked in two or three corners, of an excellent fair, deep, gold-yellow color in some, and paler in others, and of a pretty strong and resinous sweet scent.

"There is no difference between this and the single Marigold but that the flowers are single, consisting of one row of leaves of the same color; either paler or deeper yellow, standing about a great brown thrum in the middle. Our gardens are the chief places for the double flowers to grow in."

Another description is contained in the famous "Gardener's Labyrinth" by Didymus Mountain (Thomas Hill):[1]

"The Marigold, named of the herbarians *Calendula*, is so properly termed for that in every Calend and in each month this reneweth of the own accord and is found to bear flowers as well in Winter as Summer, for which cause the Italians name the same the flower of every month. But some term it the Sun's Spowse, or the follower of the Sun; and is of some named the Husbandman's Dial, in that the

[1] See p. 68.

same showeth to them both the morning and evening tide.   Others name it the Sun's Bride and
Sun's Herb, in that the flowers of the same follow
the Sun as from the rising by the South into the
West; and by a notable turning obeying to the Sun,
in such manner that what part of Heaven he pos-
sesseth they unto the same turned behold, and that
in a cloudy and thick air like directed, as if they
should be revived, quickened and moved with the
spirit of him.   Such is the love of it knowen to be
toward that royal Star, being in the night time for
desire of him as pensive and sad, they be shut or
closed together; but at the noontime of the day fully
spread abroad as if they with spread arms longed,
or diligently attended, to embrace their Bridegroom.
This Marigold is a singular kind of herb, sown in
gardens as well for the pot as for the decking of
garlands, beautifying of Nosegays and to be worn in
the bosom."

The Marigold is supposed to be the chrysanthemum or gold-flower of the Greeks, the *Heliotrope-
solsequium;* and the story goes that the flower was
originally the nymph Clytie, who gazed all day upon
the Sun with whom she had fallen in love.   At
length she was turned into the flower.   "All yellow
flowers," said St. Francis de Sales, "and above all

those that the Greeks call Heliotrope and we call
Sunflower, not only rejoice at the sight of the sun,
but follow with loving fidelity the attraction of its
rays, gazing at the Sun and turning towards it from
its rising to its setting."

Very charmingly does George Wither, a contemporary of Shakespeare, refer to this:

> When with a serious musing I behold
> The grateful and obsequious Marigold,
> How duly every morning she displays
> Her open breast when Phœbus spreads his rays;
> How she observes him in his daily walk,
> Still bending towards him her small slender stalk;
> How when he down declines she droops and mourns,
> Bedewed, as 't were, with tears till he returns;
> And how she veils her flowers when he is gone.
> When this I meditate methinks the flowers
> Have spirits far more generous than ours.

Margaret of Orleans, grandmother of Henri IV,
knowing well the legend of the flower, chose for her
device a marigold with the motto, *je ne veux suivre
que lui seul.*

In the reign of Henry VIII the marigold was often
called "Souvenir" and sentimental ladies wore
wreaths of marigolds mixed with the heartsease. To
dream of marigolds denoted prosperity, riches, suc-
cess, and a happy and a wealthy marriage. As the

marigold was a solar flower, the astrologers placed it under the sign and care of Leo.

In a wholly Elizabethan spirit Keats sang:

> Open afresh your round of starry folds,
>   Ye ardent Marigolds!
> Dry up the moisture from your golden lids,
>   For great Apollo bids
> That in these days your praises should be sung
> On many harps, which he has lately strung;
> And when again your dewyness he kisses
> Tell him I have you in my world of blisses!
> So happly when I rove in some far vale
> His mighty voice may come upon the gale.

The Shakespearian marigold must not be confused with the French marigold (*Flos Africanus*), called also Indian gilliflower, flower of Africa, and flower of Tunis. A long chapter on this marigold appears in Parkinson's book. This is the tightly rolled up little flower of irregular ragged petals, but of a rich, deep golden hue.

Parkinson also speaks of the great Peruvian sunflower, which he admires greatly and describes with enthusiasm. We know it well as our common sunflower with its dark center and yellow rays—a magnificent specimen of the floral world, worthy of the adoration of the Incas and of more than we usually accord to it.

LARKSPUR (*Delphinium*). "Lark's-heels trim," one of the flowers in the introductory song of "The Two Noble Kinsmen," is the.Delphinium, also called larkspur, lark's-claw, lark's-toes, and knight's-spur. The generic name is derived from the Greek *delphinium*, because the buds were thought to resemble the form of a dolphin.

As with many other plants, there were two kinds, the "wild" and the "tame"; and it was the wild kind that was "nourished up in gardens," according to Parkinson, who describes the plant as having "small, long, green leaves, finely cut, almost like fennel and the branches ending in a long spike of hollow flowers with a long spur behind them. They are of several colors: bluish purple, or white, or ash color, or red, paler or deeper, and parti-colored of two colors in a flower.

"They are called diversely by divers writers as *Consolida regulis*, *Calearis flos*, *Flos regius*, *Buccinum Romanorum*, and *Cuminum silvestre alterum Dioscoridis;* but the most usual name with us is *Delphinium*. But whether it be the true *Delphinium* of Dioscorides, or the Poet's Hyacinth, or the Flower of Ajax, another place is fitter to discuss than this. We call them in English Larks-heels, Larkspurs, Larkstoes, or claws, and Monks-hoods. There is no

use of any of these in Physicke in these days that I
know, but are wholly spent for their flowers sake."

A modern botanist remarks:

"The gardener's ideal has been the full-flowered
spike with a goodly range of colors on the chord of
blue. We think of larkspur as blue. Some of these
blues are pale as the sky, some pure cobalt, others
indigo and still others are a strange broken blue,
gorgeous and intense, yet impure, glittering on the
surface as if it were strewn with broken glass, and
sometimes darkened into red. The center of a larkspur is often grotesque; the hairy petals suggest a
bee at the heart of a flower, and the flower itself
looks like a little creature poised for flight. In
structure the garden race has changed very little
from the primitive type, though that type has wandered far from the simplicity of the buttercup, which
names the *Ranunculacæ*. Whatever path of evolution the larkspur has trod, it is very clear that the
goal at which it has arrived is cross-fertilization by
means of the bee. At some time along the path the
calix took on the duties of the corolla, became highly
colored, developed a spur, while at the same time
the corolla lessened both in size and in importance.
The stamens mature before the pistil and are so
placed that the bee cannot get at the honey without

covering its head with pollen which it then bears to another flower."

The name of Monk's-hood is also given to the Blue Helmet-flower, or aconite.[1]

Yellow Lark's-heels is a name our Elizabethan forefathers gave to the *Nasturtium Indicum*, a plant found in the West Indies and taken by the early Spanish explorers to Spain, whence it traveled to all parts of Europe.

"It is now very familiar in most gardens of any curiosity," says Parkinson. "The likeness of this flower, having spurs, or heels, is of so great beauty and sweetness withall that my Garden of Delight cannot be unfurnished of it. The flowers are of an excellent gold yellow color and grow all along the stalks. In the middle of each of the three lower leaves there is a little long spot, or streak, of an excellent crimson color, with a long heel, or spur, behind, hanging down. The whole flower hath a fine small scent, very pleasing, which, being placed in the middle of some Carnations, or Gilloflowers (for they are in flower at the same time), make a delicious Tussiemussie, as they call it, or Nosegay, both for sight and scent. Monardus and others call it *Flos sanguineus* of the red spots in the flower, as

[1]See p. 248.

also *Nastnerzo de las Indias*, which is *Nasturtium Indicum;* and we thereafter in English, Indian Cresses. Yet it may be called from the form of the flowers Yellow Lark's heels."

This flower is phosphorescent and is said to emit sparks, which are visible in the dark.

VII

Pansies for Thoughts and Poppies for Dreams

PANSY (*Viola tricolor*). "Pansies—that's for thoughts," exclaims *Ophelia*, as she holds out the flower that the French call *pensée* (thought). And it is the pansy that is "the little western flower" upon which "the bolt of Cupid fell" and made "purple with love's wound" and which "maidens call Love in Idleness,"—the flower that *Oberon* thus described to *Puck* when he sent him to gather it. The juice of it squeezed by *Oberon* upon *Titania's* eyelids and by *Puck* upon the Athenian youths and maidens, who were also sleeping in the enchanted wood on that midsummer night, occasioned so many fantastic happenings.

The pansy in those days was the small Johnny-Jump-Up, a variety of the violet, according to the old writers, "a little violet of three colors, blue, white and yellow." Milton noted that it was "freaked with jet." Michael Drayton showed its close relationship to the violet in the lines:

> The pansy and the violet here
> As seeming to descend
> Both from one root and very fair
> For sweetness yet contend.

Gerard wrote in 1587:

"The stalks are weak and tender, whereupon grow flowers in form and figure like the Violet and for the most part of the same bigness, of three sundry colors, whereof it took the surname Tricolor, that is to say purple, yellow and white, or blue; by reason of the beauty and bravery of which colors they are very pleasing to the eye, for smell they have little, or none at all."

The pansy was beloved of Elizabethans: the great number of popular names it had proves this. In addition to Pansy and Johnny-Jump-Up, it was called Herb Trinity, because of the three distinct petals, which made it a flower of peculiar religious significance. Another name was Three-Faces-under-a-Hood because it had such a coquettish air. Another name was Fancy Flamey, because its amethystine colors are like those seen in the flames of burning wood; and because lovers gave it to one another it had the pet names of Meet-me-at-the-Garden-Gate, Kiss-me-at-the-Garden-Gate, Kiss-me-quick, Kiss-me, Call-me-to-you, Cuddle-me-to you, Kiss-me-ere-I-rise, Pink-of-my-John, Cupid's-flower, Love-in-Idleness, and Heartsease.

There were no "wine dark pansies" in Shakespeare's time to charm the lover of flowers and none of the splendid deep purple velvets and mauves and pale amethysts and burnt orange and lemon and claret and sherry and canary hues that delight us to-day, and which are, to use the quaint old expression, "nourished up in our gardens." The modern beauties began to be developed about 1875, chiefly by the French specialists, and, as a modern writer remarks:

"Such sizes, such combinations, such weirdness of expression in quaint faces painted upon the petals were never known before. The colors now run a marvellous range; pure-white, pure yellow, deepening to orange, and darkening to brown, as well as a bewildering variety of blues and purples and violets. The lowest note is a rich and velvety shade that we speak of as black; but there is no black in flowers.

"The pansy is the flower for all. It is cheap; it is hardy; it is beautiful; and its beauty is of an unusual and personal kind. The bright, cheerful, wistful or roguish faces look up to you with so much apparent intelligence that it is hard to believe it is all a pathetic fallacy and there is nothing there."

Whether the modern pansies should be included in a Shakespeare garden is a question for each owner of a garden to decide; but there should certainly be a goodly number of the little "Johnny-Jump-Ups."

POPPY (*Papaver somniferum*). Shakespeare introduces the poppy only indirectly when he speaks of the "drowsy syrup" in "Othello." The white poppy is the flower from which the sleeping potion was made. "Of Poppies," says Parkinson, "there are a great many sorts, both wild and tame; but our garden doth entertain none but those of beauty and respect. The general known name to all is *Papaver*, Poppie. Yet our English gentlewomen in some places call it by name Joan's Silver Pin. It is not unknown, I suppose, to any that Poppies procureth sleep." Other old names for the poppy were Corn Rose and Cheese Bowl.

Scarlet poppies in the wreath of Ceres among the wheat-ears, scarlet poppies .mingled with large white-petaled daisies, and Ragged Robins belong to everybody's mental picture of midsummer days.

"We usually think of the Poppy as a coarse flower," says Ruskin, "but it is the most transparent and delicate of all the blossoms of the field. The rest, nearly all of them, depend on the texture of their surface for color. But the Poppy is painted glass; it never glows so brightly as when the sun shines *through* it. Whenever it is seen against the light, or with the light, always it is a flame and warms in the wind like a blown ruby."

"Gather a green Poppy bud, just when it shows the scarlet line at its side, break it open and unpack the Poppy. The whole flower is there compact in size and color, its stamens full grown, but all packed so closely that the fine silk of the petals is crushed into a million of wrinkles. When the flower opens, it seems a relief from torture; the two imprisoning green leaves are shaken to the ground, the aggrieved corolla smooths itself in the sun and comforts itself as best it can, but remains crushed and hurt to the end of its days."

Delicate and fine as is the above description, the sympathetic tribute to the poppy by Celia Thaxter does not suffer in proximity. She says:

"I know of no flower that has so many charming tricks and manners, none with a method of growth more picturesque and fascinating. The stalks often take a curve, a twist from some current of air, or some impediment, and the fine stems will turn and bend in all sorts of graceful ways, but the bud is always held erect when the time comes for it to blossom.   Ruskin quotes Lindley's definition of what constitutes a poppy, which he thinks 'might stand.' This is it: 'A Poppy is a flower which has either four or six petals and two or more treasuries united in one, containing a milky stupefying fluid in its stalks and leaves and always throwing away its calix when it blossoms.'

"I muse over their seed-pods, those supremely graceful urns that are wrought with such matchless elegance of shape and think what strange power they hold within.   Sleep is there and Death, his brother, imprisoned in those mystic sealed cups.   There is a hint of their mystery in their shape of somber beauty, but never a suggestion in the fluttering blossom: it is the gayest flower that blows.   In the more delicate varieties the stalks are so slender, yet so strong, like fine grass stems.   When you examine them, you wonder how they hold even the light weight of the flower so firmly and proudly erect; and they are clothed with the finest of fine hairs up and down the stalks and over the green calix.

"It is plain to see, as one gazes over the poppy-beds on some sweet evening at sunset, what buds will bloom in the joy of next morning's first sunbeams, for these will be lifting themselves heavenward, slowly and silently, but surely. To stand by the beds at sunrise and see the flowers awake is a heavenly delight. As the first long, low rays of the sun strike the buds, you know they feel the signal! A light air stirs among them; you lift your eyes, perhaps to look at a rosy cloud, or follow the flight of a carolling bird, and when you look back again, lo! the calix has fallen from the largest bud and lies on the ground, two half-transparent light green shells, leaving the flower-petal wrinked in a thousand folds, just released from their close pressure. A moment more and they are unclosing before you eyes. They flutter out on the gentle breeze like silken banners to the sun."

It would be tempting in a Shakespeare garden to include many kinds of this joyous, yet solemn, flower; and certainly as many were common in Elizabethan gardens it would not be an anachronism to have them. However, if the space be restricted and the garden lover a purist then the white poppy only should be planted.

VIII

Crow-flowers and Long Purples

CROW-FLOWERS (*Scilla nutans*). These are among the flowers *Ophelia* wove into a wreath. The queen tells the court:

> There is a willow grove ascaunt the brook,
> That shows his hoar leaves in the glassy stream.
> There, with fantastic garlands did she come
> Of crow flowers, nettles, daisies and long purples
> That liberal shepherds give a grosser name
> But our cold maids do dead men's fingers call them.[1]

Shakespeare did not select *Ophelia's* flowers at random. They typified the sorrows of the gentle victim of disappointed love whose end was first madness, then suicide. The crow-flowers signified "fair maiden"; the nettles, "stung to the quick"; the daisies, "her virgin bloom"; and the long purples, "under the cold hand of Death." Thus what Shakespeare intended to convey by this code of flowers was, "A fair maiden, stung to the quick, her virgin bloom in the cold hand of Death."

It is generally supposed that the wild blue hyacinth, or harebell (*Scilla nutans*), a flower asso-

[1] "Hamlet"; Act IV, Scene VII.

ciated with pure and faithful love, is the crow-
flower; and authority is given to this theory in the
old ballad, which, of course, Shakespeare knew,
called "The Deceased Maiden Lover":

> Then round the meddowes did she walk
> Catching each flower by the stalk,
> Such as within the meddowes grew,
> As dead man's thumb and harebell blue,
> And as she pluckt them still cried she,
> "Alas! there's none ere loved like me."

Some critics have objected to the blue harebell
because it is a spring flower, and it is midsummer
when *Ophelia* drowns herself. These authorities
suggest the Ragged Robin for *Ophelia's* crow-flower,
and others again the buttercup, also called creeping
crowfoot (*Ranunculus repens*). Bloom writes:

"It is generally assumed that the flowers are those
of the meadow and that a moist one. Why? It is
equally probable they are those of the shady hedge
bank and that the crow-flowers are the poisonous
rank *Ranunculus reptans* and its allies; that the
nettles are the ordinary *Urtica dioica* not necessarily
in flower, or if this be objected to on account of the
stinging qualities which the distraught *Ophelia*
might not be insensible to, its place could be taken
by the white dead nettle *Lamium album L.* The
daisies may be moon-daisies and the long purples

PLEACHING AND PLASHING, FROM "THE GARDENER'S LABYRINTH"

SMALL ENCLOSED GARDEN, FROM "THE GARDENER'S LABYRINTH"

Arum masculatum, another plant of baleful influence, with its mysterious dead white spadix bearing no very far fetched resemblance to a dead man's finger wrapped in its green winding-sheet and whose grosser name, cuckoo-pint, is ready at hand. With this selection we have plants of the same situation flowering at the same time and all more or less baneful in their influence."

The crow has given its name to many flowers. There are, indeed, more plants named for the crow than for any other bird: crowfoot, crow-toes, crowbells (for daffodil and bluebells) crow-berry, crow-garlick, crow-leeks, crow-needles, and many others.

LONG PURPLE (*Arum masculatam* or *Orchis mascula*) is very closely related to our woodland Jack-in-the-Pulpit. It has many names: Arum; Cookoo-pint, Cookoo-pintle, Wake-Robin, Friar's-cowl, Lords-and-Ladies, Cow-and-Calves, Ramp, Starchwort, Bloody-men's-finger, and Gethsemane, as the plant is said to have been growing at the Cross and to have received some drops of the Savior's blood. This flower is mentioned in Tennyson's "A Dirge":

> Round thee blow, self-pleached deep,
> Bramble roses, faint and pale,
> And long purples of the dale.

Dr. Forbes Watson writes:

"I use the old name Wake Robin because it is so full of poetry—to think of the bird aroused from sleep by the soundless ringing of the bell. Arum, or Lords and Ladies, is the more usual name."

The plant is under the dominion of Mars, so the astrologers said.

IX

Saffron Crocus and Cuckoo-flowers

SAFFRON CROCUS (*Crocus verus sativus Autumnalis*). Shakespeare speaks of saffron as a color—"the saffron wings of Iris" and "saffron to color the Warden [pear] pies." He never mentions the crocus from which the saffron was obtained, yet a Shakespeare garden should have this plant represented. Saffron had long been known in England; for in the time of Edward III a pilgrim from the East had brought, concealed in his staff, a root of the precious Arabic *al zahafaran*. In Shakespeare's time saffron was used for soups and sauces and to color and flavor pies, cakes, and pastry-confection. Saffron was also important medicinally, and for dyeing silks and other materials. The beautiful orange-red stigmas, the *crocei odores* of Virgil, were dried and the powder pressed into cakes and sold in the shops.

"The true saffron," writes Parkinson, "that is used in meats and medicines, shooteth out his narrow long green leaves first, and, after a while, the flowers, in the middle of them, appear about the end of August, in September and October, according to the soil and climate where they grow. These flowers are composed of six leaves apiece, of a murrey, or reddish purple color, having a show of blue in them. In the middle of these flowers there are some small yellow chives standing upright, which are unprofitable; but, besides these, each flower hath two, three, or four greater and longer chives hanging down, upon, or between, the leaves, which are of a fiery red color and are the true blades of saffron which are used physically, or otherwise, and no other."

The raising of saffron was a great industry. Old Tusser gave the good advice to

> Pare saffron plot,
>   Forget it not.
> His dwelling made trim,
>   Look shortly for him!
> When harvest is gone,
>   Then Saffron comes on;

> A little of ground
> Brings Saffron a pound.

Saffron Walden in Essex and Saffron Hill in London received their names because of the quantity of saffron crocus grown in those places.

The saffron crocus is a handsome flower, but somewhat capricious. Dr. Forbes Watson writes:

"We look at the few well selected flowers in our hand and let our mind wander in the depths of those fair-striped cups, their color so fresh, so cool, so delicate, and yet not too cool, with that central yellow stamen-column and the stigma emerging from it like a fiery orange lump. The Purple Crocus, partly from the full materials for color-contrast afforded by its interior, partly from the exceeding delicacy of tint, the lilac stripes and markings, the transparent veins and the pale watery lake which lies at the bottom of the cup, seem to bear us away to some enchanted spot, a fairy-land of color where no shadow ever falls—a land of dim eternal twilight and never fading flowers. Note, too, the differences between the Crocuses with regard to the stigma. In the Purple Crocus, where it is needed to complete the harmony of the flower, it rises long and flame-tipped out of the tall bundle of yellow stamens. Notice also the curve of the outside of the Purple

Crocus cup in a well-selected flower, and observe how quiet and solemnly beautiful it is in perfect harmony with the general expression."

According to legend, the flower derived its name from a beautiful youth, Crocus, who was transformed into the flower. His love, Smilax, was changed at the same time into the delicate vine of that name. Another legend says that the flower sprang from the blood of the infant Crocus, who was accidentally killed by a disk thrown by the god Mercury. The Egyptians encircled their wine-cups with the saffron crocus; the Greeks and Romans adorned the nuptial couch with the saffron crocus; the robes of Hymen, god of marriage, were saffron-hued; and poets called the dawn saffron, or crocus-colored. Shakespeare, therefore, had authority for "the saffron wings of Iris."

Saffron is an herb of the sun and is under the rule of Leo.

CUCKOO-FLOWER (*Lychnis Flos cuculi*): Shakespeare mentions "cuckoo-flowers" in "King Lear,"[1] in company with troublesome weeds. *Cordelia* remarks:

> Crown'd with rank fumiter and furrow-weeds,
> With burdocks, hemlocks, nettles, cuckoo-flowers,

[1] Act IV, Scene IV.

Darnel, and all the idle weeds that grow
On our sustaining corn.

Shakespeare's cuckoo-flower is identified as the Ragged Robin, so called from its finely cut blue petals which have a ragged appearance. It is also known as the meadow campion, or Meadow Pink. Parkinson says: "Feathered Campions are called *Armoraria pratensis* and *Flos cuculi.* Some call them in English Crow-flowers and Cuckowe Flowers, and some call the double hereof The Fair Maid of France."

From the above we see why it is that the Ragged Robin has been identified by some authorities as *Ophelia's* crow-flower; for even Parkinson seems to consider the crow-flower and cuckoo-flower as identical. Some of the old herbalists give the name cuckoo-flower to the lady-smock, which is called cuckoo-buds. The cuckoo's name is given to many flowers: we have the cuckoo-flower, cuckoo-buds, cuckoo's-bread (wood-sorrel), cuckoo's-meat, cuckoo-pint (*Arum maculatum*), cuckoo-grass; cuckoo-hood (blue corn-flower), etc. The cuckoo-flower (Ragged Robin) is dedicated to St. Barnabas.

X

Pomegranate and Myrtle

THE POMEGRANATE (*Punica*) is a regal flower. Its burning beauty appeals to every one who loves color, for the scarlet of the pomegranate has a depth and a quality that is all its own. The crinkled silken petals, rising from a thick, red calix and set off by bright green leaves of wondrous glossy luster and prickly thorns, delight those who love beauty. Moreover, there is something luscious and strange about the pomegranate that makes us think of Oriental queens and the splendors of Babylon and Persia, ancient Egypt and Carthage. It is a flower that Dido might have worn in her hair, or Semiramis in garlands around her neck!

Shakespeare knew perfectly well what he was doing when he placed a pomegranate beneath *Juliet's* window, amid whose leaves and flowers the nightingale sang so beautifully. The pomegranate was exactly the flower to typify the glowing passion of the youthful lovers.

"There are two kinds of pomegranate trees," writes Parkinson, "the one tame or manured, bearing fruit; the other wild, which beareth no fruit, because it beareth double flowers, like as the Cherry, Apple and Peach-tree with double blossoms.

"The wild Pomegranate (*Balustium maius sive Malus Punica*) is like unto the tame in the number of purplish branches, having thorns and shining fair green leaves, somewhat larger than the former. From the branches likewise shoot forth flowers far more beautiful than those of the tame, or manured, sort, because they are double, and as large as a double Province Rose, or rather more double, of an excellent bright crimson color, tending to a silken carnation, standing in brownish cups or husks, divided at the brims usually into four, or five, several points like unto the former, but that in this kind there never followeth any fruit, no not in the country where it is naturally wild. The wild, I think, was never seen in England before John Tradescant, my very loving good friend, brought it from the parts beyond the seas and planted it in his Lord's Garden at Canterbury. The rind of the Pomegranate is used to make the best sort of writing Ink, which is durable to the world's end."

The pomegranate was from the dawn of history a favorite with Eastern peoples. It is represented in ancient Assyrian and Egyptian sculpture and had a religious significance in connection with several Oriental cults.

The tree was abundant in ancient Egypt and the fruit was such a favorite of the Israelites that one complaint against the desert into which Moses led them was the charge that it was "no place of pomegranates," and Moses had to soothe the malcontents by promising that the pomegranate would be among the delights of Canaan, "a land of wheat and barley, vines and fig-trees and pomegranates, a land of olive oil and honey." The pomegranate was one of the commonest fruits of Canaan, and several places were named after it—Rimmon. The Jews employed the pomegranate in their religious ceremonies. On the hem of Aaron's sacred robe pomegranates were embroidered in blue and purple and scarlet alternating with golden bells,—an adornment that was copied from the ancient kings of Persia. The pomegranate was also carved on the capitals of the pillars of the Temple of Jerusalem. Solomon said to his bride, "I will cause thee to drink of spiced wine of the juice of my pomegranates." There is a tradition that the pomegranate was the fruit of the Tree of Life and that it was the pomegranate that Eve gave to Adam.

The Romans called it the Carthaginian apple. The pomegranate abounded in Carthage and derives its botanical name, *Punica*, from this place. Pliny says that the pomegranate came to Rome from Carthage; but its original home was probably Persia or Babylon. It was early introduced into Southern Europe and was taken to Spain from Africa. Granada took its name from the fruits and the Arms of the province display a split pomegranate. Around Genoa and Nice there are whole hedges of it— rising to the height sometimes of twenty feet. It was introduced into England in Henry VIII's time, carried there among others by Katharine of Aragon, who used it for her device. Gerard grew pomegranates in his garden. Many legends are connected with the pomegranate, not the least being that of Proserpine. When the distracted Ceres found her daughter had been carried off by Pluto, she begged Jupiter to restore her. Jupiter replied that he would do so if she had eaten nothing in the realms of the Underworld. Unfortunately, Pluto had given her a pomegranate and Proserpine had eaten some of the seeds. She could not return. The sorrow of Ceres was so great that a compromise was made and the beautiful maiden thereafter spent six months in the Underworld with her husband and six months with her mother above ground—a beautiful story of the life of the seed!

In nearly all the legends of the East in which the word "apple" is mentioned it is the pomegranate that is intended. It is said to have been the fruit presented by Paris to Venus, and it is always associated with love and marriage.

In Christian art the pomegranate is depicted as bursting open and showing the seeds. This is interpreted as both a promise and an emblem of hope in immortality. St. Catharine, the mystical bride of Christ, is sometimes represented with a pomegranate in her hand. The infant Savior is also often represented as holding the fruit and offering it to the Virgin: Botticelli's "Madonna of the Melagrana" is a famous example.

There is also a legend that because the pomegranate was planted on the grave of King Eteocles, the fruit has exuded blood ever since. The number of seeds has caused it to become the symbol of fecundity, generation, and wealth.

MYRTLE (*Myrtus latifolia*) was looked upon in Shakespeare's time as a delicate and refined rarity, emblem of charming beauty and denoting peacefulness, plenty, repose, and love. Shakespeare makes *Venus* and *Adonis* meet under a myrtle shade; he speaks of "the soft myrtle" in "Measure for Measure"; and he alludes "to the moon-dew on the myrtle leaf," which is as delicate a suggestion of the evening perfume as the "morning roses newly washed with dew" is of the scents at dawn.

"We nourish Myrtles with great care," says Parkinson, "for the beautiful aspect, sweet scent and rarity, as delights and ornaments for a garden of pleasure, wherein nothing should be wanting that art, care and cost might produce and preserve.

"The broad-leafed Myrtle riseth up to the height of four or five foot at the most with us, full of branches and leaves, growing like a small bush, the stem and elder branches whereof are covered with a dark colored bark, but the young with a green and some with a red, especially upon the first shooting forth, whereon are set many fresh green leaves very sweet in smell and very pleasant to behold, so near resembling the leaves of the Pomegranate tree that groweth with us that they soon deceive many that are not expert therein, being somewhat broad and long and pointed at the ends, abiding always green. At the joints of the branches, where the leaves stand, come forth the flowers upon small footstalks, every one by itself, consisting of five small white leaves,

with white threads in the middle, smelling also very
sweet."

According to the Greeks, Myrtle was a priestess
of Venus and an especial favorite of the goddess,
who, wishing to preserve her from a too ardent
suitor, turned her into this plant, which continues
odorous and green throughout the year. Having
the virtue of creating and preserving love and being
consecrated to Venus, the mrytle was symbolic of
love. Consequently it was used for the wreaths of
brides, as the orange-blossom is to-day. Venus wore
a wreath of myrtle when Paris awarded her the
Golden Apple for beauty,—perhaps in memory of
the day when she sprang from the foam of the sea
and, wafted ashore by Zephyrus, was crowned with
myrtle by the Morning Hours! Myrtle was always
planted around the temples dedicated to Venus.

Rapin writes:

> When once, as Fame reports, the Queen of Love
> In Ida's valley raised a Myrtle grove,
> Young wanton Cupids danced a summer's night
> Round the sweet place by Cynthia's silver light.
> Venus this charming green alone prefers,
> And this of all the verdant kind is hers:
> Hence the bride's brow with Myrtle wreath is graced,
> Hence in Elysian Fields are myrtles said

> To favor lovers with their friendly shade,
> There Phædra, Procris (ancient poets feign)
> And Eriphyle still of love complain
> Whose unextinguished flames e'en after death remain.

The Romans always displayed myrtle lavishly at weddings, feasts, and on all days celebrating victories. With the Hebrews the myrtle was the symbol of peace; and among many Oriental races there is a tradition that Adam brought a slip of myrtle from the Garden of Eden because he considered it the choicest of fragrant flowers.

The myrtle was early loved in England. In one of the old Roxburgh Ballads of the Fifteenth Century a lover presses his suit by promising:

> And I will make the beds of Roses,
> And a thousand fragrant posies;
> A cap of flowers and a kirtle
> Embroidered with leaves of myrtle.

In those days and long afterward there was a saying that "if you want to be sure of your myrtle taking root, then you must spread out your dress grandly and look proud" when you are planting your slip. We can imagine one of the Fifteenth Century ladies spreading her voluminous and flowing robes with majestic grace and holding her head adorned with the tall pointed cap, or *hennin*, with veil fluttering from its peak as she planted the little flower in her tiny walled Garden of Delight!

There is a saying, too, that one must never pass a sweet myrtle bush without picking a spray. The flowering myrtle is considered the luckiest of all plants to have in the window, but it must be watered every day.

Autumn

"HERBS OF GRACE" AND "DRAMS OF POISON"

I

Rosemary and Rue

ROSEMARY (*Rosmarinus officinalis*). Rosemary "delights in sea-spray," whence its name. "The cheerful Rosemary," as Spenser calls it, was in high favor in Shakespeare's day. The plant was not only allowed a corner in the kitchen-garden; but it was trained over arbors and allowed to run over the mounds and banks pretty much at its own sweet will. "As for Rosemarie," said Sir Thomas More, "I let it run all over my garden walls, not only because my bees love it, but because it is the herb sacred to remembrance, and, therefore, to friendship; whence a spray of it hath a dumb language that maketh it the chosen emblem at our funeral-wakes and in our burial-grounds."

Ophelia handed a sprig of rosemary to her brother with the words: "There's rosemary; That's for re-

"A CURIOUS-KNOTTED GARDEN," VREDEMAN DE VRIES

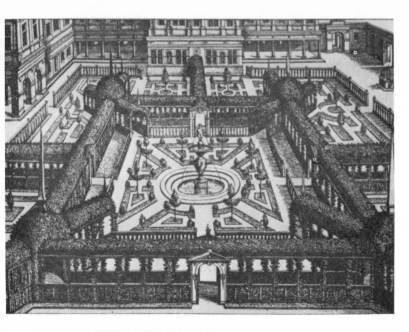

GARDEN WITH ARBORS, VREDEMAN DE VRIES

membrance; pray you, love, remember." Probably
she knew the old song in the "Handful of Pleasant
Delights" [1] where occurs the verse:

> Rosemary is for remembrance
> Between us day and night,
> Wishing that I might always have
> You present in my sight.

Rosemary was used profusely at weddings
among the decorations and the strewings on the
floor. A sprig of it was always placed in the wine
to insure the bride's happiness.

The herb was also conspicuous at funerals,
naturally enough as the herb was emblematic of remembrance. The *Friar* in "Romeo and Juliet" exclaims:

> Dry up your tears and stick your rosemary
> On this fair corse.[2]

Sometimes the plant was associated with rue as when
in "The Winter's Tale" [3] *Perdita* says,

> Give me those flowers, Dorcas:—reverend sirs,
> For you there's rosemary and rue; these keep
> Seeming and savour the whole winter through.

Most important was rosemary at Christmas-tide.
It had a place among the holly, bay, ivy, and mistle-

[1] See p. 127.
[2] Act IV, Scene V.
[3] Act IV, Scene III.

toe to which it added its peculiar and delicious perfume. Moreover, it was said that rosemary brought happiness to those who used it among the Christmas decorations.

Rosemary also garlanded that most important dish of ceremony—the boar's head, which the butler (or sewer) bore into the hall of great houses and famous institutions, like the colleges of Oxford and Cambridge and the City Companies, on a silver dish, preceded by a flourish of trumpets. The carol he sung began:

> The boar's head in hand bring I,
> With garland gay and rosemary.

Lyte said: "Rosemary comforteth the brain and restoreth speech, especially the conserve made of the flowers thereof with sugar." Worn on the person it was thought to strengthen the memory and to make the wearer successful in everything. The famous Hungary-water, so favorite a perfume in the days of Elizabeth and after, was distilled from rosemary. The leaves were used as a flavor in cooking (just as the Italians use it to-day). Placed in chests and wardrobes, rosemary preserved clothing from insidious moth. According to astrologers, rosemary was an herb of the sun.

"The common Rosemary (*Libanotis Coronaria sive Rosmarinum vulgare*) is so well known," says Parkinson, "through all our land, being in every woman's garden, that it were sufficient to name it as an ornament among other sweet herbs and flowers in our gardens, seeing every one can describe it; but that I may say something of it, it is well observed, as well in this our Land (where it hath been planted in Noblemen's and great men's gardens against brick walls) as beyond the Seas in the natural places where it groweth, that it riseth up unto a very great height, with a great and woody stem of that compass that, being cloven out into thin boards, it hath served to make lutes, or such-like instruments, and here with carpenter's rules and to divers other purposes, branching out into divers and sundry arms that extend a great way and from them again into many other smaller branches whereon are set at several distances at the joints, many very narrow long leaves, green above and whitish underneath, among which come forth toward the tops of the stalks, divers sweet gaping flowers, of a pale or bleak bluish color, many set together, standing in whitish husks. The whole plant as well, leaves as flowers, smelleth exceeding sweet.

"Rosemary is called by the ancient writers

Libanotis, but with this difference, *Stephanomatica*, that is *Coronaria*, because there were other plants called *Libanotis*, that were for other uses, as this for garlands, where flowers and sweet herbs were put together. The Latins called it *Rosmarinum*. Some would make it to be *Cueorum nigrum* of Theophrastus, as they would make Lavender to be his *Cueorum album*, but Matthiolus hath sufficiently confuted that error.

"Rosemary is almost of as great use as Bays or any other herb, both for inward and outward remedies and as well for civil as physical purposes. Inwardly for the head and heart; outwardly for the sinews and joints. For civil uses, as all do know, at weddings, funerals, etc., to bestow among friends; and the physical are so many that you might be as well tired in the reading as I in the writing, if I should set down all that might be said of it."

RUE (*Ruta graveolus*). Rue was a much valued plant in Shakespeare's time. There were many superstitions about it which seem to have been survivals from ancient days, for rue is supposed to have been the moly which Homer says Mercury gave to Ulysses to withstand the enchantments of Circe. Miraculous powers were attributed to rue: it was said to quicken the sight, to stir up the spirits, to sharpen the wit, to cure madness, and to cause the dumb to speak. It was also an excellent antidote against poison and the very smell of it insured preservation against the plague. Rue was, therefore, very popular and was much used as a disinfectant.

Parkinson tells us:

Garden Rue (*Ruta*), or Herbe Grace, groweth up with hard whitish woody stalks whereon are set divers branches of leaves being divided into many small ones, which are somewhat thick and round pointed, of a bluish-green color. The flowers stand at the tops of the stalks, consisting of four small yellow leaves, with a green button in the middle, and divers small yellow threads about it, which growing ripe, contain within them small black seeds.

"The many good properties whereunto Rue serveth hath, I think, in former times caused the English name of Herbe Grace to be given unto it. For without doubt it is a most wholesome herb, although bitter and strong. Some do wrap up a bead roll of the virtues of Rue, as Macer the poet and others, in whom you shall find them set down to be good for the head, eyes, breast, liver, heart, spleen, etc."

Gerard quaintly said:

"It is reported that if a man be anointed with the juice of rue, the bitings of serpents, scorpions, wasps, etc., will not hurt him.　When the weasel is to fight with the serpent, she armeth herself by eating rue against the might of the serpent."

Another quaint idea was that rue throve best if a clipping from the plant was stolen from a neighbor's garden.　Like rosemary, rue was considered by the astrologers as an herb of the sun and was placed under the sign of Leo.

Rue was also called the herb of grace and the "serving man's joy."　Shakespeare frequently refers to the herb o' grace: once in connection with salad in "All 's Well That Ends Well." [1]

Ophelia has rue among her flowers when she distributes appropriate blossoms to the courtiers.　She says:

> There 's rue for you; and some for me;
> We may call it herb of grace o' Sundays.
> Oh, you must wear your rue with a difference.

Again we find rue in the *Duke of York's* garden in "King Richard II."　After the sad queen and her ladies have departed, bewailing the news of the king's deposition, the gardener, looking after them, exclaims:

[1] See p. 237.

Poor queen! So that thy state might be no worse,
I would my skill were subject to thy curse.—
Here did she fall a tear; here, in this place,
I'll set a bank of rue, sour herb of grace:
Rue, even for ruth, here shortly shall be seen,
In the remembrance of a weeping queen.[1]

II

Lavender, Mints, and Fennel

LAVENDER (*Lavendula Spica*). "Hot lavender," *Perdita* calls it. Why is this? Turning to
Gerard for an explanation, we find he says: "Lavender is hot and dry in the third degree and of a substance consisting of many airy and spiritual parts."
Gerard had lavender in his garden and so did Parkinson, who says:

"It is called of some *Nardus Italica* and *Lavendula*, the greater is called *Fœmina* and the lesser
Mas. We do call them generally Lavender, or
Lavender Spike, and the Lesser Spike. Lavender
is little used in physic but outwardly: the oil for
cold and benumbed parts and is almost wholly spent
with us for to perfume linen, apparrell, gloves,
leather, etc., and the dried flowers to comfort and
dry up the moisture of a cold brain.

[1] Act III, Scene IV.

"Our ordinary Garden Lavender riseth up with a hard woody stem about the ground parted into many small branches whereon are set whitish long and narrow leaves by couples; from among which riseth up naked square stalks with two leaves at a joint and at the top divers small husks standing round about them formed in long or round heads or spikes with purple gaping flowers springing out of each of them.   The heads of the flowers are used to be put among linen and apparrell."

Because of its scent, lavender was often included in the nosegay.   Lavender was much loved by sweethearts.   In the "Handful of Pleasant Delights" (1584) it is described thus:

> Lavender is for lovers true,
>   Whichever more be saine,
> Desiring always for to have
>   Some pleasure for their pain.
> And when that they obtainèd have
>   The Love that they require,
> Then have they all their perfect joy
>   And quenched is the fire.

Lavender belongs to the crowfoot family, and therefore is related to the columbine, buttercup, and monk's-hood (aconite).   The ancients used it in their baths, whence the name from the Latin *lavare*, to wash.   The Elizabethans loved, as we do to-day, to place bags of dried lavender among the household linen.

MINTS (*Mentha*). Mints occur in *Perdita's* list with "hot lavender, thyme and savory." Although many kinds of mint were cultivated in gardens, Parkinson mentions only three:

"The Red Mint, or Brown Mint, with dark green nicked leaves, reddish flowers and of a reasonable good scent; Speare Mint, greener and paler leaves, with flowers growing in long ears, or spikes, of a pale red, or blush, color; and Parti-colored, or White Mint, with leaves more nicked, half white and half green, and flowers in long heads, close set together of a bluish color.

"Mints are oftentimes used in baths with Balm and other herbs as a help to comfort and strengthen the nerves and sinews, either outwardly applied or inwardly drunk. Applied with salt, it is a good help for the biting of a mad dog. It is used to be boiled with mackerel and other fish. Being dried, it is often and much used with pennyroyal to put into puddings, as also among pease that are boiled for pottage."

In Elizabethan days it was the custom to strew churches with mint. In an Elizabethan play, "Appius and Virginia," these lines occur:

Thou knave, but for thee ere this time of day
My lady's fair pew had been strewed full gay
With primroses, cowslips and violets sweet,
With mints, with marigold and marjoram meek.

Pliny said "the smell of mint doth stir up the mind and taste to a greedy desire of meat." This carries mint-sauce back into antiquity! Medieval writers believed that the smell of mint refreshed the head and memory; and in Medieval days the herb was dedicated to the Virgin and called *Herba Sanctæ Mariæ* and *Menthe de Notre Dame*. The ancients dedicate it to Venus; hence it was used as a garland for brides—*corona Veneris*. The old myth had it that Menthe was a nymph beloved of Pluto and transformed into an herb by Proserpina who had now become sufficiently interested in the husband who had carried her off against her will to be jealous.

FENNEL (*Fœniculum vulgare*). *Falstaff* speaks of fennel as a relish for conger in "King Henry IV";[1] and *Ophelia* presents fennel to the King to clear his sight just as she gave rosemary to *Laertes* to refresh his memory,[2] for according to a belief held by Pliny: "Fennel hath a wonderful property to

[1] Act II, Scene IV.
[2] "There's fennel for you and columbines" ("Hamlet"; Act IV, Scene V).

mundify our sight and take away the film, or web, that overcasteth and dimmeth our eyes."

"There are three sorts of Fennel," says Parkinson, "whereof two are sweet. The one of them is the ordinary sweet fennel whose seeds are larger and yellower than the common. The other sweet Fennel is not much known and called *Cardus* Fennel by those that sent it out of Italy. Fennel is of great use to trim up and strew upon fish, as also to boil, or put among fish of divers sorts, Cowcumbers pickled and other fruits, etc. The roots are used with parsley roots to be boiled in broths and drinks. The seed is much used to be put into pippin pies and divers other such baked fruits, as also into bread to give it the better relish.

"The Sweet Cardus Fennel being sent by Sir Henry Wotton to John Tradescant had likewise a large direction with it how to dress it, for they used to white it after it hath been transplanted for their uses, which by reason of the sweetness by nature and the tenderness of art causeth it to be most delightful to the taste, especially with them that are accustomed to feed on green herbs."

Another ancient belief preserved by Pliny was "that serpents eat fennel because it restored their youth by causing them to cast their old skins and they recovered their sight by eating the plant."

The flowers of the fennel are yellow.

The Greek name for fennel is *marathon*. The Battle of Marathon took its name from the plant. The story goes that a youth named Pheidippides ran to Sparta to seek aid for Athens when the Persian fleet appeared, and he was told that the Spartans could not come until after the full moon. Very disheartened, he was returning to Athens when Pan appeared to him and promised victory, giving the youth a piece of fennel as a token of his prophecy. The battle took place on a field full of fennel and was known henceforth as the Battle of Marathon (490 B. C.). Statues of the youth always represented him as holding a sprig of fennel. Browning has told the story in his "Pheidippides."

III

Sweet Marjoram, Thyme, and Savory

MARJORAM (*Origanum vulgare*) was a favorite plant in Tudor and Stuart times. An old writer informs us that "Sweet Marjoram is not only much used to please the outward sense in nosegays and in the windows of houses, as also in sweet powders.

sweet bays and sweet washing waters, but is also of much use in physic."

Perdita classes it with hot lavender and savory.[1] Shakespeare, appreciating its delicate and delightful scent, brings this out most beautifully in his "Sonnet XCIX":

The forward violet thus did I chide:—
Sweet thief, whence didst thou steal thy sweet that smells
If not from my love's breath? The purple pride
Which on thy soft cheek for complexion dwells,
In my love's veins thou hast too grossly dyed.
The lily I condemnèd for thy hand,
And buds of marjoram had stolen thy hair.

This comparison is even more lovely than Milton's description of *Sabrina* with her "loose braid of amber-dropping hair."

In Shakespeare's time several species were grown: the common, the winter, and the sweet. They were all favorite pot-herbs and were used in salads, if we may believe the *Clown* in "All's Well That Ends Well":

LAFEN. 'T was a good lady, 't was a good lady; we may pick a thousand sallets ere we light on such another herb.

CLOWN. Indeed, sir, she was the Sweet Marjoram of the sallet, or, rather, the Herb of Grace.

[1] "The Winter's Tale"; Act IV, Scene III.

LAFEN. They are not sallet-herbs, you knave, they are
nose-herbs.

CLOWN. I am no great Nebuchadnezzar; sir, I have not
much skill in grass.[1]

Parkinson writes:

"The common Sweet Marjoram (*Marierome*) is
a low herb, little above a foot high, full of branches
and small whitish, soft, roundish leaves, smelling
very sweet. At the tops of the branches stand divers
small, scaly heads, like unto knots, of a whitish
green color, out of which come, here and there, small,
white flowers, and afterward small reddish seed.
Called *Mariorama* in Latin, it is taken of most
writers to be the Amaracus, or Sampsuchum, of
Dioscorides, Theophrastus and Pliny."

According to the Greek myth a young man named
Amarakos was employed in the household of the
King of Cyprus. One day when he was carrying a
vase of perfumes he dropped it, and he was so much
humiliated by his carelessness that he fell and lost
consciousness.   The gods then changed him into
the sweet herb *amarakos*, or *amaracus*, which is the
Greek name for this plant.   Rapin thought it owed
its existence to Venus:

And tho' Sweet Marjoram will your garden paint
With no gay colors, yet preserve the plant,

[1] Act IV, Scene V.

Whose fragrance will invite your kind regard
When her known virtues have her worth declared:
On Simois' shore fair Venus raised the plant,
Which from the Goddess' touch derived her scent.

THYME (*Thymus Serpyllum*). Thyme has always been appreciated by those who delight in aromatic perfume. It was one of those plants that Lord Bacon said were so delicious when trodden upon and crushed. Thyme was the symbol for sweetness in Elizabethan days.

And sweet thyme true

was a favorite expression. "Sweet thyme true" occurs in connection with roses, "maiden pinks," and daisies in the song in "The Two Noble Kinsmen." [1]

Fairies were thought to be particularly fond of thyme, and that is one reason why Shakespeare covered the bank where *Titania* was wont to sleep with wild thyme. The other reason was that he chose the sweetest flowers for perfume for the canopy and couch of the Fairy Queen: musk-roses, eglantine, honeysuckle, violets, and wild thyme mingling the most delicious of scents. The word comes from the Greek and Latin *thymum*. Thyme

[1] Act I, Scene I.

covered Mount Hymettus and gave to the honey
produced there a particularly delicious aromatic
flavor. The "honey of Mount Hymettus" became
a proverb. Hybla in Sicily was no less famed for
its thyme, and, consequently, its honey. Thyme is
especially a "bee-plant"; and those who would see
their gardens full of bees would do well to plant
thyme with lavish hand. Ladies used to embroider
a bee hovering over a sprig of thyme on the scarves
they gave to their lovers—a symbol of action and
honor. Thyme, too, was supposed to renew the
spirits of man and beast and it was deemed a powerful antidote against melancholy.

Turning to our old friend, Parkinson, we find
that

"The ordinary garden Thyme (*Thymus vulga-
tius sive durius*) is a small, low, woody plant with
brittle branches and small, hard, green leaves, as
every one knoweth, having small white purplish
flowers standing round about the tops of the stalks.
The seed is small and brown, darker than Marjoram.
The root is woody and abideth well divers Winters.

"To set down all the particular uses whereunto
Thyme is applied were to weary both the writer and
the reader. I will but only note out a few, for besides the physical uses to many purposes for the

SHAKESPEARE GARDEN, VAN CORTLANDT HOUSE, VAN CORTLANDT PARK, COLONIAL
DAMES OF THE STATE OF NEW YORK

SHAKESPEARE GARDEN, VAN CORTLANDT HOUSE, VAN CORTLANDT PARK, COLONIAL
DAMES OF THE STATE OF NEW YORK

head, stomach, spleen, etc., there is no herb almost
of more use in the houses both of high and low, rich
and poor, both for inward and outward occasions,
—outwardly for bathings among other hot herbs
and among other sweet herbs for strewings. Inwardly in most sorts of broths, with Rosemary, as
also with other faseting (or rather farsing) herbs,[1]
and to make sauce for divers sorts, both fish and
flesh, as to stuff the belly of a goose to be roasted
and after put into the sauce and the powder with
bread to strew on meat when it is roasted, and so
likewise on roasted or fried fish. It is held by divers
to be a speedy remedy against the sting of a bee,
being bruised and laid thereon.

"The wild Thyme (*Serpyllum hortense sive
maius*), growth upright, but yet is low, with divers
slender branches and small round green leaves,
somewhat like unto small fine Marjoram, and smelling somewhat like unto it. The flowers grow in
roundels at the tops of the branches of a purplish
color. And in another of this kind they are of a
pure white color. There is another also that smelleth
somewhat like unto Musk, and therefore called
Musk Thyme, whose green leaves are not so small
as the former, but larger and longer."

[1] *Farsi,* stuffing.

SAVORY (*Satureia*). This herb is mentioned by
Perdita. It was a great favorite in the old herb-
garden and was probably introduced into England
by the Romans. It is mentioned in Anglo-Saxon
recipes as "savorie." Both the winter and summer
savory were used as seasoning for dressing and
sauces. "The Winter Savory is used as a condiment
and sauce to meat, to put into puddings, sausages
and such-like kinds of meat." So says an old writer,
who continues: "Some do use the powder of the
herb dried to mix with grated bread to bread their
meat, be it fish or flesh, to give it the quicker relish."

Parkinson writes:

"The Winter Savory (*Satureia sive Thymbra*) is
a small, low, bushy herb, very like unto hyssop, but
not above a foot high, with divers small, hard
branches and hard, dark, green leaves thereon,
thicker set together than the former by so much, and
as thick as common Hyssop, sometimes with four
leaves, or more, at a joint, of a reasonable strong
scent, yet not so strong or quick as the former.
The flowers are of a pale purplish color, set at several distances at the tops of the stalks with leaves
at the joints also with them, like the former. The
root is woody with divers small strings thereat, and
abideth all the winter with his green leaves. It is

more usually increased by slipping, or dividing, the root and new setting it, severally again in the Spring, than by sowing the seed."

IV

Sweet Balm and Camomile

SWEET BALM (*Melissa officinalis*). Sweet *Anne Page* commanded the elves to bestow good luck throughout Windsor Castle: [1]

> The several chairs of order look you scour
> With juice of balm and every precious flower.

The Greek and Latin names, *melissa*, *mellissophyllum*, and *apiastrum*, show that this was a bee-plant, which was still the case in Shakespeare's time.

"It is an herb," says Parkinson, "wherein bees do much delight"; and he also tells us that if balm is rubbed on the inside of the hive "it draweth others to resort thither." He goes on to describe it as follows:

"The Garden Balm hath divers square blackish green stalks and round, hard, dark, green pointed leaves growing thereon by couples, a little notched about the edges; of a pleasant sweet scent drawing near to the scent of a Lemon or Citron; and there-

[1] "The Merry Wives of Windsor"; Act V, Scene V.

fore of some called Citrago.   The flowers grow about
the tops of the stalks at certain distances, being small
and gaping, of a pale carnation color, almost white.
The roots fasten themselves strongly on the ground
and endure many years.   It is increased by dividing
the roots; for the leaves die down to the ground
every year, leaving no show of leaf or stalk in the
Winter.   Balm is often used among other hot and
sweet herbs to make baths and washings for men's
bodies in the Summer time.   The herb without all
question is an excellent help to comfort the heart,
as the very smell may induce any so to believe.   It
is also good to heal green wounds being made into
salve.   I verily think that our forefathers hearing
of the healing and comfortable properties of the true
natural Balm and finding this herb to be so effectual
gave it the name of Balm in imitation of his properties and virtues."

Arabian physicians recommended balm for affections of the heart and hypochondria.

CAMOMILE   (*Anthemis   nobilis*).   *Falstaff*
points a moral in the lowly camomile: "Though the
Camomile the more it is trodden on the faster it
grows, yet youth the more it is wasted the sooner
it wears." [1]   A   similar   idea   occurs   in   Lyly's

[1] "King Henry IV"; Part I, Act II, Scene IV.

"Euphues" (1588): "Though the Camomile the more it is trodden and pressed down the more it spreadeth, yet the violet the oftener it is handled and touched, the sooner it withereth and decayeth."

Emblem of patience, the camomile was often used to point a moral and to teach patience. In "The More the Merrier" (1608), a character observes:

> The Camomile shall teach thee patience,
> Which riseth best when trodden most upon.

Because its scent was brought out when trodden upon, camomile was planted in and along walks and on the edges of flower-beds. Its low growth and delicious perfume made it a very attractive border plant.

In Lawson's "New Orchard" (about 1616) there are instructions for "Large walks, broad and long, close and open like the Tempe groves in Thessaly, raised with gravel and sand, having seats and banks of Camomile: all this delights the mind and brings health to the body."

In Shakespeare's day camomile grew in "the wild field by Richmond Green."

"Our ordinary Camomill [says Parkinson] is well known to all to have many small trailing branches set with very fine small leaves and spreading thick over the ground taking root as it spreadeth; the tops of the branches have white flowers with yellow thrums in the middle, very like unto the Featherfew, but somewhat greater not so hard but more soft and gentle in handling and the whole herb is to be of a very sweet scent.

"Camomill is called *Anthemis Leucanthemis* and *Leucanthemum* of the whiteness of the flowers; and *Chamæmœlum* of the corrupted Italian name Camomilla. Some call the naked Camomill *Chrysanthemum odoratum*. The double Camomill is called by some *Chamæmœlum Romanum flore multiplici*.

"Camomill is put to divers and sundry uses both for pleasure and profit; both for inward and outward diseases, both for the sick and the sound, in bathings to comfort and strengthen the sound and to ease pains in the diseased. The flowers boiled in posset drink provoketh sweat and helpeth to expel colds, aches and other griefs. A syrup made of the juice of the double Camomill with the flowers and white wine is used by some against jaundice and dropsy."

V

Dian's Bud and Monk's-hood Blue

DIAN'S BUD (*Artemesia*). This plant is nothing more nor less than absinthe, or wormwood. It is

mentioned under its poetic name by Shakespeare in
"A Midsummer Night's Dream" when *Oberon* bids
Puck find him the "little purple flower called Love
in Idleness," the juice of which placed on sleeping
eyelids would make man, or woman, madly dote on
the first object beheld on awakening, and with which
he intended to anoint the eyelids of the sleeping
Titania. He also told the mischievous sprite that
the charm could be removed with another herb—
Dian's bud, the flower sacred to the goddess Diana.
Later in the play, touching the eyes of the spellbound fairy with this second herb, *Oberon* pro-
nounces the following incantation:

> Be as thou was wont to be,
> See as thou was wont to see;
> Dian's bud on Cupid's flower
> Hath such force and blessed power.

From the earliest times absinthe was associated
with sorcery and was used for incantations. Pliny
says the traveler who carried it about him would
never grow weary and that it would drive away any
lurking devils and counteract the evil eye. Ovid
calls it *absinthium* and speaks of its bitterness.

The Greeks also called it *artemesia* after the goddess Artemis, or Diana, and made it a moon-plant.

Very poetically, therefore, Shakespeare alludes to it as "Dian's Bud,"—and most appropriately does it appear in the moon-lit forest. Gerard, however, quaintly says that is was named for Queen Artemesia, wife of Mausolus, King of Caria, who built the Mausoleum, which was one of the "Seven Wonders of the World." The ancients liked its flavor in their wine as many people still like vermouth, one of its infusions.

In Shakespeare's time people hung up sprays of wormwood to drive away moths and fleas; and there was a homely verse:

> Whose chamber is swept and wormwood is thrown
> No flea for his life dare abide to be known.

Wormwood was also kept in drawers and closets. To dream of the plant was of good augury: happiness and domestic enjoyment were supposed to result. Mugwort is another old name for the plant.

MONK'S-HOOD (*Aconitum Napellus*). This plant has three names: monk's-hood, wolf's-bane, and aconite. Aconite is the "dram of poison" that *Romeo* calls for,[1] and Shakespeare alludes to *aconitum* in "King Henry IV," where the king, addressing *Thomas of Clarence*, compares its strength

[1] "Romeo and Juliet"; Act V, Scene I.

and that of gunpowder. "Though it do work as strong as aconitum or rash gunpowder." [1] Aconite was supposed in Elizabethan days to be an antidote against the most deadly poison. Ben Jonson in "Sejanus" makes one of his characters remark:

> I have heard that aconite
> Being timely taken hath a healing might
> Against the scorpion's sting.[2]

Lord Bacon in "Sylva" calls *Napellus* "the most powerful poison of all vegetables."

Yet despite its poisonous qualities, an English garden lover writes, "the plant has always held, and deservedly, a place among the ornamental plants of our gardens; its stately habit and its handsome leaves and flowers make it a favorite."

The ancients, who were unacquainted with mineral poisons, regarded aconite as the most deadly of all poisons and believed that Hecate had caused the plant to spring from the venomous foam frothing from the mouth of the three-headed dog, Cerberus, when Hercules took him from Pluto's dark realm on one of his Twelve Labors. Ovid describes the aconite as

[1] Part II, Act IV, Scene IV.
[2] Act III, Scene III.

A weed by sorcerers renowned
The strongest constitution to compound
Called aconite, because it can unlock
All bars and force its passage through a rock.

In Greece it was also known as Wolf's-bane (*Lycoc-tonum*), and it was thought that arrow-heads rubbed with it would kill wolves.   Turner quaintly writes in his "Herbal" (1568):

"This of all poisons is the most hastie poison, howbeit Pliny saith this herb will kill a man if he take it, except it find in a man something to kill. Let our Londoners which have of late received this blue Wolf's-bane, otherwise called Monk's Cane, take heed that the poison of the root of this herb do not more harm than the freshness of the flower hath done pleasure. Let them not say but they are warned."

Parkinson's name for it is *Napellus verus flore cœruleo* (Blue Helmet-Flower, or Monk's-hood).

"The Helmet Flower," he writes, "hath divers leaves of a fresh green color on the upper side and grayish underneath, much spread abroad and cut into many slits and notches.   The stalk riseth up two or three foot high, beset to the top with the like leaves, but smaller.   The top is sometimes divided into two or three branches, but more usually

without, whereon stand many large flowers one
above another, in form very like a hood, or open
helmet, being composed of five leaves, the upper-
most of which and the greatest is hollow, like unto
a helmet, or headpiece: two other small leaves are
at the sides of the helmet, closing it like cheeks, and
come somewhat under, and two other which are
the smallest hang down like labels, or as if a close
helmet were opened and some pieces hung by, of a
perfect, or fair, blue color (but grow darker having
stood long) which causeth it to be so nourished up
in Gardens that their flowers, as was usual in former times (and yet is in many country places)
may be laid among green herbs in windows and
rooms for the Summertime; but although their
beauty may be entertained for the uses aforesaid,
yet beware they come not near your tongue or lips,
lest they tell you to your cost, they are not so good
as they seem to be. In the middest of the flower,
when it is open and gapeth wide, are seen certain
small threads like beards, standing about a middle
head, which, when the flower is past, groweth into
three or four, or more, small blackish pods, containing in them black seeds. The roots are brownish
on the outside and white within, somewhat big and
round about and small downwards, somewhat like

unto a small, short carrot root, sometimes two being joined at the head together. It is the true *Napellus* of the ancient writers, which they so termed from the form of a turnip called *Napus* in Latin."

Generally speaking the leaf and flower of the monk's-hood resemble the larkspur; and, like the larkspur and the columbine, the plant has wandered away from its original family, the buttercup tribe. The upper sepal has developed from a spur into a hood.

Winter

"WHEN ICICLES HANG BY THE WALL"

1

Holly and Ivy

HOLLY (*Ilex aquifolium*). Holly, with its beautiful red berries and unique leaf, stiff and prickly, but highly decorative, is the chief emblem of Christmas. We are continuing very ancient traditions when we hang up our Christmas wreaths and garlands. The earliest records of the human race contain references to the custom of decorating houses and temples and evergreens on occasions of rejoicing. Holly comes to us from pagan usage. Five hundred years before the birth of Christ the Romans had been celebrating their midwinter festival—the Saturnalia—commemorating the equality supposed to have existed on earth in the golden reign of Saturn. The Saturnalia was a period of general merry-making and relaxation. People gave each other presents, wished each other "Io Saturnalia," just as we wish each other "Merry

Christmas," and decorated their houses and temples with evergreens, among which holly was conspicuous. The early Christians, who celebrated the birth of Christ during the Saturnalia, adorned their homes with holly for the purpose of safety. They would have been unpleasantly noticed had they left their homes undecorated. After a time holly became associated with the Christian festival itself. As the Christmas celebration spread throughout Europe and into Great Britain, local observances naturally became added to the original rites; and gradually to certain features taken over from the Saturnalia were added customs which the Germanic tribes, the Scandinavians, the Gauls, the Celts, and early Britons practised for the midwinter festival. "Thus," says a modern writer, "all the pagan winter festivals were transmuted and sanctified by the Christian Church into the beautiful Christmas festival that keeps the world's heart young and human. The Church also brought from ancient observances a number of lovable customs, such as the giving of presents, the lighting of candles, the burning of the Yule-log, the Boar's Head, the Christmas Tree, the mistletoe, the holly, laurel and other greens and the mince-pies."

At a season when everything was chosen to commemorate, or invoke, the spirit of growth, or fertility, the holly, mistletoe and ivy—all of which bear fruit in the winter—become particularly precious. Beautiful, cheery holly, with its glossy, prickly leaves and its coral bells, was a sacred plant in the childhood of the world and will continue to be a sacred plant as long as the world lasts. We may make garlands of laurel or bay-leaves, we may bind together ropes of crow's-foot or smilax, and we may bring into our rooms pots of poinsettia; but nothing takes, or will ever take, the place the holly occupies in our affections. In our literature holly is honored. It now symbolizes the spirit of Christmas as nothing else does.

One of the earliest Christmas carols, dating from the Fifteenth Century, describes a contest of Holly and Ivy for the chief place in the hall. Holly is the man and Ivy the woman. They have an argument (which is a kind of duet), each setting forth his or her claim to superiority. Finally, it is decided that Holly, with his beautiful red berries, shall reign in the hall instead of Ivy, whose berries are black. Moreover, many sweet birds are attracted to Holly; but only the owl loves Ivy.

Holly is, of course, the subject of many carols. A typical one of the Fifteenth Century is as follows:

Here comes Holly, that is so gent,
Alleluia!
To please all men is his intent,
Alleluia!
But lord and lady of the hall,
Alleluia!
Whosoever against Holly call,
Alleluia!
Whosoever against Holly do cry,
Alleluia!
In a lepe shall he hang full high.
Alleluia!
Whosoever against Holly do sing,
Alleluia!
He may weep and his handys wring,
Alleluia!

From the above it will be seen that it was a crime to say a derogatory word about holly. Holly was not only loved for its beauty but it was a holy plant. Witches detested it and it was a charm against their evil machinations. The name comes from the Anglo-Saxon *holegn*. The Norse word is *hulf*, or *hulver;* and as Chaucer calls it "Hulfeere" we may conclude that holly was familiar to the people of Chaucer's time under that name.

It is somewhat singular that Shakespeare has written a song of wintry wind and holly berries to be sung in the Forest of Arden. It affords, however, a delightful contrast to the sun-lit summer woodland.

TUDOR MANOR HOUSE WITH MODERN ARRANGEMENT OF GARDENS

While in it holly is not actually described, *Amiens's* song will always remain the song of songs to holly:

> Blow, blow, thou winter wind,
> Thou art not so unkind
>   As man's ingratitude;
> Thy tooth is not so keen,
> Because thou art not seen,
>   Although thy breath be rude.
> Heigh ho! sing heigh ho! unto the green holly:
> Most friendship is feigning, most loving mere folly.
>   Then heigh ho the holly!
>   This life is most jolly.
>
> Freeze, freeze, thou bitter sky,
> Thou dost not bite so nigh
>   As benefits forgot;
> Though thou the waters warp
> Thy sting is not so sharp
>   As friend remembered not.
> Heigh ho! sing, heigh ho! unto the green holly:
> Most friendship is feigning, most loving mere folly.
>   Then, heigh ho! the holly!
>   This life is most jolly.

IVY (*Hedera Helix*). Shakespeare mentions ivy twice: in "A Midsummer Night's Dream" where *Titania*, bidding *Bottom* sleep, says:

> Sleep thou and I will wind thee in my arms . . .
>   the female ivy so
> Enrings the barky fingers of the elm.[1]

[1] Act IV, Scene I.

and in "The Tempest," when *Prospero* compares
his false brother with the ivy:

> The ivy, which had hid my princely trunk,
> And suck'd my verdure out on 't.[1]

In the old carols and plays Ivy is always represented as a woman, and yet, although beloved, was
used for the outside decorations and doorways. Ivy
never had the place within that holly occupied.

As ivy clings and embraces the object near it, the
plant was chosen as an emblem of confiding love
and friendship. Tusser's commands are as follows:
"Get Ivy and Holly, women, deck up thy house."
Ivy was also used in the church decorations at Chris-
mas-tide. In the Middle Ages ivy was a favored and
most auspicious plant. An old carol says:

> Ivy is soft and meke of speech,
>   Against all bale she is bliss,
> Well is he that her may reach:—
>   *Veni, coronaberis.*
>
> Ivy is green with color bright,
>   Of all trees best she is,
> And that I prove will now be right:—
>   *Veni, coronaberis.*
>
> Ivy beareth berries black,
>   God grant us all His bliss,
> For there we shall nothing lack:—
>   *Veni, coronaberis.*

[1] Act I, Scene II.

Ivy was the crown of the Greek and Roman poets, whose myths proclaimed the plant sacred to Bacchus. Indeed the plant took its name from Bacchus (*kissos*) for it was said that the child was hidden under ivy when abandoned by his mother, Semele. The ivy was mingled with the grape in the crown of Bacchus and it enwreathed his thyrsus. Ivy berries eaten before wine was swallowed prevented intoxication, so Pliny says. Perhaps because of its association with Bacchus ivy was hung at the vintners' doors in England as well as on the Continent, and a reference to this custom is contained in Nash's "Summer's Last Will and Testament" (1600).

In Shakespeare's time ivy was considered a remedy against plague, which gave another reason for veneration.

England would almost cease to be England without the ivy that so luxuriantly covers the walls of old buildings and adds its soft beauty to the crumbling ruins. Everybody loves it—strangers as well as natives; and every one loves the poem that Dickens inserted into "The Pickwick Papers":

> Oh, a dainty plant is the Ivy green,
>   That creepeth o'er ruins old!
> On right choice food are his meals, I ween,
>   In his cell so lone and cold.

The wall must be crumbled, the stone decay'd
  To pleasure his dainty whim;
And the mouldering dust that years have made,
  Is a merry meal for him.
    Creeping where no life is seen,
    A rare old plant is the Ivy green!

First, he stealeth on, though he wears no wings,
  And a staunch old heart has he;
How closely he turneth, how close he clings,
  To his friend, the huge oak tree!
And slily he traileth along the ground,
  And his leaves he gently waves,
As he joyously hugs and crawleth round
  The rich mould of men's graves.
    Creeping where grim Death hath been,
    A rare old plant is the Ivy green!

Whole ages have fled and their works decayed,
  And nations have scattered been;
But the stout old ivy shall never fade
  From its hale and hearty green.
The brave old plant in its lonely days
  Shall fatten on the past,
For the stateliest building man can raise
  Is the ivy's food at last.
    Creeping on where Time has been
    A rare old plant is the Ivy green!

II

Mistletoe and Box

THE MISTLETOE (*Viscum album*). The mistletoe, the "all-healer," is a mysterious and mystical plant. The Greeks venerated it. Virgil gave it to Æneas for the "Golden Bough," to guide him to the Underworld. The Scandinavians dedicated it to their goddess of love, Freya (or Freyja). The mistletoe is, however, more closely associated with the Druids than with any other race. The plant was so sacred to these strange people that it was never allowed to touch the ground. At the New Year the Druids marched in solemn procession into the forest, and the high priest climbed the oak-tree and, with a golden sickle, cut the mistletoe from the branches. Other priests stood below holding a white cloth to receive the mistletoe as it fell. The sacred plant was dipped into water and then distributed among the people, to whom it was supposed to bring good luck of all kinds.

Even to-day we do not like the "Mistletoe Bough" to fall. We say it is "unlucky"; but possibly we have unconsciously inherited from our remote ancestors a spark of reverence for the "Golden Bough."

The Welsh thought the mistletoe "pure gold," believing that it had a connection with the golden fire of the sun; and they thought also that the mistletoe absorbed the life of the oak-tree to which it clung.

The Church never sanctioned the mistletoe. It never appears, therefore, among the Christmas decorations in the churches. No edicts, however, were strong enough to banish it from the decorations of the house, and the mistletoe bough is always a feature in the home where Christmas is celebrated with picturesque traditions. The precise reason for hanging up the Mistletoe Bough is lost in antiquity; but it is possible that the particular reasons were because it has supposed miraculous powers of healing sickness and averting misfortune, and great potency in promoting fertility and bestowing prosperity. For hundreds of years the mistletoe has been reverenced alike in castle, baronial hall, manor house and farmhouse in Shakespeare's country and in the homes of rich and poor in our own country.

Undoubtedly the idea of kissing under the Mistletoe Bough was derived from the fact that the plant was dedicated to the Northern goddess of love. The old saying is that the maiden who is not kissed under the mistletoe will not be married within the coming year. The ceremony of kissing is not properly performed unless a berry is plucked off and given with each kiss to the maiden. When the berries are all gone the privilege of kissing ceases.

That mistletoe grows on the oak-tree solely is a popular error. In fact, the plant prefers the apple. Most of the English mistletoe now comes from the apple orchards of Herefordshire. Normandy sends a great deal of mistletoe to England and to our country. The strange parasite is also found on the linden, poplar, and white-thorn. When once the seed is lodged, it drives its roots deep into the branch and draws sap and nourishment from the tree. The European variety is known as *Viscum album* and is much forked. In the United States the ordinary mistletoe is known as *Phoradendron* and grows on various hardwood trees in many of the Southern States.

There is something curiously interesting about the mistletoe. It is not beautiful, the leaves are irregular and often stained and broken, the berries fall almost when looked at and the plant is stiff and woody; yet for all that there is a peculiar quality in the greenish white and waxy berries and the shape of the forked twig that makes us think of divining-rods and magical words. It has a mystic fascination for us. Shakespeare's only reference speaks of it as *baleful: Tamora* says in "Titus Andronicus": [1]

> The trees, through summer, yet forlorn and lean,
> O'ercome with moss and baleful mistletoe.

BOX (*Buxus sempervirens*). Shakespeare mentions the box once—when *Sir Toby Belch* and *Sir Andrew Aguecheek* and the *Clown* are in *Olivia's* garden and *Maria*, running out to tell them that *Malvolio* is coming, excitedly cries:

> Get ye all three into the box-tree. [2]

Every one knows how important a feature the box-bush is in English gardens and in the old American gardens that were planted after English models.

So fine in color, so deep and luxuriant in foliage, so dignified and aristocratic in its atmosphere the name box is almost synonymous with old gardens. Its acrid yet aromatic scent—most delicious after rain—is one of its characteristics.

Greek myth consecrated the box to Pluto, and the plant was said to be symbolical of the life in the Underworld which continues all the year. The ancients used it to border their flower-beds, and probably the great use of box in England comes from

[1] Act II, Scene III.
[2] "Twelfth Night"; Act II, Scene V.

the Roman times. The wood was used for delicate inlay in the days of the Renaissance and also for making musical instruments.

Box is thought to be the assur-wood of the Bible. There is authority for using greenery in church decoration for in Isaiah we read: "The glory of Lebanon shall come unto thee; the fir-tree, the pine-tree, and the box together to beautify the place of my sanctuary; and I will make the places of my feet glorious." [1]

To dream of box, according to the astrologers of Shakespeare's time, signified a happy marriage, long life, and prosperity.

Box was used for decoration in the Tudor and Stuart days and succeeded the Christmas garlands, as Herrick sings in the time of Charles I, at Candlemas (February 2):

> Down with the Rosemary and Bays,
>   Down with the Mistletoe,
> Instead of Holly now upraise
>   The greener Box for show.
>
> The Holly hitherto did sway,
>   Let Box now dominere
> Until the dancing Easter Day
>   On Easter eve appear.

[1] Chap. LX, v. 13.

The youthful Box which now hath grace
    Your houses to renew,
Grown old, surrender must his place
    Unto the crispèd Yew.

When Yew is out, then Birch comes in,
    And many flowers beside,
Both of a fresh and fragrant kin
    To honor Whitsuntide.

Green rushes then and sweetest Bents,
    With cooler oaken boughs
Come in for comely ornaments
    To re-adorn the house.

Thus a constant succession of decorative flowers
and evergreens appeared in the houses of Old England.   Every season had its appropriate flowers, each
and all emblematical.   It was also the same in the
Church.   An English writer remarks:

"Mindful of the Festivals which our Church pre-
scribes, I have sought to make these objects of floral
nature the timepieces of my religious calendar and
the mementos of the hastening period of my mor-
tality.   Thus, I can light my taper to our Virgin
Mother in the blossoming of the white Snowdrop,
which opens its flower at the time of Candlemas;
the Lady's Smock and Daffodil remind me of the
Annunciation; the blue Harebell of the Festival of
St. George; the Ranunculus of the Invention of the

Cross; the Scarlet Lychnis of St. John the Baptist's
day; the White Lily of the Visitation of Our Lady;
the Virgin's Bower of the Assumption; and Michael-
mas, Martinmas, Holy Rood and Christmas have all
their appropriate decorations."

PART THREE

PRACTICAL SUGGESTIONS

THE LAY-OUT OF STATELY AND SMALL FORMAL GARDENS

I

The Stately Garden

BEFORE taking any steps to make a Shakespeare garden, it is essential to study the architectural lines of the house and the conformation of the grounds on which it is purposed to lay out the garden, or series of gardens. If the grounds are undulating, or hilly, naturally the gardens must be arrayed on different levels. The gardens can rise above the house in terraces if the house stands on the side of a hill, or beneath it; or the gardens may sink below the house, if the building crowns the summit of an elevation. On the other hand, if the house is erected on a flat plain, the gardens can open out like a series of rooms partitioned off by hedges, arbors, or walls. An artistic eye and resourceful mind will prefer to take advantage of the natural lines and work out a plan suggested by them. With nearly every kind of house the square garden accords, either perfectly square or longer than broad. Frequently the small enclosed garden looks well at the side of the house. It is essential to call in the professional gardener for advice regarding the situation of the garden, and questions of drainage, sunshine, and exposure to winds and sunshine; for all these matters aid in determining the arrangement. If a series of gardens is planned, one leading from another, it is well to consider them as outside rooms. In this case there will be little trouble in making the lay-out. The simplest plan is always the most effective. A very good example to follow is the lay-out of Montacute, Somersetshire, built in 1580-1601:

"Before the house is a walled-in forecourt, and in the forecourt a small lawn with a fountain, or pool, in the center. An entrance-gate leads into the forecourt. Before this forecourt comes a small ante-court, designed for the sake of dignity. On one side of the forecourt is the base, or bass, court, surrounded by the stables, kitchens, and other buildings; and on the other side is the ornamental pleasure-grounds, including 'my lady's garden,' a survival of the small enclosed castle garden, of the Middle Ages.

"Overlooking the garden is the Terrace—twenty

GARDEN HOUSE IN OLD ENGLISH GARDEN

or thirty feet wide—of considerable length, and protected by a balustrade of detached banisters, of
handsome design pierced in stone. From the Terrace
wide flights of steps at either end lead to the broad
sanded walks that divide the parterre into several
subdivisions, which are again divided by narrow
paths into smaller designs.

"The general shape is square, following the
antique classical garden of Pliny's time, enclosed
with trellis-work, espaliers, clipped box-hedges,
statuary, fountains, vases, and pleached alleys."

The famous Nonsuch, near Ewell, in Surrey, laid
out by Henry VIII toward the end of his life, re-
tained its appearance for more than a hundred years;
for at the time of the Parliamentary Survey (1650)
it was thus described:

"It was cut out and divided into several allies,
quarters and rounds, set about with thorn hedges;
on the north side is a kitchen garden, very commodi-
ous and surrounded with a brick wall of fourteen
feet high. On the west is a wilderness severed from
the little park by a lodge, the whole containing ten
acres. In the privy garden were pyramids, fountains
and basins of marble, one of which is set round with
six lilack trees, which trees bear no fruit, but a very
pleasant flower. Before the Palace is a neat and

handsome bowling-green surrounded with a balustrade of freestone."

Hampton Court Gardens, so beautiful to-day, were very famous in Tudor times. The old manor house was at the southwest corner of the area, and around it Cardinal Wolsey laid out his gardens and orchards. In 1599 Henry VIII seized the estate and enlarged the gardens. Ernest Law exclaims:

"What a truly delightful picture must these gardens have formed with their little walks and parterres, sheltered arbors and banquetting-houses. The largest plot was called the King's New Garden and occupied the place called the Privy Garden. Here were the gay parterres with gravel paths and little raised mounds with sun-dials on them. Here was also the Pond Garden, which is still to be seen and which, though much altered, yet retains something of its Tudor aspect; and another, known as the Little Garden, which may, perhaps, be identified with the enclosed space at the side of the Pond Garden. Studded about in various parts of the gardens and orchards were heraldic beasts on pedestals, holding vanes, or shields, bearing the King's Arms and badges; also many brass sun-dials."

Another typical garden was that of Kenilworth,

known, of course, to Shakespeare, as it is in War-wickshire:

"His Honor's the Earl of Leicester's exquisite appointment of a beautiful garden, an acre or more in quantity, that lieth on the north. Whereon all along the Castle wall is reared a pleasant terrace, ten feet high and twelve feet broad, even under foot and fresh of fine grass, as is also the side, thereof, towards the garden, in which, by sundry equal dis-tances with obelisks and spheres and white bears all of stone upon their curious bases by goodly shew, were set. To these, two fine arbors, redolent by sweet trees and flowers, at each end, one; the garden-plot under that, with fair alleys, green by grass, even voided from the borders on both sides, and some (for change) with sand, smooth and firm, pleasant to walk on, as a sea-shore when the water is avoided. Then much gracified by due proportion of four even quarters, in the midst of each upon a base of two feet square and high, seemingly bordered of itself, a square pilaster rising pyramidically fifteen feet high."

Thus Robert Laneham wrote in a letter describ-ing the pageant at Kenilworth in 1575.

The garden of varying ascents and descents was

much admired in Elizabethan days.   Sir Henry
Wotton (1568-1630), a most sensitive critic, who
wrote so beautifully of flowers, describes in his "Elements of Architecture" a garden laid out on different
levels:

"I have seen a garden for the manner perchance
incomparable into which the first access was a high
walk like a terrace, from whence might be taken a
general view of the whole Plot below.   From this,
the Beholder, descending many steps, was afterwards conveyed again by several mountings and
fallings to various entertainments of his scent and
sight.   Every one of these diversities was as if he
had been magically transported into a new garden."

The above extracts will afford suggestions for the
lay-out of fine stately gardens.   The most typical
Elizabethan estates are Montacute, Somersetshire;
Longleat, Wiltshire; Hatfield, Hardwicke, Kirby,
Penshurst, Kent; and Drayton House, Northamp-
tonshire.   All of these are models for imitation in
our own country.

II

The Small Garden

Turning now to the small enclosed garden, first
select your ground, your design, and your flowers

for borders, edging, and knots, so that you will know the effect you wish to produce.

"Making a garden," says H. H. Thomas, "may be likened to painting a picture. Just as the artist has before him the landscape which he is to depict on the canvas, the gardener should have in his mind's eye a strong impression of the kind of garden he wishes to make. There is nothing like being methodical even in gardening, so it is best to materialize one's ideas in the form of a rough sketch, or plan."

Show your gardener the diagram and have him stake off your garden and beds with the greatest accuracy. Your walks, paths, and beds must be *exact*. Next select your style of enclosure and build your brick wall, plant your green hedge, or construct your pleached alley. Each one has its own particular advantages and charm. The brick wall forms a shelter for plants that love shade and a fine support for climbing plants, especially ivy. The hedge makes a rich and distinguished wall of living green, which can be artistically clipped; and arches can be made through it. The pleached alley, formed of wooden trellis, lattice-work, or rustic, or wire arches painted an attractive color, or left in the natural wood, will, if they are covered profusely with roses, honeysuckle, rosemary, and other roving flowers, give the effect of the old leafy tunnels of greenery and blossoms.

III

Soil and Seed

Every gardener of olden times, as well as every practical worker to-day, insists upon the necessity of digging and trenching and preparing the soil before any seeds are sown, or cuttings planted. For this important preparation, the advice of the best local gardener is imperative.

Regarding seeds it is interesting to seek advice from Didymus Mountain's "The Gardener's Labyrinth." "Every gardener and owner," he says, "ought to be careful and diligently to foresee that the seeds committed to the earth be neither too old, dry, thin, withered, nor counterfeited, but rather full, new and full of juice.

"After the seeds being workmanly bestowed in the beds, the gardener's next care must be that he diligently pull up and weed away all hurtful and unprofitable herbs annoying the garden plants coming up."

All very sound advice, quaintly expressed. Old

Didymus is even quainter as he tells of the astrological influences:

"The daily experience is to the gardener as a schoolmaster to instruct him how much it availeth and hindereth that seeds to be sown, plants to be set, yea, scions to be grafted (in this or that time), having herein regard, not to the time especially of the year, as the Sun altereth the same, but also to the Moon's increase and wane, yea, to the sign she occupieth, and places both about and under the earth. To the aspects also of the other planets, whose beams and influence both quicken, comfort, preserve and maintain, or else nip, wither, dry, consume, and destroy by sundry means the tender seeds, plants, yea, and grafts; and these after their property and virtue natural or accidental."

Then he goes on to say:

"To utter here the popular help against thunder, lightnings and the dangerous hail, when the tempest approacheth through the cloud arising, as by the loud noise of guns shot here and there, with a loud sound of bells and such like noises which may happen, I think the same not necessary, nor properly available to the benefit of the garden.

"The famous learned man, Archibus, which wrote unto Antiochus, King of Syria, affirmeth that tempests shall not be harmful to plants, or fruit, if the speckled toad, enclosed in a new earthern pot, be buried in the middle of the garden."

A modern authority says:

"While no hard and fast rule can be made, a general practice is to cover seeds with double their own depth of soil under glass and four times their own depth of soil when sowing in the open ground. To protect seeds from cats, bury several bottles up to the neck in seed bed and put in each bottle a teaspoonful of liquid ammonia."

IV

The Gateway

The gate entrance was always important in Tudor times. The gate, usually of pierced ironwork, but also of wood artistically cut into balusters, was hung between two square piers of brick or stone, about ten feet apart. Each pier was surmounted by a stone ball, with or without necking, unless heraldic lions, bears, wyverns, or other emblems of the owner were used. The piers were, as a rule, two feet square and nine, or ten, feet to the top of the cornice. Gateways were also set in walls, and little gates were set in hedges, or flanked by ornamental shrubs.

V

The Garden-House

The garden-house was very important in Shakespeare's time. It was often a substantial edifice, built of brick or stone, placed at the corner of a boundary, or dividing wall, so as to afford a view of more than one part of the garden. Sometimes two buildings were constructed, one at each corner, as at Montacute. Another favorite position was at the end of a long walk ending in a vista; and another was overlooking the bowling-alley, from which visitors could watch the game. The garden-house was often fitted with handsome woodwork and even a fireplace. An outside staircase sometimes led to the roof.

The summer-house arbor was also often made of wooden lattice-work and covered with vines. Sometimes it was hollowed out of the clipped hedge, or out of a large tree properly shaped by the toparian artist. The gazebo, built at the corner of a wall overlooking the garden within and the road without, was also a popular kind of summer-house. The origin of the name is still obscure. Some people say it comes from the same root as to gaze, and refers to viewing the scenery; but there is a suggestion of the Orient in the word.   The gazebo may best be described as a kind of wall pavilion.

VI

The Mount

The mount, originally intended to enable persons to look over the enclosing wall, served both as a place to enjoy the view and as a post of outlook in time of danger.   Mounts were constructed of wood or stone, curiously adorned within and without. They were also made in the old barrow shape of earth and covered with grass.   The top of the mount was often adorned with a summer-house, or arbor.   The mount at Hampton Court, constructed in 1533 on a brick foundation, was the first specimen of its day; and the arbor upon it was a very elaborate affair, made of wooden pales and trelliswork.   Sometimes the mount, instead of being a raised and detached mound, was formed like a long bank raised against an outer wall.

VII

Rustic Arches

"Rustic arches should be in keeping with the house and grounds.   Firstly they should be in keeping with the style of the house and grounds. A white stone house with a light pillared verandah is not suited by rustic arches: it requires to be seen through vistas made up of arches as slender as the verandah pillars, of painted iron-work preferably, and the most telling contrast will be arranged if there are numerous deep evergreen shrubs.

"Rustic, or peeled oak, arches suit the modern red brick villa style of house to perfection; the trellis arch, being neat and unpretentious, is also in excellent taste. The old-fashioned country cottage, or the house built to imitate it, should not have trellis-work within half a mile. Rustic arches, or invisible ones of bent iron, are alone in keeping. By an invisible arch, I mean one consisting of a single bend of iron, or narrow woodwork upright with a cross bar—anything really that is intended only to support some evergreen climber or close grower, such as a rose that will hide the foundation at all seasons.

"Arches simply built of rustic poles are more pleasing than wire or lattice ones in any landscape; and the roughness of the wood is beneficial to the climbers that grow over them, affording an easy hold for tendrils. Whether the wood is peeled, or employed with the bark on—the latter is the more artistic method—it is an admirable plan to wash it all over with a strong solution of some insecticide and then give one or two coats of varnish. In most cases varnish alone is enough to preserve the wood.

"The use of rustic wood in a garden is always safe since its appearance cannot conflict with Nature as painted woodwork when present in excess is sure to do. From woodcutter's yards, especially those in the heart of the country, charming pieces of log of any size can be bought very cheaply and whenever a tree on an estate has to be felled portions of its trunks or branches can be turned to good account in the garden." [1]

VIII

Seats

Garden seats are of so many kinds and styles that one has much latitude in selection. Rustic seats, painted iron seats, and marble seats are all proper; but should be selected to harmonize with the house and general style of the garden or gardens.

IX

Vases, Jars, and Tubs

Marble vases, old pottery jars of simple type, and wooden tubs can be selected for individual

[1] H. H. Thomas.

plants to grow in, or for fine arrangements of ferns and other flowers. Placed at regular intervals in the garden, or on the terrace, these simple ornaments add brightness and elegance to the scene.

X

Fountains

In Elizabethan gardens the fountain was a familiar feature, and fountains were very elaborate with regard to their construction.

Bacon says:

"For fountains they are a great beauty and refreshment: the one that sprinkleth or spouteth water; the other, a fair receipt of water of some thirty or forty foot. For the first, the ornaments of images gilt, or marble, which are in use, do well. Also some steps up to it and some fine pavement about doth well. As for the other kind of fountain, which may be called a bathing-pool, it may admit much curiosity and beauty, as that the bottom be finely paved, and with images; the sides likewise and withal embellished with colored glass and such things of luster encompassed also with fine rails of low statues."

Hentzner saw three famous fountains on his visit

to England in 1592, at Hampton Court, Whitehall, and Nonsuch. He describes the one at Hampton Court as follows:

"In the middle of the first and principal court stands a fountain, splendid, high, and massy, with an ingenious water-work, by which you can, if you like, make the water to play upon the ladies and others who are standing by and give them a thorough wetting."

The one at Whitehall was also capable of playing practical jokes:

"A *jet d'eau* with a sun-dial, which, while strangers are looking at it, a quantity of water forced by a wheel, which the gardener turns at a distance through a number of little pipes, plentifully sprinkles those who are standing round."

More ornate was the fountain at the superb palace of Nonsuch in Surrey:

"In the pleasure and artificial gardens are many columns and pyramids of marble, two fountains that spout water, one round the other like a pyramid upon which are perched small birds that stream water out of their bills. In the Grove of Diana is a very agreeable fountain with Actæon turned into a stag, as he was sprinkled by the goddess and her nymphs with inscriptions. There is besides another pyramid of marble full of concealed pipes which spirt upon all who come within their reach."

In the small formal garden a fountain looks well at the intersection of the paths in the center of the quarters. It is not necessary to have an ornate fountain, for the real charm of a fountain consists in the upward plume of spray that glistens in the sunshine, that turns to pearls in the moonlight, and that always charms the eye of man and delights the neighboring flowers with its spray blown by the breeze.

XI

The Dove-cote

Every manor-house had its dove-cote, or columbary, as it was called. Here doves and pigeons aided in making a very pretty picture as they flew in and out of the architecturally designed bird-house. The right to keep them was confined to the lords of the manor, and the law was very strictly enforced.

Andrew Borde tells us that a dove-house is a necessary thing about a mansion-place. It is, therefore, quite proper to include a bird-house in the Shakespeare garden; and a pool for the birds' comfort is also a pretty as well as necessary adjunct to the dove-cote.

Birds add much to the pleasure of the garden. Pigeons and doves give a poetic touch as they strut along the paths and flutter about. Nothing gives more quality and elegance, however, than a peacock, and, to quote from a contemporary writer:

"The peacock is a bird of more beautiful feathers than any other that is. He is quickly angry, but he is goodly to behold, very good to eat, and serveth as a watch in the inner court, for that he, spying strangers to come into the lodging, he faileth not to cry out and advertise them of the house."

The peacock is as much of a joy to the garden lover as the sun-dial.

XII

The Sun-dial

The sun-dial forms a perfect ornament at the intersection of the garden paths. Every one responds to the quaint beauty and mystery of the sun-dial with its dark shadow that creeps quietly across the dial and tells the hours so softly. As Charles Lamb says: "It is the measure appropriate for sweet plants and flowers to spring by and birds to apportion their silver warblings by." Nothing has a more antique air than the sun-dial. The simple baluster

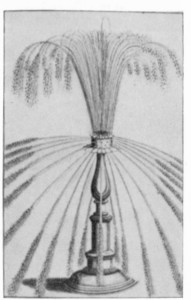

FOUNTAINS, SIXTEENTH CENTURY

pillar is a good model, and the base should be surrounded by a circle of grass.

This grassy ring is the "wabe," where Lewis Car-
roll's "slithy toves" did "gyre and gimbel" in the
immortal poem "Jabberwocky."

The sun-dial can also be placed at the end of a
path, if the path is important enough to warrant it.

In our Shakespeare garden I suggest using a
Shakespearian quotation for the inscription, such as,
for example:

> For never-resting Time leads summer on.
>
> or
>
> Nothing 'gainst Time's scythe can make defense.
>
> or
>
> Like as the waves make towards the pebbled shore,
> So do our minutes hasten to their end.
>
> or
>
> Come what, come may,
> Time and the hour runs through the roughest day.

XIII

The Terrace

The terrace is essential, if one would have the
true Elizabethan atmosphere. The terrace can be
of stone, or brick, or brick combined with stone, or
brick combined with wood. Whatever the material,

the balustrade is of the greatest importance. The designs for balusters in the old architectural books are legion, some of them of very complicated intertwining after the patterns of arabesques and *cuirs* (strap-leather work), but good taste, even in that day of complicated design, demanded that the balusters should be very widely spaced. This is obvious, because half of the effect, at least, of out-of-door architecture depends upon the open spaces for light to play its part—and a great part, too—in the design. In balustrades the spacing is, therefore, very important. The balusters should never be too crowded. The most satisfactory ones are those in which the distance from center to center almost equals the height from plinth to coping. The piers dividing the groups should not be too far apart—ten to fifteen feet is a good distance. Much, however, depends on the proportion of the balusters themselves. Frequently the balustrade is adorned with ornamental vases, or urns, set at regular intervals on the rail and on the newel-posts of the steps. As a rule, the steps lead from both ends of the terrace. Sometimes there are also steps in the center; sometimes the terrace is double. A jar, vase, or tub of growing plants, or containing one handsome plant, looks well placed on the lawn on either side of the steps. Vines can be trained gracefully along the balustrade, hand-rails, and posts of the steps. A rich border of flowers should be grown all along the side of the terrace: in the spring hosts of daffodils and in the summer larkspur, marigolds, lilies, iris, and climbing roses and honeysuckle. The terrace gains in style and beauty when the proper floral decorations are tastefully selected and well combined.

From the terrace one can enjoy a fine view of the garden as a whole; and it is a pleasant place to stroll upon and to sit. Sometimes the terrace is of two levels with several stairways.

Leaving the architectural terrace, which is an adjunct of the house bringing the house into relation with the garden, we must turn to the garden terrace made of grass, and ascended by grass steps cut in the bank, or by stone or brick steps cut in the bank, or standing outside with handrails and newel-posts. If the steps are of grass, good effects can be made by placing large jars, or tubs, filled with flowers, ferns, or a single plant, such as the pomegranate, for instance, on either side.

The grass-terrace is very charming leading up to the garden, leading from one garden to another, or leading from the lawn proper to the sunken garden.

A very attractive arrangement was at Penshurst, Kent, the home of the Sidney family. It is described thus: "Garden on south and west, ground sloping to south and west, house on a grass platform, about nine feet above the garden level. Along the south-west side of the flower-garden a broad grass-terrace, and near the house a few steps lead to the yew alley, at the end of which is a quaint old sun-dial known as the Turk's Head."

The yew alley was evidently a pleached alley.

XIV

The Pleached Alley

The "Pleached Alley," another typical feature of the Elizabethan garden (from the French *plessir*, to weave), is nothing more nor less than a thickly covered walk. In Shakespeare's time this was constructed of woven boughs and climbing vines and flowers, or a series of arbors. The old prints and pictures show them to be complete tunnels of greenery. We can make a pleached alley to-day by setting up a pergola and smothering it with flowers and vines. Ironwork arches covered with roses, honeysuckle, and other creepers will produce the proper effect. A latticework trellis covered with vines and flowers will, if properly constructed, produce the appearance of a pleached alley.

When the pleached alley is not used to enclose the garden, then a brick wall or, still better, a fine hedge should be planted.

XV

Hedges

Box makes a perfect hedge. The hedge must be clipped at the upper part narrower than at the base, otherwise the base will become bare. Privet makes an excellent hedge and so does the Osage orange, which grows luxuriantly in some parts of the United States. It is decorative to trim the hedge so that tall pyramids ornament either side of the gate, or an arch can be made to grow over the gate. A small lavender hedge is very attractive. Each autumn, after the flower-spikes have gone, trim plants for the dwarf hedge.

Roses, particularly the sweetbrier, make a charming hedge. Honeysuckle is another delightful flower for a hedge; and nothing could be more beautiful than the two combined.

If the rose and honeysuckle hedge is desired, have the carpenter make a lattice screen of the desired height, or simply construct a rustic fence and plant the creepers near it and train them so that they will make a wall of flowers and leaves.

XVI

Paths

"There is no pleasanter path than that of grass, and even the small garden ought to have a little grass-walk between the flower borders and rose beds. It adds immensely to the attractiveness of the garden and none other is so pleasant to the tread. Constant mowing and rolling are necessary and the edges must be kept neat and trim; for while a well-kept grass-path is most attractive of all, its charm is never fully realized unless it is carefully attended to." [1]

Gravel-paths must be frequently rolled and the surface of the walk made a little higher in the center than the sides with a curving outline, so that water may drain away to the sides.

The brick pathway is capable of much variety. Bricks may be laid in many patterns; and the little garden, if very small, may be entirely paved with bricks, leaving the formal flower-beds only of earth. A fountain or sun-dial looks well in the center.

[1] H. H. Thomas.

Flagged pathways are effective in certain garden arrangements. Old paving-stones are suitable, but they should first be broken up into irregular pieces.

"Build a good foundation, cover it with a thin layer of sandy loam, then lay the larger pieces flat on this. Fill the interstices with the fragments, but leave crevices filled with soil, two inches or so wide, here and there. Make up a compost of equal parts of loam, sand and leaf-mould, sweep this over the path and let it settle in the joints. Many plants can be established in the joints and a pretty effect obtained." [1]

Among the plants practical for this purpose are thrift, thyme, and camomile, and the more they are trodden on the sweeter they smell and the better they grow.

"The Gardener's Labyrinth" gives three or four feet as the width for paths between beds and one foot to one foot six inches for the cross-path.

XVII

Borders

Borders should not be confused with edgings.

"Border is the name applied to the narrow di-

[1] H. H. Thomas.

vision of the garden which usually accompanies each
side of a walk.   In fact, any bed which acts as a
boundary to a walk or grass-plot, or the main quarters of a garden may be properly described as a
border.

"Flower-borders should be well drained.   In plot-
ting them it must be remembered that if narrow no
art will impart to them an air of boldness.   If the
pleasure grounds are small, narrow borders are per-
missible.   All flower-borders should be made in proportion to the size of the garden and other surroundings.   Neatness must be the presiding deity
over flower-borders; and no application of the hoe
and rake, no removal of decayed leaves, no tying up
of straggling members can be too unremitting." [1]

According to Lawson, the borders "should be
roses, thyme, lavender, rosemary, hyssop, sage and
such like and filled with cowslips, primroses, violets,
Daffy-down-dillies,   sweet   Sissely,   Go-to-bed-at-
noon, and all sweet flowers; and, chief of all, with
gilliflowers, July-flowers, commonly called gilliflowers or clove July-flowers (I call them so because they flower in July); they have the names of
cloves of their scent.   I may well call them the King

[1] Johnson's "Gardener's Dictionary and Cultural Instructor,"
edited by Fraser and Hemsley (London, 1917).

of Flowers (except the rose). Of all flowers save the Damask Rose they are the most pleasant to sight and smell."

XVIII

Edgings

Edging is the material used for dividing beds and borders from the paths, or grass leading up to the bed, if the bed is alongside a wall, or terrace, or veranda.

Box is a formal, but charming, edging. "The growth must be regularly clipped each year. Stretch a line the whole length of the edging, so as to show the correct height; then cut evenly and neatly both at top and sides. When relaying, take up the plants, pull them to pieces and use the strong young growths, which must be clipped to one level. Box is easily grown and stands pruning with impunity." Such is the advice of an authority. Another practical gardener says: "Most amateurs clip box-edgings early in the Spring. This causes an early growth, which is just in the condition to be nipped by a sharp, late frost. The safeguard is to delay clipping until the end of August. Then comes free, healthy growth, which renders box-lined garden paths cheerful and pleasant to the eye through times of heat and drought."

Thrift (*Armeria*) is one of the best edgings as it is green all the year round and in summer is covered with bright pink flowers. A flower-lover says:

"Thrift is seen as an edging in many old English gardens. To preserve its beauty the plants must be lifted, divided and replanted once in at least four years: a rich even growth is then the reward. The tufted habit, fresh green growth and rose-purple flowers in Summer are enjoyable to look at."

Thrift requires frequent trimming.

London-pride (*Saxifraga umbrosa*) is very pretty when in flower and, therefore, makes an attractive edging.

Pansies also form a decorative edging for flower beds, large and small.

Another charming edging is the carnation, especially the white varieties. The gray-green foliage makes a beautiful border for flower-beds. Pinks are pretty, too, for bed edgings, and the sweet-william is also attractive for this purpose.

XIX

Knots

The knot should occupy a piece of ground from twenty-five to one hundred feet square. According

to "The Gardener's Labyrinth" "the flower-bed
should be kept to the size that the weeder's hands
may well reach into the middest of the bed." The
size given in this manual is twelve feet by six, "each
bed raised one foot above the ground (two feet in
marshy ground) and the edge cased in with short
planks framed into square posts with finials at the
angles with intermediate supports." A prettier
method, however, is to border the flower-bed with
an edging of box, thrift, pansies, or pinks. This
border outlines the shape of the knot. Within the
edging, or border, "the flowers are all planted in
some proportion as near one into another as it is fit
for them, which will give such grace to the garden
that the place will seem like a tapestry of flowers."

It would seem from the hundreds of designs for
knots in the old garden-books that every possible
combination of scroll and line and curve had been
exhausted; but ingenious persons liked to invent
their own. Markham tells us that "the pattern of
the design cannot be decided by rule; the one whereof is led by the hops and skips, turnings and wind-
ings of his brain; the other, by the pleasing of his
eye, according to his best fantasie."

Lawson gives the following nine designs for
knots:

Cinkfoyle	Lozenges
Flower-de-luce [1]	Cross-bow
Trefoyle	Diamond
Frette	Oval

Maze.

Here the maze is not intended as a labyrinth to walk in, but is a design for the planting of flowers.

Markham's knots are:

Straight line knots	Mixed knots
Diamond knots, single and double	Single impleate of straight line
Single knots	Plain and mixed

Direct and Circular.

Knots, formed with "a border of box, lavender, or rosemary, are eighteen inches broad at bottom and clipped so close a level at the top as to form a table for the housewife to spread clothes to dry on," are Lawson's idea.

The old garden books contain many designs for knots, some of which are astonishingly intricate. Examples occur in Markham's and Lawson's books and in Didymus Mountain's "Gardener's Labyrinth" (editions of 1557, 1594, and 1608), which are perfectly practical for use to-day.

[1] Fleur-de-lis.

In David Loggan's "Oxonia Illustrata" (Oxford, 1675, folio) several large plates show formal gardens. Among them New College Gardens and those of Jesus are extremely interesting. Loggan's companion book on Cambridge, "Cantabrigia Illustrata" (Cambridge, 1688), has splendid views of architecture and formal gardens with knots.

Typical flower-beds are also represented in Vredeman de Vries's "Hortorum Viridariorumque" (Antwerp, 1583) and Crispin de Passe's "Hortus Floridus" (Arnhem, 1614).

Theobald's as late as 1650 preserved the Tudor arrangement.

"In the great garden are nine large complete squares, or knots, lying upon a level in the middle of the said garden, whereof one is set forth with box-borders in the likeness of the King's Arms, one other plot is planted with choice flowers; the other seven knots are all grass-knots, handsomely turfed in the intervals, or little walks. A quickset hedge of white thorn, or privet, cut into a handsome fashion at every angle, a fair cherry tree and a cypress in the middle of the knots—also a marble fountain."

XX

The Rock-Garden

It is well to build a little unostentatious rock-garden in some appropriate spot where a few flowers, which you may not want in the beds, can grow. Flowers that find a congenial home in a loosely arranged pile of rocks and turf are anemones, columbines, thrift, thyme, rosemary, violets, buttercups, harebells, ferns, fennel, ivy, myrtle, pansies, and the ragged-robin (gentian).

Select weather-worn stones and pile them carelessly one above another, placing some of them as shelves. Leave plenty of room for the earth and let your flowers grow as they please.

XXI

Flowers

As I do not pretend to be a practical gardener, having had no experience, I have culled these hints from several authorities, including E. T. Cook's "The Century Book of Gardening" (London, 1901); Johnson's "Gardener's Dictionary and Cultural Instructor," edited by Fraser and Hemsley

(London, 1917); H. H. Thomas's "The Complete Gardener" (London, 1912); and Mabel Cabot Sedgwick's "The Garden Month by Month" (New York, 1907).

ANEMONE STELLATA requires a sheltered, warm position and light, sandy soil, well drained. It grows about ten inches high with star-like flowers, purple, rose-color, and white. Generally speaking, it requires the same treatment as the tulip. Anemones also flourish in the rock-garden.

BOX can be grown in almost any soil, but prefers light soil with gravelly subsoil. See page 297.

BROOM-FLOWER (*Cytisus scoparius*), a splendid flowering shrub with yellow flowers of handsome color, succeeds in dry, sandy places where most other plants fail. It can, therefore, be planted on rough dry banks. It grows from seed; and this can be sown in any sheltered place out of doors. Cuttings placed in a frame are also easy to strike.

CAMOMILE will grow in any garden soil. It is a creeping plant and grows freely in dense masses. The flowers are white and blossom from June to August. The height attained is from twelve to eighteen inches. The foliage is finely divided and has a feathery appearance. The plant makes a good border, for it loves the sun. Propagate by division and cuttings.   Camomile may be allowed to run over paving-stones, for it grows when trodden upon.

CARNATIONS.   A carnation specialist says:

"A great number of amateur cultivators of the Carnation have an idea that if they obtain seed from a variety of Carnation, the seedlings produced from such seed will be reproductions of the parent plant. This, of course, is wrong, and it is well to mention it.   Now to grow Carnations well they must have a good soil, or the plants will not produce flowers, or layers, for another season.   For the open garden, I strongly recommend seedlings.   The cultivator must not expect all the flowers to be as good as the parent, or even all double.   There will be from ten to fifteen per cent with single flowers, all the others having double flowers, some as good as, or even better than, their parents; but the majority will be of uncertain quantity.

"The seed will germinate in a hothouse well within a week from the time of sowing, and the seedlings should be pricked out in boxes as soon as large enough.   Plant in good soil and let the plants be fifteen inches apart and two feet between the rows. Seedlings are not nearly so particular in regard to soil as named varieties.   The seedling is more robust; and, given the same cultural conditions, grows more

SUNKEN GARDEN, SUNDERLAND HALL, WITH UNUSUAL TREATMENT OF HEDGES

vigorously. It is always best to dig a trench some time before the seedling is planted. This admits of the soil being aerated. The plants should be put out after a shower of good rain. I trench it eighteen inches deep, put a layer of manure at the bottom and another layer six or eight inches below the surface.

"A warning is necessary to those unacquainted with the nature of soils. It will not do to trench up soil that has not been there before. New subsoil is not adapted to grow anything until it has been well turned over two or three times and mixed with decayed manure.

"After planting, give a light dressing of manure: it keeps the roots in better condition and the plant starts more freely into growth. Carnations must not be left to themselves after planting."

Gilliflowers, pinks, and sweet-williams belong to this family.

COLUMBINES prefer a situation where the roots can obtain moisture. They also do well and look at home in a rock-garden. "Gather ripe seeds in July and sow them so that the seedlings are well established before winter," an authority says. "Such plants will bloom the next year. Aquilegias often die out after their second year, although they are classed as perennials, and should therefore be treated as biennials and raised annually from seed. Seed is produced in abundance and should be sown as soon as ripe in a shady place in the garden, or in pans in a cold frame, care being taken to sow the seed very thinly. When the seedlings are large enough to handle they should be lifted and planted out in their permanent quarters. Aquilegias growing in a garden are almost invariably cross-fertilized; and it is therefore necessary, where more than one variety is in bloom at the same time, to procure the seed from some other dependable source."

COWSLIP. This flower needs a rich, light soil, not dry. Its small, yellow cup-like flowers with ruby spots in the center blossom in the late April and late May. It grows to six or twelve inches and prefers half-shade. It must be protected in the winter. Propagate by seed. Cowslips make a charming border plant and are happy, also, in rockgardens.

CROCUS SATIVUS, the beautiful purple flower that blooms in autumn, should be planted near trees. "The cultivation of the garden crocus is so simple a matter that the merest novice may plant the bulbs with the assurance that he, or she, will reap a bright reward in the near future, provided the burrowing mouse and flower-picking sparrow do not interfere with nature. Crocuses may be propagated from seed sown as soon as ripe in light, sandy soil in pans, or pots. They reach their flowering stage in three years."

CROW-FLOWERS. Some authorities, as we have seen, identify crow-flowers as the buttercup; others, as *Scilla nutans*. The buttercup is easy to raise in almost any soil. As it should be represented, it is well to put it in the rock-garden. See Harebell.

CROWN-IMPERIAL. This plant, which the people of Shakespeare's time valued so highly, is rare in our gardens. The popularity of the flower decreased because of its unpleasant odor; but no Shakespeare garden can be without at least one representative because of *Perdita's* words. The Crown-Imperial is a very showy plant and makes a splendid effect if planted in groups. It also looks well among shrubs and in a border. The blossoms appear in March, April, and May, and are very handsome as to shape and color. The bell-shaped flowers, orange-red or reddish-orange, droop gracefully beneath an upright crown of leaves. When the foliage turns brown, the plant can be cut down. Propagate by offsets in deep, rich, well-drained soil, and divide every two or three years.

CUCKOO-FLOWERS (*Lychnis Flos cuculi*), or the Ragged-Robin, with its deeply cut petals of rich blue, makes a pretty border plant as it is an abundant bloomer. (See page 214.)

CUPID'S FLOWER. See Pansy.

DAFFODILS do better in half-shade than in full sunlight. The earlier the buds can be procured and planted the better: August is none too soon.

"Late planted bulbs must necessarily lose much of their vigor by being kept out of the ground too long, and the longer the period of root-growth the stronger the flower-spikes. As regards soil one that is fairly retentive of moisture is more suited to the requirements than a light staple that soon dries up. They should be covered to the depth of one and a half times the depth of the bulb measured from base to shoulder. A bulb two inches deep can be covered to a depth of three inches, and so on in proportion. In light soil the bulbs should be placed a little deeper and in heavy soil not quite so deep."

DAISY. In the spring florists have plenty of English daisies to sell in little pots. Propagate by seed in spring or division in September. This daisy is pink and white; the little rays tipped with pink sometimes almost cover the yellow center. The plant requires rich soil and plenty of sunshine. It blooms in mid-April to mid-June and grows to a height of three to six inches. The daisy must be protected in the winter. It is most desirable for borders and makes a charming edging.

DIAN'S BUD, *Artemesia,* or wormwood, is a bushy foliage plant of small globe-shaped, drooping flowers of whitish yellow. The leaves are finely divided. Propagate by division. This grows in a poor soil and likes sunshine.

FENNEL, though regarded as a weed, can be utilized so that it makes a decorative appearance, for its foliage is light and a brilliant green. The tiny flowers are yellow and grow in flat-tipped clusters on branching stalks. They blossom in July. The plant rises to a good height and prefers rich, deep, open soil and plenty of sunlight. Plant fresh seeds and make the plants grow in bold groups.

FERNS are effective planted in pots, jars, or tubs, and look well at the sides of the steps and on the newel-posts of the steps. They look well in a rock-garden.

FLOWER-DE-LUCE (*fleur-de-lis*). There are many native American flags, or irises; but the plants nearest to those described by Parkinson are the *Iris florentina,* the *Iris pseudacorus,* and the great purple Turkey flag.

The *Iris florentina* grows from one to two feet, blooms in May and June, with large, delicately scented white flowers tinted blue and streaked with purple veins and having orange-yellow beards. The fragrant rootstock is the orris-root. Propagate by division in soil not too dry. This is an excellent border plant and prefers half-shade.

Iris pseudacorus grows from one and a half to three feet and blossoms in late May and late June. It forms luxuriant clumps, having many stems, which bear large broad-petaled flowers, yellow veined with brown. The leaves—long, stiff, and gray-green—are handsome. This is a beautiful plant for the margin of water, and is very pretty around a bird-bath. Propagate by division. This iris likes the sun.

The great purple Turkey flag will grow in either sun, or half-shade. The height is from two to four feet. The large fragrant flowers bloom in May, June, and July. This iris is very handsome in large groups and in the border. Propagate by division. It is a gross feeder, but grows well in any garden soil.

GILLIFLOWERS. See Carnations.

HAREBELL. This lovely jewel of the English woodland has drooping bell-shaped flowers, fragrant, and blue in color. The bells hang from tall stems. The leaves are long and grass-like. The height is from eight to twelve inches. It is bulbous. Propagate by offsets and give it occasionally a top dressing of manure. *Scilla nutans* blooms in May and June and prefers half-shade. There are varieties, white, pink, and purple.

HOLLY should be used for hedges and ornamental bushes. Some varieties grow very well in certain parts of the United States.

HONEYSUCKLE grows easily in any garden. It is a luxuriant creeper and is generous with its blossoms and lavish in fragrance. Use it for hedges and to climb over walls, arbors, trellises, gates and wire screens.

IVY. English ivy is a climbing and trailing evergreen sub-shrub, with beautiful large, dark-green leaves, richly veined, and of graceful heart-shape. The flowers are inconspicuous, but the berries, almost jet-black, are decorative. Propagate by half-ripe cuttings in rich, damp soil and protect in winter. Ivy prefers shade. It blossoms in June and July.

LADY'S-SMOCK (*Cardamine pretensis*) will grow in sun, or shade, but prefers a moist soil. Propagate by division. Its blossoms are pinkish lilac in terminal clusters and appear in June. The foliage is deeply cut. Lady's-smocks will grow in rock-gardens and are excellent border-plants.

LARK'S-HEELS. See Nasturtium.

LARKSPUR is a glorious flower, noble in masses of bloom and fine in growth, highly decorative, and lasts well besides. "Delphiniums are very easy to grow and can be planted at almost any time, but the best seasons are early autumn and spring when new growth commences. The great point is to plant them in rich well-dug and manured soil and strew coal-ashes about for the reason that slugs are very partial to these plants. Ample space must be left for full development as with age the roots increase greatly, so that two and a half feet apart is none too much. The plant needs a rather rich ground, for its growth is strong. Larkspur looks well planted in the back row of the mixed border."

LAVENDER is a precious, fragrant, hardy bush. Its sweet-smelling leaves and blue flowers are ever welcome, whether in the border, or as a low hedge, or standing alone. A very light soil and sunshine are essential. Propagate by cuttings in early autumn out of doors in a sheltered, but not shady, place and plant out when rooted, or divide in March, planting out the rooted slips one foot apart in light soil.

Lavender may be used to beautify walks. Bushes in some sunny corner of the garden are pretty for picturesque growth and color. Lavender can be grouped so as to give a touch of silvery gray to the border. It permits itself to be clipped, and it must be cared for, or it will grow twisted and gnarled. If flower-spikes are desired, the lavender must be clipped in autumn; if the gray leaf is all that is desired then it must be clipped in the spring before the young twigs have begun to grow.

LILIES. The lily bed should be deep—three feet if possible,—the soil open and porous without being light. There cannot be a better material than sound fibrous loam with which leaf-mold has been mixed. Lilies are rarely benefited by animal manure. The bed should be sheltered from boisterous winds, for lilies lose half their beauty if it becomes necessary to stake their graceful stems, and partially shaded so that the sun does not parch the ground, or prematurely wither their dainty petals. In times of drought the beds should be given a copious *soaking of an hour or two's duration.*

The Madonna Lily is a great favorite and is very effective in small clumps against a background of shrubs and in borders. Unfortunately it is subject to disease. It is bulbous. Propagate by offsets, scales, or very slowly by seed. It likes rich, well-dressed soil and half-shade. Avoid contact with manure. The Madonna Lily flowers in June and July with white blossoms.

The Martagon has much reflexed flowers on long spire-like racemes and is light-purple with darker spots. The *Martagon dalmaticum* grows from six to seven feet. It has dark purple flowers. There is also a white kind. Both are very hardy and succeed in open borders.

The *Chalcedonicum*, or Scarlet Turk's-Cap, grows from three to four feet high and has waxy flowers of bright vermilion. This is the *brightest* of all lilies. It is very hardy and easy to cultivate.

Lily-of-the-Valley flourishes in the shade and also where there is a little (but not too much) sunlight. It thrives beneath shade trees and near a wall. *Room for development it must have;* otherwise it becomes crowded to such an extent that the plants deteriorate and fail to bloom. The Lily-of-the-Valley should be planted in September or October. Prepare the soil by deep digging and mix in a plentiful supply of decayed manure. Leaf-soil and road sweepings may be added to heavy soil. Plant crowns about three inches apart to allow room for future development. Bury the crowns just below the surface and make them moderately firm. When all are planted mulch with rolled manure and leaf-soil in equal parts, covering the bed to a depth of two inches.

LONG PURPLES. This Arum, being a plant of the woods, does well in the rock-garden. The best plan is to remove a Jack-in-the-Pulpit from the woods with some of its native soil and transplant it in the garden. It grows in shade and sun alike.

MARIGOLD. For marigolds choose a light, dry, *poor* soil and a sunny spot. Sow seed any time from February to June. Seeds sown in the spring will produce flowers in June. Sow in drills ten inches apart and water moderately. Thin the seedlings and remove into rows ten inches apart. In rich soil the plant grows too large and fails to blossom well. H. H. Thomas in "The Complete Gardener" says:

"The ordinary reader understands Marigold to refer to the French, African and Pot Marigolds. The botanical name *Calendula* is said to imply that the plant keeps pace with the calendar. In other words that it is nearly always in bloom. And really this is not very far from the truth. Once introduce the Pot Marigold into your garden and you will rarely be without flowers. It is hardy and seeds itself very freely.   Seed may be sown out of doors where the plants are to bloom, choosing for preference poor ground, otherwise the plants will grow freely enough, but blooms will be scarce."

The French marigold is deep yellow, orange, or pale yellow striped or marked with brown, and crinkled.   It grows from twelve to fifteen inches high.   "The Gentleman's Labyrinth" gives quaint instructions for the growth of the Marigold:

"The seeds of this flower are commonly bestowed in a husbandly and well-dressed earth, but this rather done by the counsel of the skilful in the increase of the Moon, whereby the flowers may grow the bigger and broader.   But to procure the flowers to grow the doubler, bigger and broader the owner ought to remove the plants and set them in new beds, lying in sunny places herein considering at those times of removing that the Moon be increasing so nigh as you can.   These, after certain leaves spring up, if they be often removed and clipped by the course of the Moon, yield a better, broader and fairer flower, and they yield always more flowers in the harvest than in the spring time."

MARJORAM is a branching plant with flowers in clusters, purplish pink.   Propagate by seed and division in early spring in any garden soil.   Sweet marjoram must be treated as an annual, for winter kills it. The leaves are deliciously fragrant and are useful in cookery.

MINT (*Mentha spicata*, spearmint) has purplish flowers that bloom in July and August. These blossoms appear in slender spikes. The leaves have a pleasant taste and are used for flavoring. Spearmint will grow in any ordinary soil, but it likes the sun. It grows from one to two feet high.

Mentha rotundifolia has round leaves, variegated, and pale yellow flowers that appear in June and July. Propagate by division. The height is from one to two feet. The flowers are unimportant; but the foliage is sufficiently interesting to use as an edging, and this variety is useful to cover waste places.

MONK'S-HOOD has large showy helmet-shaped flowers of deep purple-blue growing on racemes on erect stems. The leaves are deeply cut. The plant is suited to borders and rough places. Propagate by division in rich soil. Monk's-hood likes sun or shade. It blooms in late summer or early autumn. The roots and flowers are poisonous. It grows from three to four feet.

MYRTLE (*Myrtus latifolia*). This plant has charming foliage and pure white flowers. Both leaves and flowers are fragrant. The fragrance of the foliage is caused by an oil, which is secreted in the leaves. Myrtle is quite hardy. Propagate by cuttings, or partially ripened shoots. Myrtle looks well in large pots.

NASTURTIUM. *Tropæolum* is the botanical name, meaning trophy, for the leaves suggest a buckler and the flowers a helmet. Treat as a hardy annual. Sow seeds in the spring. Nasturtium is a splendid climber over rocks, stones, or latticework, and a prolific bloomer.

OXLIP. Propagate by fresh seed, divisions, or cuttings in rich, light soil, not dry. *Protect in winter*. The oxlip grows from eight to twelve inches and likes half-shade. It resembles the primrose, but has larger flowers. These open in May and are yellow. The leaves are broad and flat and wrinkled.

PANSY. Heart's-ease and Johnny-Jump-Up are other names for the *Viola tricolor*, which has a wonderful length of blossoming, for the flowers continue from mid-April to mid-September. The flowers must be constantly picked, or the plant deteriorates. This precious little plant is very easy to raise, provided it is protected from the noonday sun. Propagate by seed or division in any garden soil, and in half-shade or morning sunlight. Protect it from the hot noon-day sun. Pansies look well in a bed by themselves and make a beautiful border plant.

PINKS. See Carnations.

POMEGRANATE is a highly decorative shrub, particularly the beautiful double scarlet variety (*Punica rubrum florepleno*), which flowers in August. Plant cutting in a big pot, jar, or tub, or buy plants. Stand these plants in pairs in some conspicuous place in the garden and they will add great elegance.

POPPY. The common garden herbaceous poppy flowers in May and June, in sun or half-shade, rising from two to three feet. It has large flowers and handsome divided foliage. For a Shakespeare garden select the white. Propagate by dividing in early autumn. The poppy is a gross feeder and likes rather moist loam enriched with cow manure.

PRIMROSE. This flower blooms from mid-April to mid-June. It has several solitary pale yellow blossoms on naked stem. It grows from six to nine inches high. *Protect in winter.* Propagate by seeds and offsets in rich, light soil, not dry.

ROSE. "How to plant a rose may seem a simple matter, but many have laid the foundation of failure through bad planting," writes a rose cultivator. "Never plant in a very wet soil, nor allow crude

manures to come into direct contact with the roots.
See that the roots are spread out properly and naturally, not pressed into a small hole and cramped
or distorted from the first. Plant dwarf kinds two
inches deeper than the junction of the rose and stock,
and standards three inches below the original root.
To place a small grower side by side with one of
three or four times the strength is a great mistake;
the weaker grower has no chance whatever. For
medium growers three feet is a good distance, while
plants of greater vigor will need to be from four
feet to six feet apart. Do not plant *against* a wall;
but leave some four or six inches between the wall
and the base of the plant. "It should not be difficult
to obtain the roses familiar to Shakespeare. The
old Hundred-Leaved and Damask are easy to procure. The *Rosa alba*, or white rose, has two familiar
varieties called "Maiden's Blush" and "Madame
Plantier."

The Musk-Rose may give some trouble, but E. T.
Cook gives us a good clue as well as instructions
for growing it. He says:

"These are very old roses, certainly known in
England three hundred years ago. The flowers are
insignificant individually, but collectively are pleasing and appear late in August. They require good

KNOTS FROM MARKHAM

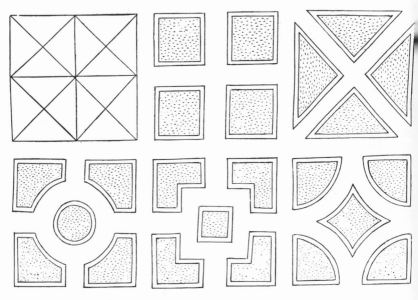

SIMPLE GARDEN BEDS

culture, and very little, if any, pruning. As pillar roses they are seen at their best. 'Fringed' is very pretty and strikes freely from cuttings. Its color is white shaded sulphur. All the Musk-Roses have a peculiar musk-like odor, but this is distilled only on still damp mornings or evenings. 'Eliza Verry' is white, very free, the flowers appearing in large corymbs. 'Rivers Musk' is a pretty pink variety, well worth cultivating. Of the Hybrid Musks the 'Garland' is of rampant growth. It has immense corymbs of tiny white flowers with innumerable little buff colored buds, peering out among them. 'Madame d' Arblay' is another. 'Nivea' is a beautiful kind for a pergola, or fence."

The "Noisette" is also a hybrid musk, named for a French gardener of Charleston, South Carolina, who took the seed from the musk-rose in 1817.

There is a difference between the Eglantine, or Sweetbrier, and the Dog-rose, although they are difficult to distinguish.

"The 'Dog Rose' sends up long arching branches some six to nine feet high and perhaps more; the 'Sweetbrier' is content with branches three or four feet in length. And whereas in the 'Dog Rose' the branch continues single the 'Sweetbrier' sends out side growths, or branchlets quickly forming a dense

bush.   Note also the prickles.   To a certain extent
they are stout and hooked like those of the 'Dog
Rose,' but more irregularly placed.   On the young
root-shoots there is a marked difference, for whilst
on the 'Sweetbrier' this young growth is covered
with *setæ*, some of them very small, tipped with
glands, in the 'Dog Rose' they are totally absent." [1]

ROSEMARY.   Tender, aromatic sub-shrub with
small flowers in short racemes.   Propagate by seeds,
cuttings, or layers in dry, light soil.   The flowers
are purple and bluish.   Rosemary is valued in
cookery as a flavoring.   It can be allowed to wander
all over the garden.   It was always a favorite border-
plant in old-fashioned gardens.

RUE.   The "herb of grace" is not very pretty.
It has much divided leaves and panicles of small
fragrant flowers, yellowish-green, or greenish-yel-
low.   Propagate by seed and division.   Rue needs
a sheltered position and protection in winter.   Its
height is about two feet.

SAVORY.   Sow in open ground at the end of
March, or early April, in light, rich soil.   Thin the
seedlings moderately; they may remain where they
are, or be transplanted.   Sown along the outside of

[1] Pemberton, "Roses" (London, 1908).

beds, savory makes a good edging. It is useful in cookery.

SWEET BALM. *Melissa officinalis* is the botanical name. Sweet balm is loved for its fragrance. The yellowish white flowers bloom in June, July, and August. It grows about two feet and loves the sun. Propagate by seed and division.

SWEET-WILLIAM is a valuable little garden plant, for it blooms profusely in June and July and is vigorous and rapidly spreading. The flowers are in double clusters, pink, white, red, and party-colored, single and double. Propagate by seed in any soil. See Carnations.

THYME. This aromatic herb is of dense growth with small, pale-lilac flowers in terminal spikes. Its pale, bright-green foliage makes it an attractive creeper for banks. Thyme also grows well in a rock-garden and makes a good border-plant also. Propagate by seed and division. The plant grows in any soil. It attains a height of from one to two inches and blossoms in June and July. Every one knows the value of dried thyme for flavoring in cookery.

VIOLETS prefer shady places. They are at home in the rock-garden, and they are very charming if planted on a little bank. They can be sown on the grassy slope of a terrace. In that case, let them come up of their own sweet will. The graceful heart-shaped leaves of the *Viola odorata* and its purple blossoms that open in late April and May are known and loved by every one. Propagate by seed or division, selecting a loose, rich, sandy soil.

XXII

Potpourri

As the ladies of Shakespeare's time were so fond of making *potpourri*, I think it may be of value to place here an old recipe, which any one who has a garden can follow:

"Many fragrant flowers and leaves can be used in the making of an old-fashioned bowl of *potpourri*. Those usually employed are rose-petals, lavender, lemon-plant, verbena, myrtle, rosemary, bay, mignonette, violets, pinks and syringa. Thyme, mint and other sweet herbs should be used, if available. Shred the larger leaves and dry all in the sun. Mix an ounce of orris-root, allspice, bay-salt and cloves and mix freely with about twelve handfuls of the dried petals and leaves and store in a jar, or bowl. A small quantity of essence of lemon and spirits of lavender may be added, but are not necessary. Should the mixture become too moist, add more powdered orris-root."

A MASKE OF FLOWERS

A MASKE OF FLOWERS

IT seems to me that nothing more appropriate could be placed here as an epilogue to this book on the Shakespeare garden than the contemporary description of "A Maske of Flowers by the Gentlemen of Gray's Inn at Whitehall on Twelfth Night, 1613, being the last of the solemnities and magnificences which were performed at the marriage of the Earl of Somerset and Lady Frances, daughter of the Earl of Suffolk, Lord Chamberlain."

This was printed in 1614; and I have quoted it from the "History of Gardening in England" by the Hon. Alicia Amherst (London, 1895), who copied it from a very rare original.

This description not only presents a perfect picture of a Shakespearian garden but will be a revelation to those persons who think that only crude stage-setting existed in Elizabethan and Jacobean days. Although elaborate stage-setting was restricted to private entertainments, the designers of the period knew how to produce splendid effects. There is nothing more elaborate in the theater today than this ornate and brilliantly lighted scene:

"When the Dance ended, the loud music sounded. The curtains being drawn was seen a Garden of a glorious and strange beauty, cast into four Quarters with a cross-walk and alleys compassing each Quarter. In the middle of the cross-walk stood a goodly Fountain, raised on four columns of silver. On the tops whereof strode four statues of silver which supported a bowl in circuit containing four and twenty foot and was raised from the ground nine foot in height, in the middle whereof, upon scrolls of silver and gold, was placed a globe garnished with four golden mask heads, out of which issued water into the bowl; above stood a golden Neptune, in height three foot, holding in his hand a trident.

"The Garden walls were of brick, artificially painted in perspective, all along which were placed fruit-trees with artificial leaves and fruits. The Garden within the walls was railed about with rails of three foot high, adorned with balusters of silver, between which were placed pedestals beautified with transparent lights of variable colors. Upon the pedestals stood silver columns, upon the tops whereof were personages of gold, lions of gold and unicorns of silver. Every personage and beast did hold a torchet burning, that gave light and luster to the whole fabric.

"Every Quarter of the Garden was finely hedged about with a low hedge of cypress and juniper; the Knots within set with artificial flowers. In the two first Quarters were two Pyramids, garnished with gold and silver and glittering with transparent lights resembling carbuncles, sapphires and rubies.

"In every corner of each Quarter were great pots of gilliflowers which shadowed certain lights placed behind them and made resplendent and admirable luster. The two farther Quarters were beautified with tulips of divers colors, and in the middle and in the corners of the said Quarters were set great tufts of several kinds of flowers receiving luster from secret lights placed behind them.

"At the farther end of the Garden was a Mount, raised by degrees resembling banks of earth covered with grass. On the top of the Mount stood a goodly Arbor, substantially made and covered with artificial trees and with arbor flowers such as eglantine, honeysuckles and the like. The Arbor was in length three and thirty foot, in height one and twenty, supported with termes of gold and silver. It was divided into six arches and three doors answerable to the three walks of the Garden.

"In the middle of the Arbor rose a goodly large turret and at either end a smaller. Upon the top of the Mount in the front thereof was a bank of flowers, curiously painted behind, while within the arches the maskers sat unseen.

"Behind the Garden, over the top of the Arbor, were set artificial trees appearing like an Orchard joining to the Garden; and over all was drawn in perspective a Firmament like the skies in a clear night. Upon a grassy seat under the Arbor sat the Garden Gods in number twelve, apparrelled in long robes of green rich taffeta, caps on their heads and chaplets of flowers. In the midst of them sat Primaura, at whose entreaty they descended to the stage, and, marching up to the King, sung to lutes and theorbos." [1]

[1] The tenor lute.

COMPLETE LIST OF SHAKESPEARIAN FLOW-
ERS WITH BOTANICAL IDENTIFICATIONS

Anemone (*Anemone purpurea striata stellata*).
Box (*Buxus sempervirens*).
Broom-flower (*Cytisus scoparius*).
Camomile (*Anthemis nobilis*).
Carnation (*Dianthus caryophyllus*).
Columbine (*Aquilegia vulgaris*).
Cowslip (*Paralysis vulgaris pratensis*).
Crocus (*Crocus verus sativus autumnalis*).
Crow-flower (*Scilla nutans*).
Crown-imperial (*Fritillaria imperalis*).
Cuckoo-buds (*Ranunculus*).
Cuckoo-flowers (*Lychnis Flos cuculi*).
Daffodil (*Narcissus pseudo-narcissus*).
Daisy (*Bellis perennis*).
Diana's-bud (*Artemesia*).
Fennel (*Fœniculum vulgare*).
Fern (*Pteris aquilina*).
Flower-de-luce (*Iris pseudacorus*).
Gilliflower (*Caryophyllus major*).
Harebell (*Scilla nutans*).
Holly (*Ilex aquifolium*).
Honeysuckle (*Lonicera perfolium*).
Ivy (*Hedera helix*).
Lady-smocks (*Cardamine pratensis*).
Lark's-heels, Nasturtium.

Larkspur (*Delphinium*).
Lavender (*Lavendula spica*).
Lily (*Lilium candidum*).
Long purples (*Arum masculata*).
Marigold (*Calendula officinalis*).
Marjorum (*Origanum vulgare*).
Mint (*Mentha*).
Mistletoe (*Viscum album*).
Monks-hood (*Aconitum Napellus*).
Myrtle (*Myrtus latifolia*).
Oxlip (*Primula eliator*).
Pansy (*Viola tricolor*).
Pomegranate (*Punica*).
Poppy (*Papaver somniferum*).
Primrose (*Primula vulgaris*).
Rose (*Rosa*).
Rosemary (*Rosmarinus officinalis*).
Rue (*Ruta graveolus*).
Savory (*Satureia*).
Sweet Balm (*Melissa officinalis*).
Thyme (*Thymus serpyllum*).
Violet (*Viola odorata*).

APPENDIX

T WO reports made in the spring of 1920, one by Frederick C. Wellstood, secretary and librarian of the Trustees and Guardians of Shakespeare's Birthplace, and the other by Ernest Law, C.B., one of the trustees, will doubtless be of interest to the reader. They have been made available through the courtesy of Mr. Law.

Mr. Wellstood, writing on Easter, 1920, in his report says:

"The appeal of the Trustees and Guardians of Shakespeare's Birthplace, &c. issued three months ago, for gifts of Elizabethan plants and flowers, wherewith to stock his 'Great Garden' at Stratford-upon-Avon, has had a very gratifying response. The King and Queen, Queen Alexandra and the Prince of Wales, have graciously interested themselves in the project, and have given practical support by valuable contributions of old-fashioned roses and other flowers.

"From the gardens of all the Royal Palaces, which were known to Shakespeare, ample parcels of the same sorts of flowers as grew in them when he visited them have been forwarded to Stratford-upon-Avon. Thus, from Greenwich, where we know that he appeared as an actor before Queen Elizabeth at Christmas, 1594; from Windsor, where his Company performed before the same Queen—probably in "The Merry Wives of Windsor"—as well as from Frogmore, which that play proves his acquaintance with; from Hampton Court—out of the Old Tudor Garden, 'circum-mured with brick,' which he must have visited when he and his fellows of the 'King's Company of Actors' spent ten days there during the Christmastide of 1603-4, presenting six plays before King James and his Court—from the gardens of all these places large consignments of plants have reached Shakespeare's Garden.

"From Wilton, likewise, where Shakespeare and his Company first acted before King James, a large number of specimens of every plant and flower wanted by the Trustees, has been sent by the present owner—the lineal descendant of the one, and the kinsman and representative of the other, of the two 'most noble and incomparable Paire of Brethren, William Earle of Pembroke and Philip Earle of Montgomery . . . who prosequuted the Author living with so much favor'—to quote the words of the famous 'First Folio,' which was dedicated to them.

"Similarly, from the gardens of other places, which Shakespeare must have known well, have come very welcome gifts, notably from Charlecote, close to Stratford—the beautiful home of the Lucys for 750 years, where Shakespeare is said when a youth to have poached the deer of Sir Thomas Lucy, who had him whipped for his offense—whence now comes a charming collection of the poet's favorite flowers from the direct lineal descendant and heiress of the original 'Justice Shallow.'

"The trustees have also received choice batches of old-fashioned flowers from the gardens of medieval Castles mentioned in the plays—Glamis and Cawdor, for instance—and some which were probably well known to Shakespeare, such as Berkeley Castle; and from the great Tudor houses also, which he knew well, at any rate by repute, such as Knole, Burghley House, and Cobham Hall. The owner of Cobham Hall sends specimens of the famous 'Cobham' Rose, known to have been grown in the garden there for four or five hundred years. From Esher Place also—the 'Aster House' of 'King Henry VIII' —come many beautiful flowers and herbs.

"The sentiment, which has prompted such generosity, has equally appealed to many possessors of more modern gardens; while the authorities of Kew Gardens, regarding the scheme as one of national concern, have cordially aided the Trustees both with counsel and with contributions.

"Last, but by no means least, are the many small gifts from quite small gardens, even of cottagers; while, in some ways, the most pleasing of all, are the subscriptions from school children of some of the poorest districts in the East End of London—for instance, of the Mansford Street Central, and Pritchard's Road Schools, Bethnal Green—for the purchase of favorite flowers of the dramatist, whose plays they have so often witnessed with delight at the 'Old Vic.' and elsewhere.

"Thus, effect has been given to a prime desire of the Trustees, that as large as possible a number of people in every section of the community should be associated with this tribute to Shakespeare's memory.

"Most of the plants needful to furnish forth Shakespeare's garden in the style of his own time have been forthcoming in sufficient quantities—yet there are some important gaps still to be supplied. These are:—Box, dwarf Box, both the ordinary and the 'Gilded' variety; Thrift; Thyme, the Golden and Glaucous, as well as the Wild; and that pretty herb, known under its simple old English name as 'Lavender Cotton.' Of all of these, thousands of plants are still needed. Similarly of Pinks, 'Streaked Gillyflowers'; 'Spike Lavender'; and of Pansies—'Love in Idleness,'—pale and dark 'purple with Love's wound.' Of 'Eglantine'—Sweet Briar —a few scores would be very welcome.

"Such shortages are mainly due to the large quantities of these plants required for the purpose of filling the intricate-patterned beds of the 'Curious Knotted Garden.' That kind of garden was an invariable adjunct to every house of importance in Shakespeare's time, and the Trustees are laying one out on what is believed to be the exact site of the poet's own 'knotted garden,' modeling it on the designs printed in the contemporary books on gardening—the designs being followed with a fidelity and completeness unattempted, it is believed, for two hundred and eighty years. At the same time, suggestions have naturally been sought in Bacon's famous Essay 'On Gardens.' . . ."

SHAKESPEARE'S GARDEN RESTORED

Mr. Law's report, which is dated "Shakespeare's Birthday, A. D. 1920," says:

"The project of laying out the ground attached to Shakespeare's home in his later years as an Elizabethan garden, to be stocked with all the old-fashioned flowers mentioned by him in his plays or well known in his time, first took practical shape last winter.

THE LONG BORDERS

"The first step was to lay out the long, narrow strip of ground by the side of the wall parallel with Chapel Lane as a border for summer and autumn flowers—hollyhocks, canterbury-bells, lupins, larkspurs, crown imperials, lilies, and so on. As a background for these—and also to hide the ugly, cast-iron railings that disfigure the top of the wall—there was planted a row of yew trees. This border of some 300 feet long has been treated in the formal fashion of the olden time . . . being divided into compartments, separated by 'buttresses' supporting 'pillars' or 'columns' surmounted by 'balls.'

"On the path side the beds are edged with box—

'dwarfe boxe, of excellent use to border up a knott or long beds in a garden.'

"The beds ranging with these, on the other side of the gravel walk, are at present entirely occupied with spring flowers—largely gifts, like the others, from contributors all over the kingdom. In the summer they will be furnished with the low-growing flowers known to the gardeners of the early years of James the First's reign—carnations, 'our streaked gillyvors,' pansies, stocks, fox-gloves, sweet-williams, snapdragons, and so on. . . .

THE WILD BANK OF HEATH

"At the eastern or lower end of the garden the aim has been to carry out, so far as the space available admits, Bacon's idea, expressed in his famous essay 'Of Gardens,' of a 'heath or desert, in the going forth, framed, as much as may be, to a natural wild-ness.' With this object, there has been thrown up an irregular bank, whereon have already been planted most of the flowers and herbs mentioned by Shake-speare in his writings; and where, it is hoped, every species known in his time will eventually find a place.

"In doing this the great natural philosopher's pre-cepts have been faithfully followed, modified by hints derived from the greater poet. 'Some thickets,' says Bacon, 'I would have made only in sweetbriar (eglantine) and honeysuckle (woodbine); and the ground set with violets and primroses (oxlips); for these be sweet and prosper in the shade.' This has been done: and with wild thyme—many square yards of it—added, and also musk-roses—a few procured with great difficulty, so unaccountably neglected are they in our too-pretentious modern gardens—they will form here, in effect, Titania's Bower—

"I know a bank whereon the wild thyme blows,
 Where oxlips and the nodding violet grows,
 Quite over-canopied with luscious woodbine,
 With sweet musk-roses and with eglantine.
 There sleeps Titania some time of the night,
 Lull'd in these flowers, with dances and delight.

"Bacon, of course, often witnessed the performances of Shakespeare's plays at Court, as well as in the public theaters; and reminiscent echoes of that beautiful passage were probably ringing in his ears when he penned the sentences quoted above.

"With passages in plays other than 'The Dream,' Bacon has also parallels. His essay happens to have been published exactly twelve months after the production of 'A Winter's Tale' at Court, and in his

somewhat arid enumeration therein of the seasonal
succession of flowering plants, we seem to hear echoes
of those exquisite verses in Peredita's speeches—the
most beautiful expression of the intimate love of
flowers in all literature—

> ". . . Daffodils,
> That come before the swallow dares, and take
> The winds of March with beauty; violets dim,
> But sweeter than the lids of Juno's eyes,
> Or Cytherea's breath; pale primroses,
> That die unmarried ere they can behold
> Bright Phœbus in his strength.

" 'For March,' writes Bacon, 'there come violets,
especially the single blue, which are the earliest . . .
and which, above all other flowers, yields the sweetest smell in the air; also the yellow daffodil.' 'Lilies
of all sorts, the flowre-de-luce being one,' says Perdita. 'Flower-de-Luces, and lilies of all natures,'
echoes Bacon.

"Near the Wild Bank later on there may, perhaps,
be planted some of those specimens of the topiary
art, which were so general in Jacobean gardens.
Even Bacon would admit them into his 'Princely
Garden.' 'Little low hedges (of box or yew),' he
writes, 'round like welts, with some pretty pyramids,
I like well, and in some places fair columns.' But he

would confine them to geometric patterns: 'I, for my part, do not like images cut out in juniper or other garden stuff, they be for children.' But then Shakespeare had children and grandchildren; and, besides, many children of the present day will visit his garden, much taken, we may be sure, with such curious devices, and delighting in our simple sweet old English flowers—very few of them, it is to be hoped, serious little prigs, bursting with botany. . . .

THE "KNOTT GARDEN"

"It is now necessary to say a few words about the 'Knott Garden'—an enclosure which, being an invariable adjunct to every house of importance in Shakespeare's time, is the most essential part of the reconstruction, on Elizabethan lines, of the ground about New Place. It need not, however, engage us long: for M. Forestier's beautiful drawing of it represents it as it is to be, better than any amount of wordy description.

"The whole is closely modeled on the designs and views shown in the contemporary books on gardening; and for every feature there is unimpeachable warrant. The enclosing palisade—a very favorite device of the Jacobean gardeners—of

Warwickshire oak, cleft, is exactly copied from the one in the famous tapestry of the 'Seven Deadly Sins' at Hampton Court. And here again Bacon's advice has been useful: 'The garden is best to be square, encompassed on all four sides with a stately arched hedge, the arches on pillars of carpenter's work, of some 10 foot high, and 6 foot broad.' The 'tunnel,' or 'pleachéd bower, where honeysuckles, ripened by the sun, forbid the sun to enter'—follows ancient models, especially the one shown in the old contemporary picture in New Place Museum.

"The dwarf wall, of old-fashioned bricks—hand-made, sun-dried, sand-finished, with occasional 'flarers,' laid in the Tudor bond, with wide mortar joints—is based on similar ones, still extant, of the period. The balustrade is identical, in its smallest details, with one figured in Didymus Mountain's 'Gardener's Labyrinth,' published in 1577—a book Shakespeare must certainly have consulted when laying out his own Knott Garden. The paths are to be of old stone from Wilmcote, the home of Shakespeare's mother. The intricate, interlacing patterns of the Knott beds—'the Knottes so enknotted it cannot be expressed,' as Cavendish says of Wolsey's garden—are taken, one from Mountain's book; two from Gervase Markham's 'Country Housewife's

Garden' (1613); and one from William Lawson's
'New Orchard and Garden' (1618); and they are
composed, as enjoined by those authorities, of box,
thrift, lavender-cotton, and thyme, with their inter-
spaces filled in with flowers.

ROYAL ROSES FOR THE KNOTTED BEDS

"In one point the Trustees have been able to 'go
one better' than Shakespeare in his own 'curious
knotted garden'—to use his own expression in
'Love's Labour's Lost.' For neither King James, nor
his Queen, Anne of Denmark, nor Henry Prince of
Wales sent him—so far as we know—any flowers
for his garden. On his 356th birthday, however,
there will be planted four old-fashioned English
rose-trees—one in the center of each of the four
'knotted' beds—from King George, Queen Mary,
Queen Alexandra, and the Prince of Wales. Surely
Shakespeare, could he have known it, would have
been touched by this tribute!

"They will be planted by Lady Fairfax-Lucy, the
heiress of Charlecote, and the direct lineal descendant of the Sir Thomas Lucy whose deer he is said
to have poached, and who is supposed to have had
him whipped for his offense, and who is believed to

be satirized in the character of 'Justice Shallow.' This also might well have moved him!

"Here, in the restored 'Knott Garden,' as every-where in the grounds about New Place, flowers—Shakespeare's Flowers—will clothe and wreathe and perfume everything, all else being merely devised to set them off—musk-roses, climbing-roses, crab-apples, wild cherries, clematis, honeysuckle, sweet-briar, and many more.

"By next year, the Trustees expect to have some 200,000 individual plants—including, of course, the crocuses, 'bold oxlips,' 'nodding violets,' 'winking marybuds,' 'pale primroses,' and 'azured harebells,' on the wild bank and lawn—decking, in succession through the months, the ground whereon the poet trod, their millions of blossoms, with every breath of air doing reverence, waving banners of gorgeous hue, and flinging the incense of their delicious fragrance in homage to the memory of William Shakespeare."

INDEX